BARABBAS

AN AUTOBIOGRAPHY

IAN LINDSAY

Published in 2013 by FeedARead.com Publishing –
Arts Council funded
Copyright © Ian Lindsay

With thanks to Margaret
and Cate.

To Begin With the Ending:

I'm just a tired old Jew, who should have been dead years ago, and soon will be anyway. So I could understand you asking why anyone should listen to anything that I have to say - who am I to tell you anything? I have never held high office or performed great feats in my life and can think of no particular reason why you would ever have heard of me. But once upon a time I stood at the edge of certain events, an unimportant figure in the background, someone you wouldn't notice - a hanger on.

It was in that position that I saw some of the things that are now being talked about so much, I just didn't realise how important they were, or I might have paid closer attention. But one of my few gifts in this life has always been to have a good memory, and when I hear some of the strange stories being told about those times, it makes me angry to see things being twisted by people who should know better. Some of the wilder versions are being told by people who weren't even there, but have now decided they want to be part of it.

Well I was there, and I saw, and I remember, and I might be the last person on earth who can honestly say that. So unless what actually happened is recorded, then the truth will sink beneath the lies. Although I have long been able to read and write for myself, my grammar and spelling aren't really good enough for a work of this sort, so my friend Chloe is writing down my words. Whilst my native tongue was and remains Aramaic, by virtue of my travels I have become fluent in the international language of Greek, and it is in that language that my story is being told. For this reason

5

you may notice that although my birth name in Aramaic was Yeshua, and that was what my mother and family called me, for the purposes of this narrative my name, and those of the other characters, will usually be shown in the Greek fashion.

With that stipulation, I therefore state that my name is Jesus Barabbas, and although I have been in plenty of courts in my life, this is the first time I have ever been a witness. That fact alone would give some people a laugh. Since I started to tell Chloe my story I have been embarrassed, but only slightly, by the realisation of just how unpleasant I once was, and perhaps still am, but it's far too late to try and change that now. I was what I was, I am what I am. So for what it's worth this is what happened, and how it looked to me at the time.

CHAPTER ONE

I was born and grew up in Kerioth in southern Judea, about a half day's journey south of Hebron. The place is still today what it always has been, a typical small Judean hill town, bigger than a village, but with no pretensions to being anything more than quietly provincial. It only really exists as the meeting place of three roads, one each: north, east and south, with a large main square with two wells and another smaller square with one well. There's a new synagogue with attached administrative offices and three resting places, scarcely inns, for the passing travellers on the road down to Masada and the Salt Sea. Apart from the usual range of trades like butchers, bakers and wine merchants the only other thing of note is the small Legion barracks. There isn't a permanent garrison and it only gets used when the Tenth have some reason to be in the area, or to put it another way: when there's trouble.

For all the rest of the time, when there isn't any trouble, the town just sits there in the sunshine, a collection of one and two story, flat roofed, mud brick buildings, sprawling over two hillsides, with the surrounding scrub covered landscape rising and falling monotonously out of sight in every direction. The sun comes up in the morning, becomes too hot to work in by noon, and sinks again in the evening, and that makes our daily round. Even the so called 'highway' to the Salt Sea is a little travelled country track - in short nobody visits Kerioth for the excitement.

I thought it must be the dullest place in the world, partly because it was true, and partly because I was young. Lots of young men think their home town is boring and want to see the world, and I was no exception. There had been a variety of minor scrapes with the law, and several occasions when I was caught in some minor misdemeanour and suffered the penalty, it all added to my sense of dissatisfaction.

For most young men, this means going to spend a few months hustling for pennies on the busy and uncaring streets of Jerusalem, before admitting defeat and going home, thinner and dirtier, to marry the girl your mother told you to marry in the first place. If I'd been luckier, or maybe brighter, that would have happened to me.

Instead, even after realising that I didn't have enough to eat and wasn't impressing anyone in Jerusalem, I still didn't come to my senses. I arrived back home, uncomfortably aware of my failure in the city but still quite sure that Kerioth wasn't big enough for me - an unhappy combination.

My mother arranged for my apprenticeship to Jacob the tent maker, who was, like half the people in town, some sort of distant relative. For four years I worked, learning all there is to know about the joys of tent making, and even more importantly how to deal with a Legionary Quartermaster. It's no good making tents if you can't sell them. The Legions might be a curse and a foreign intrusion but since they'd decided to ignore my opinion and come anyway, we should try to turn a profit on the situation.

There had been two or three occasions during this period when my dissatisfaction with life, a general feeling of, *is this all there is?* had bubbled to the surface. An incident when a young Legionary officer, instead of just signing for two tents I was delivering, had insisted that I should erect them so that he could inspect them first. He wasn't much older than me and so I told him, "If you're that interested in looking at them -

you put them up." It turned out that I'd misjudged the man, for instead of shouting at me he just hit me, hard enough to send me flying.

"Right." I said warningly, as I scrambled back to my feet, but two troopers standing nearby put their hands on their sword hilts, even more warningly. I suppose that I was lucky to have been stopped because I was hot headed enough to have taken a swing at the man, which would have been a very serious mistake. Even more galling than being hit was the fact that the officer in question regarded me as so insignificant that he didn't bother reporting my behaviour to Jacob, I didn't even need to lie my way out of trouble.

Then there was Miriam the tanner's daughter. She was only young and a bit simple minded, but she was very trusting and had the breasts and backside of a grown woman. She was a disaster waiting to happen. And sure enough I happened to her, frequently. The inevitable pregnancy was quickly identified as my doing and I was faced with a demand to marry her. Her father quoted the old law which said that in the case of the rape of an unbetrothed virgin, I must not only pay a fine in silver, but that the father could insist on me marrying the girl, and that such a forced marriage could never be dissolved.

"And you can forget any idea of a dowry." He finished off, pointing his finger in my face as he spoke. I thought of running, but that hadn't been a great success the last time I tried, so I took a deep breath and relied on talking my way out of trouble.

"If we're going to discuss the law," I said, pointing a finger right back at him, "then we should remember it says that any girl raped within a town boundary who fails to cry for help is equally guilty with the man. And the reason no one heard her cry out was because she didn't, the only sounds she made were those of pleasure.

9

Your daughter was no virgin and I think you set her on me deliberately to get her married off, because no one else would take her. She's a danger to herself and anyone else around, she should be locked up to ensure the safety of decent men."

Her father, a powerfully built man, stared at me with such hostility that a lesser man than me would have wilted, but I stared right back at him. He had made the mistake of bringing one of the rabbis with him as a witness to the law, and as I spoke he had been nodding sagely, as if he agreed with me. I was cock a hoop, and my smug expression must have showed this.

The Rabbi looked at Miriam. "Tell me honestly girl, did you lead this man on?"

She looked at him puzzled. "Lead him on? I don't know about that." Then she suddenly smiled. "But he's a very nice man."

The Rabbi looked helplessly at the father; this was going nowhere.

That's the good thing about simple girls like her, no one's ever quite sure if they're telling the truth. Even I was half convinced of my innocence, I thought that when she'd had this baby I might give her another. She was cheap fun and had just been publicly branded a slut, no one could possibly object to what happened to her now.

Each time there was another problem, there always seemed to be some way out, I was quick on my feet and fast with my mouth, and so against all the odds the apprenticeship ran its full course.

With my time completed and a full man's pay now my right, together with the expectation that some respect might accompany the pay rise, I should have been content. I had come to man's estate and should now reap my reward. Unfortunately, like so many things in my life, it didn't quite work out that way. At

10

the time I blamed Jacob for being unreasonable, but that now seems foolish. You don't blame a rabid dog for biting you, that's what rabid dogs do - you don't blame it, you take your stick to it. Jacob was an old man, frightened of losing trade when the Tenth Fretensis Legion moved back to their main base up to Syria, unwilling to relinquish control to me and unable to find a new outlet for our products.

As things stood the business was fairly steady, just about holding its own, with a half and half split between supplying new tents and repairing old ones. It was profitable but only sufficiently so for one master, there wasn't enough meat on the bone for two good wages, it seemed to me that Jacob should have foreseen this problem and done something other than moaning about it.

My need for an increase in pay at the end of my apprenticeship was clearly the last straw for him, but I wasn't in an understanding mood. His decision to get rid of our one remaining apprentice, supposedly to save money, meant that even though I was now a time served man all the small acts of drudgery still fell to me. Every time I swept the workshop I took it as a personal affront, and came daily closer to boiling over.

On that final day, Jacob had taken exception to one of my seams and was berating me as though I were a child. In tent making it's all about the seams, they have to be folded and bound, and the seam is always on the inside of the tent, so all you can see on the outside is a simple folded join. Otherwise there's no hope of them ever staying watertight. The tenth Legion's motto is Ever Ready, and that means getting a good night's sleep, in the dry.

Goat skin isn't the worst material to work with, it's a lot more pliable than ox leather, but it's still hard work. The standard Roman eight man infantry unit, what they

11

call the contubernium, uses a tent called a papilio, because it looks like a butterfly when it's spread out. It's nine cubits long, by six and a half wide, so with the side walls and flaps it's a lot of stitching. The only way you have a chance of achieving any speed is if you use a boy to hold the ends of the strips of material, lying along the ground, he keeps them aligned while you tack them together before the detailed stitching. Jacob was having none of that, he reckoned that as we'd got rid of the boy, I should somehow be able to do it all myself. Now whilst it's true that I'm good with my hands, it's also true that I have only one pair of them.

It wasn't that he was a bad tentmaker himself, but he was by then a frightened old man and unwilling to take the good advice I was giving him. He should have known that it was his fault the work was going so slowly, and in a perfect world I might have made some allowance for the responsibility he could no longer cope with. But what actually happened was that my patience finally snapped. His finger jabbed my chest once too often and I swung an angry fist at him.

The blow sent him reeling backwards, against a work bench, there was more astonishment than hurt in his face. Then he collected himself, he was the master and, time served or not, I was the junior. All remaining traces of warmth between us were suddenly gone, as was his previous confusion.

"You ungrateful dog - you'll never work for anyone in this town again, or anywhere else that does business with the legions. I'll break you - just watch me."

It was immediately obvious what must happen next, and once I'd realised that I never hesitated. There had been a Zealot raid on a nearby farm only two weeks earlier. They had killed the farmer, raped his young daughters and stolen all his livestock. The word in town had been that they'd accused him of being too close to the Romans. Well you can't get much closer than supplying their tents, it was time for another raid. I picked up one of the iron bars we used for beating the skins and took two paces towards him. The swing was as natural as if I were knocking in a tent peg, smoothly back and swiftly down. At the last minute he realised that he'd pushed me too far and vainly tried lifting his arms in a defensive gesture, but it was a waste of time. The flying end of the bar struck him across the head and he went down.

I dragged a half sewn tent over to the workshop fire, pushing enough of it into the flames to make a good blaze, and then swept all the tools onto the floor. I ripped my tunic, smeared dirt across my face and then hit myself on the cheek with a wooden bar. It was harder than I'd intended, but so much the better for realism. I would stagger out of the burning premises the brave survivor of another raid. In all these preparations I didn't forget to empty his purse, he owed me the money anyway.

All men think they're unique, though the differences are usually just in the details, but this was no detail. I was aware that my complete lack of excitement or emotion at the deed marked me as different, and knew this was to my credit, a sign of my superiority. As I worked at covering my tracks it never occurred to me that I couldn't, or wouldn't, fool the Temple guards who would be round to investigate. They meant well but they were old, they would believe me, people generally did.

It was plain bad luck, no one could possibly have foreseen it, to discover that along with the Temple guards the designated civil representative for the month was Ben Amal the tanner, the unhappy father of Miriam. It wasn't as if I'd done his daughter any lasting harm, she might have been simple and no more than thirteen years old but she was still ready for a man; if it hadn't been me, it would have been someone else. By her own account she thought I was a very nice man, and had clearly enjoyed herself; and as for the baby - if they were lucky it would inherit her looks and my brains. But her father was still bearing a grievance, still keeping the memory of his daughter's lost maidenhood as a thing to be avenged rather than celebrated. As I had assumed, the Temple guards were happy enough with my story, but he wasn't, and he wouldn't let it go. He knew for sure that there was something to dig out, and that he was the one to do it.

For a while he made no progress, all I had to do was stick to my story, the damage to the workshop and my face supported my version of events, and the two guards were clearly beginning to lose patience with his demands that I should keep on repeating the same story, over and over. They were happy to accept that it was what it looked like, another Zealot raid, but they couldn't do that, not until he agreed with them. Unfortunately for me, he then had a bright idea, the one thing I hadn't counted on.

He went over to Jacob's body and began to search through his clothing, but whatever he was looking for he couldn't find it. Then with a hard look at me he went over to the tent cutting floor, where I said we'd been attacked, and walked slowly around, looking at the ground.

With a small cry of triumph, he stooped down to pick up Jacob's purse, lying just where I'd dropped it. He must have known from the feel that it was empty, but in order to make a show of things he carried it carefully back, to stand in front of me. With a flourish he turned it inside out, then held it at arm's length and shook it.

"As I thought - empty, and I know for a fact that he was paid for a saddle this morning." His voice was triumphant. The guards looked puzzled, they still hadn't worked out where this was going next.

"Of course it's empty, they must have taken his money when they stole everything else they could lay their hands on." Even as I spoke it was obvious that I was standing on the edge of a very high cliff. Then he pushed me off.

Turning to the guards he said. "Seize him, and search him."

The four coins were wrapped in my belt, the first place they would look, and there was no innocent explanation for them.

They would have obeyed him, but the order had taken them by surprise and they needed a second or two to realise that I had changed from being a victim, into the main suspect. Happily I needed no such breathing space and snatched the staff from the man standing next to me, hitting him round the side of the head with it. He collapsed backwards, out of things for as long as made any difference. I was younger, I was faster and I was stronger, and I knew that Ben Amal was the danger - so I charged him. That wiped the triumph off his face.

Despite being well past forty he was built like an ox, tanning hides is a job demanding mule like strength, but not much speed. It was important to put him down before he managed to get his massive arms wrapped round me, he could crush me to death without raising a sweat and would probably enjoy doing so.

Even though he managed to catch the end of the staff in both hands as it hit him in the face, it wasn't enough to stop himself being dumped backwards onto the ground. I let him cling on to the staff - with him on his back and dazed for a moment it wasn't a problem. As he lay there, uselessly floundering, I kicked his head, hard.

Then again, and again, and again. With each impact his head flew away from my foot and blood came out of his half open mouth. The pig.

The remaining Temple guard finally managed to seize my arm, but it was a long time since he'd done any fighting and he'd forgotten how important the first few blows were. I was used to fighting and broke his neck.

As I stood, gasping for breath, as much at the surprise as the exertion, and surveying the result of Ben Amal's good idea, I knew what I had to do. If only he'd kept his mouth shut, what possible difference had it made to him? And now he'd put me into a position where I had no alternative but to get rid of the witnesses. I went and fetched one of the trimming knives and dealt with the surviving guard, before plunging it into Ben Amal's belly. I honestly think that he was dead already, from the kicking, but he'd seriously annoyed me and it made me feel better.

It was late in the afternoon by the time I'd finished, not far from dusk, the early evening crowds around the various wells would have receded, with most people at home by now for their evening meal. It was a good time to move without meeting too many people and too many questions. I ran to tell my mother that I was the sole survivor of a Zealot raid on the tent workshop, and that despite my bravery Jacob had perished. Her first reaction was to tend to my supposed injuries, it's what mothers do. I brushed her off, explaining that as the bandits left they had vowed to return with reinforcements and finish me off for having dared to defy them.

As a story it was pathetic and wouldn't survive scrutiny, and neither would I. But what it might do was establish sufficient doubt to slow down any immediate pursuit. I told her that I was going to move out of town

16

for two or three days to avoid the supposed retribution, and packed a knapsack with food and clothing; my mother didn't have anything of enough value to be worth stealing. Then taking a heavy cloak and my fathers old sword I kissed her goodbye.

My two younger cousins lived only a short distance away, and had always looked up to me, as boys often will, as someone sufficiently older than than them to be interesting, but not yet old enough to be like their parents. They were fifteen and sixteen, old enough to swing a sword or a cudgel, but not yet old enough to know better. They would jump at the chance, anything to get out of boring old Kerioth, I remembered the feeling.

CHAPTER TWO

And that's how we began our career as highway robbers, it wasn't exactly planned, but life sometimes gives you a helping hand. At all events it was easier than tent making, and a lot more fun. We made our camp in that rough hill country which lies to the west of the Hebron to Beersheba road, and would drop down on any group of travellers we felt able to cope with. The road curved round most of the hills, keeping to the flat ground on the valley floor, this made it easier for us to watch them approaching and size up their numbers and likely strength, to decide whether or not they were a soft enough target. Just as in the fight with the Temple guards, it was all about speed and brutality. Decent people need time and provocation to act brutally, a good highway robber or a good soldier, which is almost the same thing, can produce it on demand. And it's that first few seconds that decides the fight, after that it's too late to get angry because you're already down on the ground with a cracked skull.

There was the money, the jewellery, the provisions and any goods they were carrying - and don't forget the women. They were a special bonus, and it was always my turn first. We even recruited two more members to our little band, a couple of bonded servants who were already thinking of running. When we turned up they actually helped us take their master captive, saying they knew someone who would ransom him. They were mostly happy days, all decisions were mine and all the credit for our continuing success was mine. I was the undisputed master, it seemed that life was finally rewarding my efforts.

The only small cloud to mar my tranquillity was an event that I should have been able to cope with, it was only a small thing and I was surprised it bothered me. Our normal routine was to start our attack on a group of travellers with the maximum of noise and violence, a ruthless display of brutality at the outset usually cowed the survivors into docility. Once you've made it clear that any resistance will be crushed you can get on with the business of removing their valuables without further disturbance. As far as the women were concerned, if there was time, we generally took our turn with any good looking ones at the roadside, it was more trouble than it was worth to drag them back to camp. I never bothered about killing all the witnesses, people knew who we were, their problem lay in catching us.

All of which meant that after the initial attack, and brief display of blood letting there was usually no more killing, we concentrated on the robbery. Those who survived that first rush could generally count on getting out of it alive: bruised, poorer and possibly violated - but still alive.

Which is why that one particular day stuck in my mind. There was a family group, father, mother, two small girls and four servants. They shouldn't have been travelling unaccompanied, but they were, and that made them fair game. Two of the servants were hacked down immediately, and the other two fled to escape our screaming and sword slashing rush; they ran and kept on running, without a backward glance. The children were too young even for our attentions and clung to their mother's skirts as we emptied their luggage panniers onto the ground. Then in a sudden burst of recognition the father pointed a finger at me

"Jesus Barabbas of Kerioth, I know you, and I knew your donkey shagging father too."

Why do otherwise sensible people say and do such stupid things? His wife eventually managed to shut him up, but it was too late, the words were out. First, one of the two new recruits began to laugh, and then the other. From the man's face he was appalled at his own rush of bravado. It was the sort of remark that would pass without notice if made amongst men at an inn, but this wasn't an inn and the laughter left me with no alternative, I had to maintain discipline.

My sword was still in my hand and I took a short step towards him to plunge it into his belly, stepping forwards after it to maintain the thrust, and stand face to face with him as he sank dying to the ground. The children were silent, but the wife screamed and came for me, her arms flying. I dragged the blade free from his falling dead weight and did the same to her.

My two cousins stood there unmoving during this performance, but as I was striking down the woman, the two new recruits who had done the laughing, raised their own swords over the children, and then looked questioningly at me.

I had an eyeblink of time to decide which way to jump, I could have behaved reasonably and shaken my head, but their laughter had cut through my surface bluster and drawn blood. They had laughed at me and now I needed to show that I was more brutal than them. "Kill them." I said - they hesitated. But if they hadn't been sure then why had they raised their swords over the children in the first place? This way they were loading all the responsibility onto me, without leaving me any choice. "Kill them." I snarled, this time pointing my own still dripping sword at one of the men. The children never moved or made any sound as the blades swept down on them.

A stronger man than me would have laughed at the hot-tempered man and his comments, or simply hit him, instead I had allowed my actions to be decided by someone else's laughter, and that was weakness not strength. None of the others thought there was anything wrong, but I knew that this had been a significant step. I suppose there's no real difference between killing adults and killing children, the Commandments don't make any such difference and anyway I don't take any notice of the Commandments.

Children had been killed at our hand previously, perhaps even at my hand, but that had always been in the confused mayhem of the first attack, as we rushed to impose our control over a group of frightened travellers. I had crossed a significant bridge and it would be difficult to maintain my own view of myself as someone who had been forced into this life by the unreasonable behaviour of others.

"That's what happens to people who cross me." Is what I said to the men, but even as the words left my mouth I was aware that the people who had crossed me had not been the children, but the two new recruits who had laughed at me.

However, in the natural way of things with the succession of passing days the episode of the hot tempered man began to fade; there were more travellers, there was more murder, rape and robbery, we were highwaymen and we did what highwaymen do. My authority was complete and unchallenged, and in time I came to see that my distaste at killing the children had been no more than a passing disturbance, like an upset stomach.

The routine for converting our stolen property into cash was my little secret, in fact it was more than a little secret, it was the key to the whole operation. My dealer was a man called Zachary, and I took great care that none of the others ever knew his name or exactly where to find him, it seemed more likely that I would lead a long and happy life if it stayed that way. I kept half of everything we took and had no intention of anyone getting the idea that with me gone they could split my share. Zachary was a camel trader at Debir, on the same main caravan route that we preyed on, and I knew him from the tent business. He was able to move the stolen goods through a network of friendly drovers and caravan masters. He would warn me which parties to leave alone and in return my property, which had recently been someone else's, was transported sufficiently far from the area to be unrecognised. Then fifteen or twenty days later there would be a purse of money waiting for me, perhaps surprisingly, in the eleven or twelve months of our dealings I never felt that he was cheating me, well, no more than anyone else would.

I remember the rest of that summer as one long sunny afternoon, there was food and wine in plenty, there was money and there was sex. It was the happy time. Just occasionally I would have bad dreams in the night, about two small girls being hacked to death, but they never lasted long and always disappeared with the dawn. Problems like that can be shrugged away.

The Tenth Legion were supposed to keep the main roads clear of bandits, but they were never a serious problem. As far as they were concerned if the towns stayed orderly and no one raised his hand against a Roman official or preached sedition, then nothing else really mattered. They were in Judea to make sure the province stayed quiet, stayed Roman and paid its taxes, internal affairs like highway security were not a high priority. Once every three or four weeks a mounted patrol would undertake a sweep along the road, but they never strayed far off each side, and we made sure we kept our distance. It was like a ritual dance, with the two parties circling each other, but never touching.

Even when the weather closed in for the winter, it was no great problem, we simply set ourselves up in an abandoned shepherd's hut and kept the fire high. The winters in southern Judea, particularly in the hills, can be hard and we even had some snow, but they don't last for long and within a couple of months we had passed the worst of it. To allow for the reduced frequency of travellers, and thus exercise, I made sure we all kept fit by repeated sword and staff drill. We had become hardened fighting men by now and I wanted us to stay that way.

But with the first glimpses of spring came the reckoning, it seems that our success was not just an aggravation to honest travellers, it was also upsetting someone considerably nastier. I can't remember which way the saying works, is it that there is honour among thieves, or that there is no honour among thieves? Well whichever way it is I had grown to depend on my arrangement with Zachary, and was even happy for him to take his cut. I felt that as long as he was making a reasonable living out of me, then my continued wellbeing would be in his interest. Perhaps that was why I'd let my guard drop.

My normal routine was to travel down to see him by mule, leading a second beast with the booty in panniers, always taking care to arrive at his house in the night. Because of his business the house was at the camel stockades, just outside the main part of the town, which meant that people and animals were coming and going at all hours, a perfect cover. I would take two of my men, to stop me being robbed myself, until I was close by and then tell them to wait at the Rashid oasis whilst I completed the journey and did the business. Tonight it went differently.

I tied both my mules to the rail beside the house, a burly watchman was loitering by the door, I hadn't seen him before, but he had to be one of Zachary's men. I nodded to him as I entered, the fact that he took no notice didn't trouble me, I was above seeking the friendship of night watchmen. Zachary gave a start as he saw me, and came rapidly to his feet which was a change from his usual languid air.

"Ah, Jesus," he said, as if surprised at my presence, "come in, come in." As he spoke his eyes flicked briefly behind me, I turned to look and saw that the watchman had followed me in. Vaguely disturbed I turned back to query this, but he was already walking towards the low doorway through to the back storeroom. He beckoned me to follow.

"There is someone important you must meet, come this way. Please come in." He disappeared into the back room. I looked behind me again, the watchman was not only burly he looked hard. He looked about as hard as I'd thought I was - until I saw him, and he was blocking the way out. Not having a lot of choice I followed Zachary into the back room.

There was a small table with an oil lamp on it, the rest of the room retreated into a surrounding darkness. Two men sat facing each other across the table, their faces glowing yellow in the lamp light, resting on the table in front of each man was a curved dagger. With a sudden sick feeling in my stomach, as if I'd just been dropped off a cliff, I knew who they were. Or to be more precise, not who they were, but what they were. I turned to look at Zachary, he must be part of this. But he had vanished, and in his place stood the burly watchman, just an arm's length behind me. The man was so sure of himself that he hadn't even bothered to draw his own dagger, I wasn't a sufficient threat to merit that. Strangely, that fact alone frightened me as much as anything else. Looking back on it, I should have made a run for it, even if that had meant getting stabbed in the process.

The two men tuned to look at me, and one of them spoke.

"Your presence in this countryside is an offense to the Lord, and a hindrance to his work. Judea is the homeland of the Jewish people and there is no room for criminals like you."

"Who are you, are you with the Zealots?" I asked, struggling to keep the fear from my voice.

"My name is Jairus, and my companions and I are those who are zealous in God's service." By which he meant: Yes. Which in turn meant that I had picked the wrong stretch of road for my activities. These people were supposed to be working to end Roman rule, but in practice this usually seemed to involve killing other Jews. The general idea was that they would frighten people into refusing to cooperate with the occupation forces. This had always struck me as a cowardly if sensible way to confront the occupiers, kill the shopkeepers who trade with them, because it's too dangerous to confront them directly. It was just the way I would have done it, but it was hardly the sort of thing I could actually say.

"What do you want with me? I haven't interfered with your work, in fact I support your activities."

"One year ago, Jesus Barabbas, you said that we attacked the tent maker Jacob of Kerioth, didn't you?"

"No, absolutely not, I just said that some armed men had attacked us, I didn't know who they were. It's the Temple guards you should talk to, it was them who blamed the Zealots."

A hand grasped my hair from behind, the burly watchman. He was so close behind me that when he pulled my hair backwards I couldn't step back to go with it, instead my head was pulled back, my chin went

up and his knife blade was stuck into my throat. As the
two men at the table watched he slid the point of his
knife into the side of my throat and slid it down a finger
length.

My hands were shaking from the effort of keeping
my arms at my sides, because I knew that if I tried to
grab the knife he would move it across my throat, rather
than down it. I very much wanted him to stick to
frightening me and not to start killing me. His face was
just behind my right ear, I could smell his breath, I
could hear it and I could feel it. He was breathing
calmly, he wasn't excited, this was just everyday
business for him. As we stood there, pressed together, I
felt a trickle of blood begin to run down my neck and
into my tunic. I was light headed with fear.

One of the men at the table asked me the same
question again. "Who did you say had attacked the tent
maker?"

"I said it was the Zealots." My voice was strained
from the angle of my neck.

"You thought it would be convenient to blame the
servants of God for your own criminality?"

"I'm sorry I meant no harm, but it wasn't my idea.
Family relationships are very important to me and
Jacob was actually killed by my young cousin Nathan,
all I wanted was to protect him. The shame of it would
have killed his mother if she'd known. This whole gang
business was his idea, one of the other members is his
brother - he's completely mad and we're all terrified of
him. Two of them are waiting for me at the Rashid
oasis, they didn't trust me to come on my own, and I
can lead you to the rest of them. You can do what you
like with them - just let me live and I'll be your man. I'll
be so glad to be out of it that I'll do anything you want -
anything."

As I spoke I meant every word, a successful liar always does. Once you've convinced yourself, you're half way there. But it doesn't always work, because the next thing I knew was that I'd been thrown to the floor and the man had stepped forward to kick me. I curled up and tried to cover my head, but after three or four heavy kicks he stepped back.

"Stand up."

I did so, facing the table. There was a long silence as they stared at me, I didn't know what to say and didn't want to stare back at them so I just looked into the darkness beyond them.

"Luckily for you, the work of God requires to be paid for, and for this purpose we have decided to levy a tax on travellers using the Hebron to Beersheba road. You will be our chosen instrument to collect this."

He recited an oath, and I repeated it line by line, swearing on my father's grave, my own soul and the blood of my children that I would be true to my new masters, and obey them until death.

My father's grave I didn't care about, my soul I didn't know about and any children I'd fathered on the idiot girl with the big tits could go to hell - but I recognised the threat of death when I saw it. They meant business and they were powerful enough and far reaching enough to put their threats into action, I should have kept my head down.

When we had finished the oath, the watchman took my right hand and grasping the forefinger jabbed it painfully into the wound in my neck, and then he spoke for the first and only time. "Make your mark on the document."

I scrawled my mark in my own blood where he pointed.

"The goods on your pack mule have been accepted as your first payment, you will return here in two weeks with the same amount, anything more than that you can keep. When you return you will bring your two cousins with you, they will also be required to take the same oath."

I was then led outside, to where a group of some twenty men had gathered. As I stood there, oil lamps were held up to illuminate me and one of the men from the table addressed the group. "This is Jesus Barabbas that I spoke of, remember his face, if he runs it will be your job to track him." After some close scrutiny the group dispersed and I was left in the darkness with just my mules for company.

CHAPTER THREE

In the days following my encounter with the Zealots I thought of running, at first I almost convinced myself that I could do it. But the more I thought about it the more certain I was that it would end in death. The oil lamps that had illuminated me to the Zealots had also illuminated them to me, and they were all in the same category as the burly watchmen, hard professionals, probably mercenaries. I would be easy meat to them, and the rest of my little gang wouldn't be much use, not against that lot.

As it says in the book I would be a lamb to the slaughter, my body thrown into the nearest ditch. Could I go down into Egypt and escape that way? It had worked for Moses. Not a chance, they had obviously been watching me for some time, and the first thing they would do if I tried to run would be to cover the roads.

In the absence of anything more helpful, I increased the frequency of our raids, taking more chances on the size of group that we should attack. The others grumbled but I persuaded them that now we were more experienced it was time for us to stop being so cautious and start to make some serious money. Incredibly, we succeeded. We really were harder than last year, and my desperation must have spread itself to the rest of them. We were hitting fairly large groups of travellers now, even those with professional guards. We had became more ruthless, more merciless, anyone who failed to obey immediately was butchered on the spot. That soon brought the rest of them into line.

As our spoils piled up, so my fear lifted, slowly and not dramatically, the outlook was no longer quite so gloomy. All I had to do now was to let the cousins join me on my next trip to see Zachary, they'd been campaigning to meet him for months.

I waited until I was alone with Nathan, the older of the two, and raised the subject with him. "I think that you and your brother have served your time as juniors, and it's time I trusted you with all the details of our work, we shouldn't have any secrets between us."

He tried to look serious as he nodded his agreement, but you could see how pleased he was. "Would the two of you like to come with me to meet our dealer? It's only fair that you should be fully involved."

"So we'll be on exactly the same level as you?"

"Yes, I just want you to be in the same position as me, would you like that?"

"Thank you Barabbas, that's good of you."

I hoped they stayed that grateful.

It looked as if there was going to be a surplus from the amount we needed to pay the Zealots, not what we were used to, but enough to keep us going for a while. Then we could recruit another one or two gang members, and perhaps I should get the Zealots to swear them all in, that way I wouldn't be the only one in fear of his life.

As I thought about our future I even began to wonder if there was any prospect of me transferring from the front line, the cutting edge, into the senior ranks of the Zealots. They had come to me because they needed the organisation that I had built, and that I had run. Perhaps the blood oath, and the group of men staring into my face was no more than their way to try and hide the fact that they needed me more than I needed them. It certainly made sense. It could be time for me to stop being so frightened, I had something they wanted.

I might have been ignored the last time I tried to make it in Jerusalem, but if I turned up as Jesus Barabbas of the Zealots then the boot would be on the other foot. I could still remember some of the people who had laughed at me as being no more than just another simple country boy, this would change their attitude.

When the day arrived for our next delivery to the camel yard, I carefully rolled our surplus wealth, a mixture of cash and jewellery, into a roll of canvas and hid it under some rocks near the camp. Then carrying just the specified amount, the three of us made our way down to the scruffy little town of Debir. We didn't have enough mules for all of us to ride, and I didn't want to single myself out as the leader, so all of us walked, leading the pack mules behind us. It was amusing to think what a shock they were about to get when the hard faced men with daggers emerged from the shadows, and they were required to make their marks in their own blood.

The camel stockades smelt as rank as usual, and if you ignored the snuffling, grunting and occasional crying like a child noise that camels sometimes make in the night, they were oddly quiet. There were the usual muffled figures lying in small groups round the remnants of fires, but hardly anyone was moving as we approached the house. So much the better, this wasn't the kind of thing we needed an audience for. The same watchman was standing at the door and I tied the pack mule to the rail beside him. There didn't seem to be much to say so I simply led the boys into the house, it felt like leading dumb animals to the slaughterhouse.

This time Zachary was nowhere to be seen, but one of the two men who had been sat at the table last time beckoned us into the back room. I ushered the boys ahead of me and followed them in. As we went through there was a clatter behind us and figures appeared in the front door, I swung round in alarm to see what was happening, as I did the boys cried out and tried to turn back. There was a confused, but very brief struggle, and then it was over.

The men entering the house behind us were legionaries, and the men in the inside room that the boys had tried to run from were more legionaries. We were caught, bound and thrown to the floor, and then we were ignored. Nobody kicked us, beat us or questioned us, once they had secured out feet and hands they lost interest in us.

The group of legionaries who had secured us trooped out into the night and a centurion appeared. He and the two Zealots sat down at the table, one of the Zealots produced a flagon of wine and filled three beakers, then they silently toasted each other and drank.

One of the few things I knew for certain about the people in the room was that Zealots and Romans were sworn enemies, they didn't sit down and drink together and they didn't toast each other. In fact, as far as I was aware, Zealots didn't drink at all. The men at the table were talking Aramaic, which was lucky because at that time I didn't speak much Greek, and so could follow their conversation.

"How many are there in total?" Asked the Centurion.

"There's only another two, and they don't count, when these three don't come back they'll run away. Your people can pick them up in the nearest town, they're escaped slaves so there'll be a reward."

"I wouldn't have thought a bunch of ill fed runts like this could cause so much trouble, even the Prefect was asking questions."

"Does Pilate think we're involved?"

The Centurion sighed. "Of course he does: he sees the hand of the Zealot everywhere. But will that one," he pointed at me, "pass as a leader?"

"He'll pass as anything you want to call him. People will just be glad that you're catching more robbers; we'll put the word out that one of our senior people has been captured, so you can claim maximum credit. Then we'll threaten the usual reprisals, and a couple of prominent citizens will be killed on their way to the Temple, to prove how angry we are."

The Centurion nodded and took another drink. "You lot had better make yourselves scarce, by dawn this is going to have been a purely legionary affair."

But the two Zealots made no move to go, instead the talkative one raised his eyebrows in a question. "I hadn't forgotten." Said the Centurion with a smile, and then pulled out a leather purse which he slid across the table. It was bulging with coins, we were obviously worth something to somebody. Once the purse had been picked up, the three of them stood, that was clearly the end of the matter.

"Expect another message this time next month." Said one of the Zealots, and then with an exchange of clasped hands they were gone. The two boys, lying beside me on the dirt floor, were weeping in despair, they knew where this would lead. They were probably thinking that if only they'd stayed in boring old Kerioth then none of this would have happened. I couldn't think of an argument to that, so I said nothing. Gripped by the sickening certainty of hideous death I was beyond tears and spent the remaining hours till dawn staring numbly into the darkness. All our worst nightmares were about to come true.

With the morning our feet were untied and we were fed and given water. The boys had fouled themselves in the night, at least I had managed to avoid that indignity.

But none of this bothered our guards, they were professionals and we were their prisoners, they had no interest in inflicting any more pain than our situation was already going to produce. Their job was to deliver us to the goalers in Jerusalem in good enough condition to be tortured and crucified, and that was what they were going to do. We were no more than livestock, for now.

We could have made it in two, but because of the slow pace of some recaptured slaves it took us three days to trudge the dusty miles north through Hebron and Bethlehem until we finally sighted Jerusalem, sitting solidly on its hilltop. I had managed to shut out reality and concentrated on the simple act of walking, one foot in front of another, I wished it would go on for ever because of what would happen when it stopped. On the first morning the two boys had been full of accusations about my responsibility. About how they were going to tell the authorities that it was me who'd killed Jacob, and it was me who'd killed Ben Amal and the Temple guards, and it was me who'd organised the highway robbery and murder, and it was me who'd led the rape of the captured women and girls. I almost laughed at them.

"You stupid children, do you seriously think any of that matters? Do you seriously think that anyone cares? You can tell them what you like and it will make no difference - we're all going to die whatever you say."

Our guards took no steps to silence us, they had probably heard all this sort of desperate blame shifting from the last lot of prisoners they took to Jerusalem, and would hear it again from the next lot. Like I said; none of it mattered and they didn't care. In another few days neither they nor anyone else would remember our names or faces.

The roof tops and towers of Jerusalem were an unwelcome sight, this place didn't just represent the power of Rome but an entire society that I had failed to make any impression on. I hated the place and everyone in it. From that final hill we dropped down into the valley of Hinnom and up the last slope to the South Gate. That's one of the things about reaching Jerusalem, you're always going uphill to enter the city, the walls tower over you. This place wants you to know that it's more important than you.

We were marched through the noisy squalor of the Lower City, I'd forgotten how crowded it all was, how noisy and furiously busy. If I hadn't been here before, and if I hadn't got bigger things to worry about, then it might just have frightened me a little. At every gap between the buildings and the trader's awnings I could see the massive square shape of the Temple walls visible ahead of us. The Temple is Jerusalem and Jerusalem is the Temple, the one thing means the other. It's typical of the place that when you actually get there it costs you a fortune. What little money isn't taken from you by the money changers for an unblemished sacrifice, will probably be stolen by the crowds of thieves who inhabit the place like rats. As I said I hate everything about it.

But we weren't bound for the Temple, we marched the full length of its western wall, passing under the bridge of Zion and the other approach ramps from the city. The sun was on our backs, the towering white wall on our right, and there ahead of us one of the towers of our destination, the Antonia Fortress. The main function of the Antonia was as the Legionary barracks, Jerusalem base of the Tenth, but it was also the local residence of the Roman Prefect; the man in whose name I would probably die.

In the fortress courtyard we were surrounded by the daily life of legionary logistics and the Prefect's household, with tradesmen and servants pushing their way past us and round us, shouting and laughing at each other. After being kept waiting for an age, squatting in the sun, our hands were untied and we were led to an anvil near the blacksmith's forge. Shackles were put on our wrists and ankles, the leg irons allowed just enough movement to walk slowly, but any attempt at running would be very short lived. Once that was done the legionaries simply turned and left, they walked casually away, chatting to each other - whether they were going to their barracks or a tavern it didn't involve us.

Then with the accompaniment of lashes from a whip, we were herded down wide stone steps and into the dungeons. All my earlier attempts to shut out reality ended here. Coming in from the sun it was both dark and cold, there was smoke from the rush lamps and the stench was almost solid enough to touch - it was like a cess pit, in fact it probably was a cess pit. The legionaries had been professional soldiers, in other circumstances you could imagine talking to them or drinking with them, but the gaolers were a different breed. A man only takes a job like this because he likes to hurt people, or knows that he can never hold his own amongst decent men. We were kicked and thrown into a cell with a dozen other prisoners and the door slammed behind us. I lost sight of the boys and sank to the ground, my back against the wall. Would they bother with a trial, or would they just take us out and nail us up? How stupid to discover at this stage that I didn't know how these things were done, it had never occurred to me that I would need to know. I looked at the other wretched creatures surrounding me but couldn't face asking them. For some reason this didn't seem like a suitable place to confess my ignorance and anyway they probably knew no more than me.

I think I was there for eight days, it's difficult to be sure in the dark, just long enough to begin to imagine that I'd been forgotten, that I would live out my days manacled and hidden, in some stinking underground corner. But then I was dragged out, dazed and dazzled by the early morning sun, to join a group of other prisoners in the courtyard. My two cousins were there, I hadn't seen them in the dungeon gloom and hadn't felt like searching them out, but there they were, looking starved and filthy - like wild animals dragged from a cave.

One of the gaolers stood facing us, hands on hips. "Listen to me, very carefully. You're going before the Prefect, he's going to judge you and he's going to sentence you. You will speak only if spoken to. You're all in the shit anyway, so don't think you can try any of this appealing to Caesar nonsense, this one won't stand for it. As far as you're concerned he's God and don't you forget it. Just remember that in the days between the sentence being passed and carried out you'll be in my charge, one word out of place and you'll be begging them to crucify you."

Then one of the blacksmiths came forward to remove our shackles and leg irons. They tied our wrists together with leather straps, but there was no possibility of running, there were guards everywhere. The gaoler turned to bark some orders to his men and we were herded forwards, none of us spoke, we just kept our heads down and shuffled hopelessly forward. The men I was with were a mixture of the dejected filthy wretches from my cell and some relatively clean newcomers, but we were all equally subdued. Down in Judea, on my home territory I might have chanced a beating to call out some obscenity or blasphemy to raise a laugh from the others, but not here. All I could think was: what's the point? The outcome wasn't in doubt.

As we were marshalled into the basement of another wing of the building, I thought I'd heard my name mentioned by the two men next to me, but they were talking about another Jesus, some preacher from Galilee who'd fallen foul of the law. I asked them if I'd heard the name properly.

"Did you call the preacher Jesus Barabbas?"

"You can take your pick, he goes by Jesus Barabbas the Son of the Father, or Jesus the Christ, or just the Son of God, you know what these people are like, they want to cover all the angles. Why, d'you know him?"

"No it's just that Jesus Barabbas is my name as well. I wondered what he'd done to end up in jail. Country preachers aren't much of a threat to anyone."

The man gave a brief laugh. "This one took his various names a step too far, I heard they caught him going round calling himself the King of the Jews, and saying that we shouldn't pay taxes to Caesar."

I shook my head. "Can't see much profit in that - unless he was telling people to pay the taxes to himself."

"No, apparently he's one of these desert types, not interested in money or stuff, he caused a major riot in the Temple the other day, trying to close down the money changers."

Having sorted out the mystery of the name I'd lost interest in passing holy men, and wanted to know more about today. "What's the Prefect like, is there any chance of mercy?

The man turned his head to look at me, a surprised expression on his face. "His name's Pilate and he's a bastard, a Roman bastard, and they're the worst sort. Maybe the King of the Jews can help you - because nobody else will."

We had arrived in a basement, presumably below the judgement area. Immediately the first group of three men were led up the stairs, their unwillingness to be judged, together with their poor physical state, making for slow progress. Within minutes they came down again, despair across their faces. Then it was another two men, with the same result, and then it was our turn. I was pointed at and told to come forward, and the two cousins dragged out to join me. We made our way up the stairs, neither looking at, nor speaking to each other.

We were brought out into another open courtyard, but its arrangement was such that it might as well have been a large chamber. There was a raised dais forming one end of the judgement area, to one side of it was a long table covered in a blue cloth, scribes sat there looking busy with documents. In the centre of the dais sat a bored looking man in a gleaming white toga, alone on the judgement seat - no table in front of him, just the outspread human throng milling below him. From his expression he didn't look pleased to be sat outside in the thin cold air of dawn, when he could have still been in bed. I assumed the outdoor location was because the priests would be ritually unclean and unable to eat the Passover meal if they had entered a Gentile building at this time. Having to defer to a Jewish practice in this way could have been an additional reason for a high born Roman to be unhappy. Behind his chair stood a sharp faced assistant or secretary of some kind, staring down at a solitary prisoner in the centre of the courtyard.

The prisoner, who hadn't been with us in the basement, was still being judged as we arrived and we had to wait at the back. He was standing in a cleared space in front of the judge. Crowds of people formed rough edges to the space, some standing and quietly talking together, others sat at trestle tables with documents strewn untidily before them.

The prisoner, a thin man in a torn and bloodstained robe, was standing in the middle of the cleared space facing the dais, a symbolic rope noose was hanging round his neck. Near him stood a harassed looking rabbi. You could tell the rabbi was quite senior because he was wearing a phylactery, the prayer box, on his forehead and another on his arm; where I came from most rabbis didn't bother.

"Are you trying to tell me that you can't produce a single witness to support your charges?" The man that I presumed to be Pilate was addressing the rabbi, and was in no mood to respect his position, whatever that was.

"One moment if you please sir." The rabbi was trying to retain his dignity in public, but it looked like hard work. He scurried across to one of the side tables and had a head to head discussion with the clerk sitting there. Then he came back to stand near the prisoner, not next to him that would be undignified, just near him.

"I'm sorry to say sir, but . . ."

"What - speak up, I can't hear you."

"I'm sorry to say sir, but we are unable to produce the witnesses at the moment, however you do have their sworn statements before you."

Pilate waved a document, unimpressed. "This is useless - worse than useless, Roman law is most precise on this point, it requires the witnesses to appear in person except in the case of a properly notarised dying confession. Are you trying to tell me that all your witnesses are dead - is that what you're saying?" You could see a dangerous mixture of boredom, tiredness and irritability in his every action. He had a long hot day ahead of him, and already he'd had enough. This was not a man likely to be interested in prisoner's pleadings.

"No sir, but in such an important case as this, where public order is at risk, and claims have been made against the legitimacy of the civil power, the Sanhedrin have instructed me to humbly request your cooperation."

Pilate turned his head to one side as an indication for his assistant, standing behind the chair, to make some comment. The man leaned forward and whispered in Pilate's ear. Pilate nodded, and then they both glared at the Rabbi. From the looks of them they knew that the word 'humbly' was a lie, but at least he'd been asked in the right way. With a sigh he acceded.

"Very well, in response to your humble request, and despite the absence of witnesses I shall pursue the case." He shifted his glare to one side, to focus on the prisoner.

"You, what have you got to say for yourself?"

There was no reply, even though the prisoner was looking directly at Pilate, he said nothing. That took some nerve. A guard stepped forward, his staff ready to prod the man, but Pilate waved him back. Something about the man had caught his interest.

"You should understand that I have the power of life and death, so tell me what have you got to say for yourself?"

There was still no reply, and by now the exchange, or lack of it, had the attention of the whole room. Although I could only see the side of the man's face it was as if he had smiled at Pilate's mention of the power of life and death. That really did take nerve. Pilate sat back in his seat, apparently puzzled, still staring at the man.

"Very well, I'm a busy man so we shall make this short. The Sanhedrin have charged you with various counts of blasphemy, none of which concern Rome, or me. You are here to answer a charge of sedition. These documents," he waved them about, "quote you as claiming to be the King of the Jews, and that is a capital offence. Did you say that?"

Again there was no answer, but by this time he had taken Pilate past the point of interest, this time Pilate was annoyed.

"Are you the King of the Jews?" He shouted.

"You say so." At last the man had spoken, a calm steady and unafraid voice, but that was all he said, no denial or argument, just 'You say so'.

"Jesus of Galilee you are convicted from your own mouth of sedition. Sentence flogging and crucifixion. Take him away."

Then it was our turn and we were led forward to stand where the preacher had been. A clerk came to stand next to us, he held a scroll up in front of himself and, facing the dais, read out the charges against us.

"Jesus Barabbas of Kerioth is a senior commander of . . ."

"What did you call him?"

"Jesus Barabbas, sir."

"That was the last man's name, wasn't it, or are these documents wrong again?"

"No sir, both men share the same name, which is why I referred to this one as coming from Kerioth - the last one came from Galilee." Pilate shook his head at the stupidity of it all, but waved the man to continue.

"Jesus Barabbas of Kerioth is a senior commander of the Zealots in southern Judea. In this position, he has been directly responsible for attacks on several tax collectors and two Roman magistrates. He controls over two hundred armed and desperate men who have conducted a reign of terror across the countryside for the last five years. His capture, and the killing of most of his men, represents a major triumph of Roman will in a particularly lawless area. I understand that word has already been sent to Rome giving news of this success."

Pilate nodded. "Good, very good, and the witnesses - they're not dead as well are they?" A small ripple of polite laughter greeted this comment.

"Certainly not sir, all *our* witnesses are here in court your Excellency."

"Very well, then you'd better start to call them."

Until this point Pilate had never so much as looked at me, and having made his joke about the witnesses he looked about distractedly, vaguely wondering if there was anything that might be worth his attention. The whole spectacle was unreal, it was a performance between the Prefect and the court officials, entirely for their own benefit. I was already a dead man and everyone in the room knew it, so having worked out that it was all a complete waste of time, I did what I had been told not to, and spoke out.

"Excuse me sir, but you don't need the witnesses, we did it."

My two cousins turned to me and started to shout something, but I didn't care and the attendants soon shut them up.

"You did what?" Pilate had finally looked directly at me.

"Whatever it is they say sir."

"You admit to all the charges against you?"

"Yes sir."

Once again Pilate turned his head slightly to one side, inviting comment from his assistant. This was duly given, and then they both shrugged. I was clearly simple minded but at least it reduced the time they were going to have spend out here.

He looked at the two boys. "And you two, do you admit it too?"

They didn't know what to say, but after a long and baffled pause, they both eventually accepted the futility of it all and simply said, "Yes sir."

The sentence on us was the same as it had been for the preacher: flogging and crucifixion. Then with no further delay we were on our way out. And that was it, the sum total of my earthly existence, I had managed to reach the magnificent age of twenty five, before being sentenced to a very nasty death. What an achievement, and I wasn't even leaving a wife or family to mourn me.

CHAPTER FOUR

As we came down to the lower level they had the preacher, my namesake, tied to a pillar and were flogging him. We had to stand and watch until it was our turn, the two boys screamed their heads off but I was so numb from the whole process that I hardly felt a thing.

It was at this time still early, no more than the third hour, and we had already been tried, convicted, sentenced and flogged. What I hadn't known was that the whole process was being rushed through to allow for the immediate crucifixion of the four of us, that same day. I had thought they would keep us prisoner over the Sabbath, but no, this was it, they were getting ready to take us out immediately. There are always lots of strangers and country people in Jerusalem for the Passover, the Romans wanted our writhing agonised bodies on public display to act as a warning. Stay calm and keep the peace - this is what happens to troublemakers.

Jesus the preacher, the two boys and myself were kept to one side as the other prisoners went back to the cells, they were being kept until next week. They were going to walk us through the streets, carrying or dragging the parts of our own crosses, so that everyone could see us and know where we were going and why. The Jews execute people by stoning them to death, and that's all there is to it, no matter how slowly it goes it can't last for more than quarter of an hour. But the Romans want to extract the maximum publicity from each death, hence the procession through the city centre, with the jeering and the name calling; then the

47

crucifixion itself which can sometimes take two or three days to kill a man.

As we were stood there, penned against a wall by the guards, waiting to be called; it came to me. I almost laughed at how obvious it all was. I had given the order to kill those two children by the roadside, simply to demonstrate my control over my own men. I had been laughed at, and the easiest way to reassert my control had been to kill the children, and now here I was waiting to be crucified. Even a blind man could see the connection.

I rested my head back against the cold stone wall behind me, at least I knew why I was going to die. The dead children had been in my nightmares, not all the time, just often enough to let me know that they hadn't left me. And now they were waiting for me, somewhere in the coming darkness they were waiting for me, I shivered. Knowing this didn't make me feel any better, in fact it felt much worse, but it did make an awful kind of sense.

Two soldiers came to our group, one of them was carrying something which he placed on the preacher's head. It was a twisted circle of thorn branches, with the spikes pointing in all directions. With some degree of care it was adjusted to sit square on the head, but even handling it with care the soldier winced as he pricked himself. The preacher endured in silence, even though fresh trickles of blood began to run down his brow and cheeks. The two men stood back to admire their work, smiling at the effect. "Hail, King of the Jews." Said one sarcastically, bowing down in front of him, and then turned to call over some of his colleagues to see the joke. It's the sort of thing that soldiers do; coarse, brutal and not particularly funny - but that's soldiers for you. The man himself was unmoved, not resigned to his fate like me, but genuinely unmoved; it was as if he were a willing participant.

Then, from somewhere outside the basement, there came the sound of a crowd roaring and cheering. The preacher was lost in his own thoughts and pain, his lips moving slightly in some internal dialogue or prayer, the other three of us looked at each other baffled; we couldn't make out any details, just the sound of a mob giving voice to some emotion. Shortly after that a harassed looking centurion came down the steps, he looked around the poorly lit area until he saw us, then he came over.

"Jesus Barabbas." He demanded. For some reason it didn't sound like the expected summons to my death, and yet I still hesitated. No possible good could come of anything in this place. As I hesitated, Jesus the Preacher took a step towards me, holding out his bound hands until they rested on my arm.

"You have been given time to find repentance, now go in peace." It's just the sort of meaningless rubbish that preachers are always coming out with, but as he said it, his brown eyes were looking straight into mine and I was gripped by the foolish thought that he meant it. Strangely, for a while, nothing else around me was visible - just him. Even more strangely, for a moment the twisted circlet of thorns actually looked like a crown.

There's no accounting for it - the way exhaustion can take you. In the last two weeks I had been betrayed by my friends, imprisoned by the Romans, condemned to a lingering death by Pilate and now flogged until the blood ran down my back. Waiting to be crucified must be about as low as a man can get, yet as the preacher touched me, a glow of warmth flowed through my body. It was as if the sunshine had suddenly penetrated through the stones and into this basement. Not eating or sleeping properly for this length of time had all been too much. One kind word from a stranger and I nearly fall over.

He turned to the boys and spoke quietly. "Have strength, for today you will see glory." As I watched they were changed in some way, where they had been cringing they were now standing upright, and he hadn't even touched them.

The Centurion grasped my shoulder. "Are you Jesus Barabbas?"

Still unable to speak, I simply nodded, not even turning my head towards him. My attention was still on Jesus the Preacher. The Centurion spun me round so that I was facing him and then using his short sword, cut through my wrist straps. Then he pushed me away to one side. "Get out of here - disappear."

I took a step backwards not understanding what he meant. More soldiers had followed him down the steps, and they surrounded the three remaining condemned men, their spears were held pointing forwards, ready for any last minute resistance. The Centurion gave me a final push to one side and then turned his attention to the execution party.

"Move them forwards, at the double." There was a moment's hesitation. "I said move them forward - NOW." He bellowed, and the whole group of them started towards the steps leading up to ground level. I was still standing, dumbstruck and incapable of movement. As the group disappeared from view I found myself alone, still unable to understand what had just happened.

I looked around, two clerks came through a doorway, walking in my direction, I waited for them to give me an order, but they were unconcerned by my presence and simply walked past me, not caring, not interested. I still stood there. Eventually someone else, perhaps more senior then the first two, came into the basement. He stopped when he saw me, his face expressing annoyance. "What are you doing here, looking for something to steal? You've no business down here, get out. Go on with you, get out." He stood watching me, his hands on his hips, as I made my confused way back up to the courtyard and the sunshine. A few minutes later I found myself somehow back on the street, just another citizen in a mob of other citizens, with nothing but the blood on my back to show that I was in any way remarkable.

I had been lined up for execution, but then mysteriously released, that was astonishing in itself, that isn't how the Romans work. Yet there was something even more astonishing than that. Jesus the Preacher had looked at me and seen me in some way that other men couldn't. Did he know; could he have any idea of the sheer quantity and nature of my sins? There is nothing forbidden by the Law that I have not done, and done regularly. But these things aren't written on a man's face, are they? He couldn't possibly have known, and yet when he looked at me, in some way - *he had known.* And then, when he spoke to me and said those words about being given time to find repentance, how could he have known that would mean anything to me? How could he have known that I would even care. The Centurion who released me must have been mad, and now it seems, so was I.

CHAPTER FIVE

Unable to think why I'd been released and not knowing what I should do or where I should go, I walked as you might expect a dead man to walk - aimlessly. After a while, driven by thirst, I spent some time sitting by a well in one of the courtyards near the Old Wall. I couldn't remember the last time I'd had any sort of a drink and the simple well water tasted delicious and made me light headed, as though I were drinking wine. It had also been a long time since I'd eaten, but that didn't seem so important, and I certainly wasn't hungry. In the bustle of the city nobody looks at the odd stranger, the loner, everyone is far too busy looking out for their own interests. If the thieves decide you have nothing to steal and the merchants that you aren't going to buy anything - you just disappear and life makes its way around you, without including you in its calculations.

With my ragged appearance and torn and bloodstained clothing I must have looked like what I was, a man who had just escaped from jail. Some woman came up to me and asked if I needed any help, I told her to mind her own business, but she persisted - so I told her to go to hell.

However, after some hours of being carefully avoided by both the honest and the dishonest citizens I realised that I couldn't sit by the well for the rest of the day, I knew that before it was too late there was something I had to do. It felt strange to acknowledge a duty, because duty wasn't something that I gave much thought to in the average day. Yet still it had to be done.

I asked a shopkeeper where the crucifixions were held.

"The Hill of Skulls, outside the Damascus Gate." Was the short reply, accompanied by a casual nod of the head, to indicate the general direction I should take. So I took it, slowly and unwillingly.

Since that day people have often asked me how it felt to be on the point of death and then suddenly released, and I never know how to answer them honestly, so I usually lie: giving them the sort of answer they expect. In fact I don't think that I had any feelings, or perhaps I had so many feelings that none could stand out. I was like a man recovering from a great blow to the head: What am I? Where am I? Who am I? and even on that day; Why am I?

There wasn't a big crowd, executions are such a routine event around this city, even when I'd lived here I had never gone out of my way to watch them. The three crosses were on a small rise overlooking the main road near the Damascus Gate. The bodies were hanging, not yet limp, still vaguely struggling and gasping for air, as their outstretched arms pulled their chests too tight to breathe. There were a few soldiers on guard duty standing a little way off, from their slouched posture they were bored, and expected to carry on being bored. There was nobody in the crowd mocking or throwing things, which sometimes happens, so there was no need for them to keep order - they just had to be there.

I had expected some of the Preacher's followers to be present, it could have been interesting to ask them something about the man, but nobody nearby seemed to fit such a description. Until I saw someone I recognised, someone from Kerioth. It was Judas the son of Simon, he was several years older than me but I'd known his younger brother and had no trouble in recognising him. I went up and introduced myself, thinking he might be good for some money.

He seemed to be even more shocked by the day's events than me, and for a moment had trouble remembering who I was, but then collected his thoughts and acknowledged me as his one time compatriot.

"I'm sorry but nobody here calls me the son of Simon any more, I am always known as Judas of Kerioth."

"I heard that you'd become a priest." He was still distracted by the sight of the crucifixion, and kept turning to look at it, but my question roused him to a response.

"A priest? Yes for what it's worth I'm holy man, a sanctified man, a priest." He sounded disgusted by the idea and was talking to himself than to me, I was doing no more than bringing his thoughts to the surface.

"Why are you here, did you know this Jesus - the Preacher?"

He swung round to face me directly, he looked so wild I thought he was going to hit me. For a moment he struggled to find the words, and I took half a step backwards. He grasped my arm and pointed to the central one of the three men on the crosses. "That man is the Messiah, the one the prophets spoke of - come to save his people Israel."

Despite having been drawn to this place I had been reluctant to look too closely at the hanging figures, it was still unbelievable that I wasn't one of them. But now I followed his outstretched arm and stared at them openly, no longer caring if anyone associated me with them. Even after just two or three hours my cousins were all but unrecognisable, their bodies twisted from the pain, their heads slumped downwards. The central figure, Jesus the preacher, looked equally forlorn but over his head was fastened a rough notice, which I was able to make out said 'the King of the Jews'. Even a country boy like me knew that this was Pilate's gesture of contempt: not for the man himself, but for all Jews. If this is what we think of your King - imagine what we think of you.

Judas still held my arm, as if he needed someone to listen to him. "I was the only one he could trust to do it properly, to keep his nerve. That's why I was chosen out of all the twelve - that's why I stayed faithful while the rest of them scattered like chaff in the wind."

He was speaking urgently and insistently, he wanted to convince himself as much as me, if not more so; whereas I just wanted him to let go of my arm.

"Where are they now, where have they gone?"

"Where are *who*, Judas?"

"The rest of the twelve, the other disciples - where are they now?" He stared wildly around us at the small and straggling crowd.

"I don't know. Perhaps if the Romans wanted their leader dead they would feel the same about his friends. Two of those men up there are my followers, you could call them my disciples, and they still got nailed up."

"No, you don't understand - it was written that one of us would betray him, and he knew that I was the only one who could be trusted to fulfil the prophecy. That was why it was always me that was first among the twelve." He clearly needed to get this out of his system, and with his friend dying before his eyes I suppose I could understand that, so I went along with it.

"Are you telling me that you betrayed him in some way to the Romans?"

"No, not the Romans. they don't matter."

"Believe me Judas - those are Roman nails."

"That's not the point, I betrayed him to the priests, to his own people. This is their doing, in fact this is my doing."

I shivered, the sky had darkened above us, the sun had gone, and I was cold and exhausted. There was a storm coming. Still clutching at my arm Judas looked up at the mounting black clouds, he looked like a man running out of time. Then he stared hard at me.

"First must come the betrayal and then he will reveal himself in glory and save his people; but one of us had to help him." There was a sudden crack and a peal of thunder, I was startled but he continued. "I'm his helper, the one he can rely on, I'm his witness."

"Judas, he doesn't need anyone to be his witness, he's dying - just like my friends. And when you're dead, you're dead, that's all there is. Never mind what the Pharisees say - in a few hours their bodies will be thrown to the dogs. There is no more truth than that."

It was now even darker and the next peal of thunder shook us both. Cold flickers of rain were blowing against the side of my face. Judas's face was also wet but in his case I think it was more from the tears he was crying. He turned to stand directly in front of me, this time grasping both my arms.

"No, you're wrong. He will come again in glory, he will lead his people to glory and I will be there." His eyes were wide, his voice desperate, the man was beside himself. Someone or something had helped me today and for once in my life I felt an unfamiliar need to return the favour; to help straighten out Judas's disordered thoughts.

"Judas, it's not me that doesn't understand - it's you. The rule is that rats leave a sinking ship - they don't climb back onboard. That's why none of your friends are here. Whatever you had with this man is over, it dies with him, it's finished."

I found that I'd been shouting and people had turned to look at us. I couldn't pay them any attention, it was all too late. I was now swaying, I'd run my course and was close to collapse, it was only his madman's grip that held me upright. Then there were some women standing beside us, they took hold of us both, to calm him and support me. I was shivering violently, uncontrollably, one of the women put a cloak around my shoulders which helped. Unknown hands led me away, I think the women stayed at the hill but I followed my helpers back into the city. The last thing I heard as I was led away was Judas shouting through his tears: "But it was never supposed to end like this."

I was taken to a house where the wounds on my back were dressed and I was given food and drink. I must have lain down and slept then, because that's all I can remember.

*****

The next morning I awoke to find myself in the house of a young man who was called in full John Mark, but more simply Mark by his friends. He shared a house with his mother, Mary, and both were clearly disciples of Jesus; though whether Mark was one of the twelve that Judas had spoken of I didn't know. Despite the salve on my back, the wounds were throbbing and my head was aching, from the way I felt it was a miracle that I had managed to walk anywhere yesterday. Mary was a widow and said little, leaving most of the conversation to Mark, who turned out to be a plain and direct young man. Even when he discovered my background and the fact that I had been released instead of his master he still allowed me to stay under their roof and share their food.

The notion of kindness to a stranger, without visible profit, might be well known to orthodox Judaism but it was completely unknown to me and I wondered where the catch might lie. Partly because of my foul mood and partly to test his patience I explained the full circumstances of my previous life to him, in great and blood stained detail. He listened to me with politeness and even sympathy, rather than the expected shock and disgust. I even told him of my readiness to sell out my two young cousins to the Zealots to save my own life, a plan only thwarted by the Zealot's complete lack of interest in anything I had to say. This still failed to move him to outrage, and I began to wonder if anything ever would.

"Do you repent of your early life?" Was his only question, it surprised me I and considered the point.

"Not really, my one time master, Jacob, left me little choice in the matter. It was his stubbornness and his refusal to pay me my dues that forced my hand."

"And you still believe that you had no choice, but to kill him?"

"I didn't plan to kill him, and I didn't want to, but he caused the situation where it happened. He made me do it" His bland suggestion that I was somehow to blame for Jacob's stupidity was beginning to annoy me, as was his permanently understanding manner. But I was penniless and a long way from home, a home to which I could never return, so it seemed sensible to keep my mouth shut.

"I can see from your face that you dislike my questions but don't like to say so for fear of losing the roof over your head." He shook his head in sad disbelief as he saw my face begin to frame a denial, and it didn't seem worth pursuing that particular point. Despite that I found myself unable to let the matter rest.

"I've already been judged by Pilate, is your life so perfect that you wish to judge me a second time?" His face dropped, by lucky chance I'd hit an exposed nerve, it was as if I'd stabbed him with a dagger.

"No, my life is nowhere near perfect - I'm as deep in sin as you. Only two days ago in the garden at Gethsemane when they came to arrest my own master, I deserted him and ran to save my life. So don't worry, I won't throw you out, if nothing else I think that in your own way you've been honest with me, and that's always a good start."

He didn't make it clear exactly what it was a good start *to*, and I didn't ask. He then left me to my thoughts and my sore back as he and the two other men living with him discussed the death of their master, they were confused by this disaster and struggling to make sense of the events. From the sound of them, they were even more frightened than me. And more than just fear - there was shame mixed in with it, but for what cause I couldn't tell. By noon another seven or eight of them had arrived, and this lot certainly acted as though they were part of the inner group that Judas had spoken of.

They were a very mixed group of men, from rough fishermen to middle ranking officials and one was even a doctor, but none of them wore the air of big city sophistication that Judas carried. I didn't think this just because I knew him slightly and we shared a home town, I thought it because it was true: he was educated - he was a priest. Most of this bunch were a clear step down from that.

Yesterday, at the crucifixion, Judas had been panicked and wild, but then I knew just how he felt - it had been a very narrow escape for me as well. That sort of thing can upset a man. Even so, looking round at this group I didn't have much doubt that if Judas turned up he was going to be the dominant character in the room. When he'd told me that he was Jesus' senior disciple it made perfect sense.

Owing to the fact that the house had only two rooms at ground level and a single room on the roof, there was nowhere else for me to go. I could scarcely go wandering the city streets on the Sabbath, in my condition I would have been picked up in no time and was pretty sure that this lot didn't want me blabbing to the authorities about the location of the preacher's disciples. There had been various surprised looks and raised eyebrows when my own identity was revealed to the new arrivals, and I had the impression that my presence was straining their notion of hospitality to its limit. It was generally agreed that more suitable accommodation would be found for me tomorrow, which would, as they phrased it, help me to stand on my own feet.

For today, however, it remained the case that any discussions they had were necessarily in front of me. I just wished they'd been talking about something more interesting. As it was they mainly kept on and on about 'How could this be? How could our Lord leave us like this?' Then for a change they would worry about whether the Temple authorities would be looking for them. There were times when I felt like joining in, somebody needed to bang their heads together.

It being the Sabbath we ate some cold salt fish and olives with pieces of yesterday's bread for the midday meal, and the conversation continued to meander pointlessly this way and that. Despite the day, no one made any mention of visiting the synagogue, which seemed strange for such religious people, perhaps they were frightened to show themselves. However, their basic problem wasn't simply that they were scared, that I could understand, but that they were leaderless. If one of their number had stepped forward and taken control, had said 'What we need to do is *this*.' they would all have followed and been grateful for it. As it was, different voices spoke uncertainly. One of the other men living with Mark, Thomas, suggested that they should all go back to Galilee, where most of their preaching had been done and they had most supporters. The third member of Mark's household, Matthew, suggested waiting for a few days to see what happened, and Mark said they should do nothing until they had talked things over with the women. "Remember," he said, "that nothing we've done so far has been accomplished without their presence, and this would be the worst possible time to split our group. In fact it would be helpful to have their counsel today of all days."

There was a general murmur of agreement at this, but then one called James broke in. "He chose to call us, to act as his disciples, whoever else our Lord sought comfort and counsel from was for him alone. Above all we must never forget that we are Jews, any success we might ever achieve will be within the Rabbinical tradition. Our Lord said that he came to uphold the law - not to overturn it. Today is the Sabbath, and the worship and prayers of men and women should be offered separately."

This was greeted with silence, not the silence of assent, more the baffled silence of people who didn't wish to agree with him but didn't know where to start the argument. James struck me as a man filled with his own self importance, I could never have imagined him taking a murderer into his house. And as for the worship and prayer, there hadn't been a lot of either visible today, they were a lot closer to panic than that.

What this bunch seemed unwilling to face was that humanity was flawed, from top to bottom, and that included them. One of my great strengths is to know that I'm morally worthless - you should expect nothing from me, and then you won't be surprised when that's what you get. James seemed to think that he was different, but I'd heard him speak and knew that he was more like me than he could ever admit. Most people are, it's just the way of things.

Mark was unwilling to allow the moment to pass without his own comment. "Today is indeed the Sabbath and we shall respect that, as always, however, tomorrow will no longer be the Sabbath and then we shall respect our Lord's instruction as to who shall take up his work." Partly because of his hospitality and partly because he was the only one to stand up to James' pomposity I found myself drawn to Mark

There was a power struggle brewing, with various disciples positioning themselves, or some favoured colleague, to take over from the executed preacher. James and Mark were obviously in different camps, but I still didn't know who their preferred candidates were, only that it seemed to involve the women. This was turning into the most interesting part of the day, and with luck might even turn into a fight.

But then the one called Simon Peter, who some called simply Peter, took a hand. He wanted to close down the growing argument and so did exactly what I would have done, he changed the rules of the game. He found an outside enemy and pointed them in that direction, and in doing so, effectively put them all on his side.

"As our brother James reminded us, some of us here are the Lord's disciples, but there are now only eleven, there is no twelfth. I will never break bread with a traitor." Nobody else spoke, they all just looked at him, it was as if they'd all been wondering which way this particular cat was going to jump. If Judas had been here he could have spoken for himself, he could have explained his behaviour in the way he had started to do with me yesterday. But he wasn't here and that left the floor open to Peter. It was too good an opportunity to miss.

"Judas took a purse of silver from the Council and he betrayed our Lord, God's judgment will be on him."

Another voice, from a man whose name I had yet to learn, responded. "The Lord knew of the arrangement and did nothing to prevent it. He even spoke of it in the upper room and pointed to Judas. What happened was no more than a fulfilment of the Prophets."

"Whatever the Prophets might have written, no man could do as he did unless there was evil in him."

Yet another voice. "Surely our Lord needed someone to perform this function? One of us had to do it."

"It was an unclean function carried out by an unclean soul. Would you welcome the man who drove the nails through his hands and feet? And yet that was also foretold by the Prophets."

There was an amount of unhappy foot shuffling, no one was quite sure how to deal with such a persuasive point. And in the end no one did; a final voice ended the discussion. "It's not in our power to forgive such a betrayal, the judgment will be God's."

That did it, there was a subdued but unmistakeable murmur of agreement, they had damned Judas by passing the responsibility on to a higher level and Peter had won the point. It's a good ploy if you can do it, I used it myself with my little band, find an outside enemy who's uglier and nastier than you and then direct everyone's attention to that. If you've got the skill, most mobs can be led by the nose. And this lot fulfilled my definition of a mob; restive, scared and leaderless.

That was their only decisive moment, and they soon returned to their original worry, would they all end up on the Hill of Skulls themselves - were the authorities planning to round them up - should they flee for their lives? It struck me as unlikely, with their leader dead they weren't important enough to bother with, but as nobody asked for my opinion I didn't bother giving it.

Other than Mark's admission to me that he deserted his master when they came to arrest him, none of the others mentioned exactly where they had been during the actual crucifixion. I knew they hadn't been at the Hill of Skulls because I'd been there myself. The only ones of the preacher's followers to show themselves had been a distraught Judas and the group of women who'd helped me, the very people they were all now agreed they could do without. Judas might or might not deserve their condemnation, I had no idea, but he had at least turned up to say that it had all gone wrong. 'It was never supposed to end like this', had been his plaintive cry.

Throughout the afternoon a few more of their frightened and puzzled friends arrived at the house, but to no great effect, and there was no sign of the women, whoever they were. By sunset I had heard all the agonised talking I could cope with and was more than ready to crawl into a corner, wrap myself in a blanket and close my eyes. And so, not having anything better to do, I did just that.

CHAPTER SIX

The first day of the week had to be an improvement on what had gone before, almost anything would be. As the first streaks of yellow and red were showing themselves in the sky above the Temple I made myself useful by coaxing the fire back into life for Mary to bake our morning bread, and then took a pitcher to the well for her. Having lived by my own wits in the desert I had no problems with performing women's work. Life as a bandit might involve dirty work, but whatever the work is - everyone has to do it; and despite the unfolding drama all around me life's daily routine needed to be maintained. But even while we, the five of us who were staying at the house, were finishing our breakfast, there was an urgent arrival.

As the householder it was Mark who greeted our visitor, a patrician Jewish lady called Joanna. From her manner and accent, rather than her plain dress, she was a woman accustomed to wealth and servants, and yet she had a directness of approach which made her less formidable than such women so often are.

She and Mark were old friends and she greeted both him and his mother with a warm embrace. I think he was trying to ask her something polite about how she was, but she was too excited and had something much more important to say.

"The three Marys and I went to the tomb this morning, with spices for his body, but he was gone."

"Gone? How d'you mean gone?"

Joanna, still out of breath from running, took a moment to answer. "The stone had been rolled back from the tomb and there were two angels, dressed in shining white; they told us that he was no longer there - that he had risen. All that was left in the tomb were the linen wrappings."

"He is risen?" Mark was not just astonished, he was ecstatic, but Joanna hadn't finished. She clutched at Mark, almost shaking him in her excitement. "I saw him, all of us saw him. He appeared to us in the garden, and spoke to us." I might as well have been in another country, they had eyes only for each other.

"He greeted us and told us not to be afraid, but said that we should tell the brethren to go to Galilee, and that we would all see him there, as he promised." The two of them were holding on to each other now and practically dancing with excitement. "He is risen, he is risen." They kept on shouting and by now, Thomas and Matthew had come down from the upper room and joined in.

I stood to one side, watching this astonishing performance, unwilling to believe the evidence of my ears about what exactly was meant by 'risen'. Meanwhile they were frantically rushing through all sorts of subsidiary questions about the angels and about who rolled the massive entrance stone aside. None of it made sense, there must be some part of the story with which I was unfamiliar. When the first excitement had calmed slightly, Joanna turned to me, perhaps sorry to see me excluded from the general rejoicing.

"Jesus Barabbas, I'm pleased to see you again, we saw you in our sadness at the Hill of Skulls, and now you are here to witness our joy. Are you recovered from your own ordeal?"

I thought this was very polite of her, my ordeal, as she called it, hardly matched that undergone by almost everyone else involved on that day. But then that's one of the marks of the upper classes, they always remember to ask after the underling's children or their goats or their club foot - or whatever. It's a type of behaviour bred into them from childhood.

It gradually became unavoidable that the phrase so constantly used; 'He is risen', referred to the fact that they believed their master had in fact risen from the dead, and was now wandering the earth alive and well. This was what I had thought and hoped that I was mistaken, if only for their own sanity. But there was no doubt about it, I had listened carefully and that was precisely what they believed.

It must be obvious that I have never been a religious man, quite the opposite, I'm a blasphemer and sinner of the blackest hue - but that doesn't mean that I despise religious people. I just know that I'm not one of them. Their willingness to follow the law and move in predictable ways has always made my own life so much easier, it has never been in my interest to mock them. I look upon religious people as a shepherd looks upon his sheep, simple trusting creatures that exist to provide his livelihood, and be slaughtered in due time.

Yet this belief; that because someone had moved a dead body from where they thought they'd left it, must mean that the body had got up and started to walk around was astonishing, even from a religious point of view. What they thought the Temple priests would make of this I couldn't imagine. Nonetheless, despite wanting to tell them not to be so gullible I managed to keep my peace: though I did feel like mentioning that the resurrected leader's first questions to his disciples would probably be: Where were you while I was being executed? Where were you when I needed you?

One further inconsequential thought was that this should sort out any discussion over which of them was to be the next leader, if they'd just got their old one back, then perhaps they didn't need a new one.

Apparently another of the women had gone to break the news to the remaining disciples, while Mark, Matthew and Thomas had rushed off to look at the empty tomb for themselves. Which left me, as the unwanted outsider, with the woman Joanna. Despite the fact that I am only ever violent in pursuit of personal gain, and occasionally for fun, most women, and quite a few men would have been visibly nervous to be left alone with me in this fashion. Joanna wasn't one of them, she met my eye with perfect confidence and treated me as almost her equal. Even the small extent to which she did look down on me was, I suspect, caused more by the fact that I was a man than the slightly less common occurrence that I was a thief and murderer. If the men in this group were strange - the women were even stranger.

Saying that she didn't wish to leave me alone, she took me with her to, as she put it, meet the three Marys.

"Three more Marys, as well as Mark's mother Mary - how many are there?"

"Probably lots," she laughed, "but the three I visited the tomb with are central to our movement, and they'll be pleased to welcome you to their home until you can make your way back to your own people."

"Unfortunately, my own people back in Kerioth, would probably stone me as soon as they saw me, and the two cousins who were arrested with me were executed with your master. But I can find someone to stay with in the old town and they will help me to find work, I can see that you need your privacy. I'm just grateful to you for helping me at the Hill of Skulls, and to John Mark for taking me in like that."

We were by now making our way along the crowded streets, surrounded by shopkeepers and housewives, all equally busy - and both of us had to raise our voices to be heard. After yesterday's confinement and endless

70

blame shifting, the simple normality of this morning's noise and colour made my survival seem even more magical. The executions were ancient history by now and already forgotten, the Romans had demonstrated their authority and that was that, life had moved on.

As a woman of breeding Joanna swept unstoppably through the market bustle, confident that people would make way for her, and surprisingly they did. I followed like a dog on a rope.

"The others will wish to see you again, to confirm you have everything you need before trying to start your life again." She called over her shoulder, and I thought that sounded like a good idea: that someone should wish to see that I had everything I needed. I moved a little faster to make sure she didn't lose me in the crowd.

The house we came to was larger than Mark's, though still comparatively modest. It was not made clear whose house it was but, as promised, there were three Marys. The first to be introduced was Mary the mother of the dead, though possibly raised Jesus, then there was a Mary Magdalen and finally a somewhat older lady called Mary Cleopas. With a politeness and generosity that continued to surprise me they made me welcome, and all with a sincerity that would have humbled a better and more sensitive man than me. There were three or four other women with them at the house, who might or might not have been called Mary, all still buzzing with excitement at the news of Jesus' resurrection.

The three Marys had been with Joanna that morning when they arrived at Jesus' tomb, which they said was in a garden not far from the Hill of Skulls. It had been their intention to anoint the body with spices and to prepare it properly for burial, in a way that hadn't been possible during the rush on the evening of the crucifixion, before the Sabbath halted all such work. They repeated Joanna's story about arriving in the faint pre dawn light to find that the heavy stone blocking the entrance had been rolled to one side, then seeing the angels and finally Jesus their risen leader. The whole thing was almost too much for them to cope with, going from deepest mourning to sudden joy; it somehow outshone even my own last minute reprieve, which I had previously thought to be a quite a large miracle all on its own.

I no longer had the slightest idea what to think and just allowed myself to be carried along with the general euphoria. That's one of the things about us Jews, we have a constant supply of Messiahs forever emerging from our rocky soil, when one dies another takes his place. The big difference about this one seemed to be that he didn't know when to give up; when it finally comes, death is usually the end of things for most of us.

The women, who might well have been as gloomy as the men yesterday, were warm and welcoming to the strange intruder that Joanna brought with her. Why they bothered with me was a mystery, in their place I would have told the lucky escaper, me, to be happy with his lot and disappear. But that wasn't enough for them, they wanted to include me in their celebrations, despite the fact that the best emotion I could manage was slight puzzlement.

It took me a long time to decide if I was more attracted to Mary Magdalen than I was in awe of her. As surely as smoke rises and water falls she compelled my attention, it was a process beyond rational control. I knew immediately that if I ever somehow found the nerve to approach her, she was far beyond my grubby reach. It wasn't her behaviour that produced this feeling, more my instinctive awareness of how the world worked. On that day, the first time she ever spoke to me, she was practical and business-like, she took one look at me and shook her head in disgust. "Are they the best that Mark could find for you? They're far too big." She was looking at my tunic and cloak, and I agreed, they were too big.

"I don't mind, it's just that my own clothes were torn and filthy, and soaked in blood. They had to be thrown away." I didn't know what else to say.

"It's alright, I've dealt with men released from prison before, their clothes are always filthy and lice ridden. The only thing to do is burn them. But what about you, have you bathed?"

"Yes, Mark insisted, even though it was the Sabbath."

She nodded approvingly. "Necessity comes before observance."

From her Galilean accent she might once have been a country girl, but she was more than that now. I just wasn't sure in what way - I couldn't pin her down. Whereas Joanna was the opposite, everything about her said that she came from noble stock, and money, and yet even with an escaped convict like me she acted as though she were on my level.

After rummaging around in linen chests some more suitably sized items were produced and I was sent to another room to change. Then when dressed to their satisfaction I was told to sit down and given warm bread and a beaker of wine. It was as if I'd just come home, only it was unlike any actual home that had ever existed in my own life.

As they dealt with the requirements of my personal comforts, the conversation continued unchecked above and around me, and it was all about Jesus. Although I still thought of the dead man simply as The Preacher, which was the way he had first been described to me, everyone else called him either Our Lord or simply

Jesus, and referred to me as Jesus Barabbas. As the man was the constant subject of every conversation I eventually accepted that amongst such people I would never just be Jesus, that was always going to be his name first, with me a poor second.

Apparently, the dead man had not just been a wandering preacher, with a useful line in rousing rhetoric, who could enthuse the crowds and perform the occasional small miracle - the usual stuff. The village squares of Palestine were regularly visited by passing holy men offering to cure cripples, it was almost a routine event. Unusually for such people, however, this one had been a Temple trained Rabbi, and his particular angle was that God had sent him personally to spread the word of a new agreement between God and man, replacing that announced by Moses. It was even said, however improbably, that he was promising a life after death, where all believers would join him in Paradise. It made a change from the usual anti Roman rhetoric these preachers normally produced, but it wasn't such an obvious crowd pleaser and I couldn't work out what was in it for him?

Why this sort of thing bothered the Romans enough to crucify him was even less obvious. Me, they should have killed while they had the chance, because that's a mistake they're going to pay for - but this one didn't seem to make much difference.

The most interesting thing in this establishment was the hierarchy amongst the women. A reasonable assumption would have placed Mary the mother of Jesus as the dominant figure, that's how Jewish families usually work. But as I watched and listened to them, it proved to be more subtle than that. In fact the more I heard, the more complex the situation turned out to be.

It seemed that Mary Magdalen, the one who had provided me with new clothing, and about whom I had wondered earlier had been one of Jesus' constant companions throughout his travels, which in itself was unusual as most such disciples are men. She was a good looking woman, but clearly not interested: her smile and her welcome were entirely genuine but comradely rather than feminine, almost masculine in their lack of eyebrow fluttering coyness. Although we were approaching things from different angles, life on the road had put the same sort of steel into her soul that it had put into mine. There was an unforced natural authority to the woman, just the sort of thing that I had always struggled to achieve myself.

She and Jesus' mother were equally matched, and had what was clearly a long standing relationship where they each deferred to the other, often flicking a private glance to confirm agreement to some statement or suggestion. Even allowing for the fact that they now believed their master to have risen from the dead, there was no hint of the panic stricken vacillation that I had encountered yesterday.

I had only been at the house for a few minutes before Mark, Matthew and Thomas came rushing in, all out of breath and bright with excitement.

"It's just as you said, the stone had been rolled to one side, and all that's left in the tomb are the linen shrouds he was wrapped in. There were guards in the garden all night to prevent anyone moving the body, but someone or something frightened them into running for their lives at dawn this morning. All that anyone heard them say was about seeing two shining white figures."
Mark's words were almost tumbling over themselves, he was so keen to get them out.

We all looked at each other, I was beginning to merge in with the crowd, at least in their eyes. Whether the story was true or not, all that mattered was that these people believed it was.

"Tell me again," he said to the group of women, "when you saw Jesus, exactly what did he say?"

Jesus' mother answered, in the same rustic Galilean accent that so many of the group shared. "He said that we should not be afraid, and that we should tell the others to go to Galilee where he would see you again, as he promised."

"But you're not to worry Mark; he made no mention of you fleeing naked on the night of his arrest." Said Mary Magdalen with a smile, the other women laughed at his embarrassment and Joanna turned to me.

"In the confusion of the arrest at Gethsemane, it was dark and there was a scuffle, some blood was shed and then more guards began to appear. Our Lord wanted there to be no violence and so it was understandable that his companions should have left the scene as quickly as possible. In his haste, Mark somehow lost his loincloth and was last seen running naked through the trees." There was more laughter, and yet she managed to describe the scene without implying any sort of blame at what could be seen as his cowardice.

Despite my views on the basic frailty of mankind, from the lack of malice in her comment it seemed that she and some of the others in this group were trying to improve on their base natures. It will almost certainly be a failure, it invariably is, such a suspension of the natural instinct to put down another person must involve some level of self deception. You can take it from me, all charity is dishonest, there isn't any other sort. Even if the charity is not openly corrupt, it will primarily be designed to make the charitable person look or feel better than they really are. No man is ever more honest than when serving his own interests. And that makes me a very honest man indeed.

There was a commotion at the door, as another group of men arrived. This time the group included

James and Peter, and they entered the house without any of the excitement all the rest had shared. Awestruck, but still businesslike might describe them. They might not have acted quite like men come to discuss renting a field, but there was a noticeable lack of ecstasy on display.

"The tomb is certainly empty, and not from the hand of man, it seems our Lord has truly risen. Praise be to God." Said Peter, sounding shocked but not overwhelmed.

A chorus of 'Praise be' from the assembled group echoed the sentiment. "But there is something I can't understand," he continued, "surely our Lord would choose to show himself first to his own disciples. Surely he would come first to those closest to him?" And then turning to Mary Magdalen he asked. "Are you quite sure that it was the Lord you spoke to and not another angel, a different angel?"

This came very close to calling the three women liars, and I wondered how she would respond. But it was Jesus' mother who answered, quietly and with certainty. "Simon Peter, I know my own son." Then even more tellingly Mark added his own comment.

"Perhaps he did appear first to those closest to him."

There was a deadly silence, no one wanted to speak, and things could have gone either way. He could have stormed out of there in a fit of anger, taking his supporters with him, or he could have swallowed the rebuke. If, at that moment, he had he chosen the former then the small community of Jesus' followers would have been split down the middle and disappeared for ever. Such an uncertain and fledgling group would not have survived so fundamental a split. Instead he sank down onto a chair, put his elbows on the table, put his head in his hands and sobbed.

We're an emotional people, it's in our blood. We're up and down with every perceived insult, that's why the Romans have so much trouble with us, there's a riot every other week in Jerusalem. But this sort of sobbing, from a man who had just been ready to call his closest friends liars, was not to my taste.

I looked at the women, but they were filled with compassion - well they would be wouldn't they? Apparently that's how it works with this lot, Joanna had told me that you have to love your enemy and forgive every man his sins. I can't see that working as a system. If you love your enemy, then what d'you do to your friends, and if you love everybody then what's the point in having enemies in the first place?

"I've failed again, I was never there for him, I denied him and now I've failed again." I didn't understand the background to his comments, but Jesus' mother presumably did and she sat next to him and put her arm round his shoulder. One of the men who had come in with him, I think his name was Andrew, sat with them at the table. But more interesting was the behaviour of James. I had by now discovered that there were two followers of that name, one they called the son of Zebedee, and one the son of Alphaeus. It was the son of Alphaeus who interested me. He was the one who had yesterday dismissed the call to involve the women in their deliberations, and I wondered how he was feeling about today's developments. There was a guarded look on his face and unlike yesterday when he pushed himself forward, today he was holding back. I had the impression that things weren't going his way.

I was invisible in the crowd, everybody knew who I was by now, and they also knew that I didn't matter, that I could be ignored. I was the only one here who could stare at another person without it being significant or even noticed; and so now, discretely, I watched James. If you want to know what's going on in a man's head you don't listen to what he says, you watch how he acts.

James was standing very still, unnaturally so, which meant that he didn't wish to draw attention to himself. There must have been twenty five people or more in that big downstairs room by then, and the others were talking and moving about, as people do, but James was holding himself separate. Then without any words being exchanged his eyes met those of another of the disciples, a man called Simon the Zealot. They exchanged what I would call a meaningful glance, what that meaning was I had no way of knowing, all I could say for sure was that there was some hidden understanding about these events that was shared by the two men. Then even more strangely he looked at Mary Cleopas, and another blank unreadable look was exchanged. I might have known nothing about the dead Jesus, but I knew a great deal about low plotting, and that was what I was looking at. I had always known there would be a worm in the bud.

CHAPTER SEVEN

By midday the group at Mary's house had begun to break up, the first to leave had been Peter accompanied by Andrew, who I now knew to be his brother, together with two of their friends. Soon after, both the men called James had left along with Simon. The instruction from the risen Jesus had been for his followers to go to Galilee where they would see him again, and so most of them were starting to make plans for the three day journey. At about this point, if I'd had any tact I would have left with them. There were some people in the old town with whom I could find temporary shelter, and maybe some labouring work, if I had to. Just to pay my way - until I found something more interesting. But frankly I was hanging on to see what else they might have to offer me. So far I'd had a new cloak, a new tunic and new sandals, but Joanna had spoken of seeing if there was anything else I needed, and that sounded like a fairly broad category to me.

The conversation had moved onto the immediate future for what they called The Church in Jerusalem. At first I thought this meant a particular building, but they were actually using the term to describe the whole movement. Their master had given instructions that following his death, an event he had apparently foreseen in some detail, leadership of the church was to pass to Mary Magdalen. From having observed the people involved this sounded a natural order of succession; she had by all accounts been one of his constant companions for the last two years, and according to Mark she was sometimes referred to by Jesus as his *beloved disciple.* And when everything had seemed to be lost and their man was dying, it was only the women, and Judas, who had found the courage to show themselves.

James's point about the group working within Rabbinical tradition, and excluding women as leaders didn't strike me as relevant. Considering that they were planning to start a whole new church, I reckoned they could appoint anyone they wanted, an opinion it seems the other Jesus had agreed with.

As they were talking about the arrangements to be made, about who should travel to Galilee and when, I suddenly realised what was going on. It was as obvious as the nose on your face, the only reason I hadn't spotted it sooner was that I wasn't all that interested; by this time tomorrow I would probably never see any of them again. More importantly it was nothing to do with me, and so on the basis that you should never volunteer for anything, I decided to keep what I'd seen to myself.

Mark, Matthew and Thomas had stayed on at what they all called Mary's house, by which I assumed they meant it belonged to Jesus' mother, but I never asked. As there's a limit to how long you can talk about one subject, even a thing so amazing as someone rising from the dead, the conversation eventually wandered into other areas, and with their scrupulous concern for others, it finally settled on me.

Mark turned to me, a serious look on his face, I reckoned this was going to be the conversation Joanna had promised: about me getting back on my own feet.

"Jesus Barabbas, we've been talking about your future, and we're all agreed on how important it is to keep you from sliding back to your earlier ways. The sort of chance that you've been given won't happen twice in anyone's life, and it would be a sin if we allowed you to waste it." I thought that sort of thing was probably best left for me to decide, but as I had yet to discover the full extent of their generosity I let him continue.

"We understand that you're a time served tent maker, is that correct?"

"Yes, I served four years in Kerioth, under Jacob. Most of our work was for the Legion."

"Well, I have a cousin who is also a tent maker and I understand he has room for an extra pair of hands, the pay would be standard guild rates for a junior. Are you interested?"

I was astonished, and immediately dismissive. "When word gets round that he has me on the payroll, no one will touch his tents - he won't be able to give them away. Even in a city the size of Jerusalem there's sure to be someone who recognises me. A man who kills his own master is finished - for good."

"Just answer the question, do you want to speak to him about it, and would you be true to your new master if he took you on?"

The standard guild rate was exactly what I'd wanted Jacob to pay me, but there had to be more to this, for once I was unable to see the catch, but everyone was staring at me and I had to make some reply. "If it can be organised in some way, then yes I would be glad of the work, and yes, I would be true to my new master." I was accustomed to making bold promises, they were a cheap currency.

"As I understand it, there is unlikely to be a problem with you being recognised, the work won't be in Jerusalem. You have no family, well none that will talk to you, do you?"

"No."

"Then a little travelling shouldn't bother you, and a life of honest toil should prepare your mind for repentance. Are you sincere in your desire to take such work?"

"I am." And I almost meant it. He clasped my hand and looked me in the eye for a long moment. "Very well, then we shall go back to my house and I'll try to arrange a meeting with my cousin, this afternoon if possible."

"Could you give me a moment please, I want to thank Joanna for bringing me here this morning."

"There's really no need." She said, having heard my comment. But I shook my head, now that things were different, even if only temporarily, she needed to be told something - the thing I'd spotted earlier. I was well aware that opening my mouth could be a mistake, but her treatment of me, as if I were almost an equal had affected me. I walked over and took her hand, the rest of them continued their previous conversations, perhaps a little self consciously. In such crowded quarters as these, people try to give each other some small scraps of privacy.

"Joanna, I'm not only grateful for the kindness I've received from you and the others, but there's something you need to know." I had spoken quietly, not being sure who else might be involved in what I had to say. I paused for a moment, I knew what needed saying, it was just that I wasn't sure how to phrase it. If in doubt, go for the throat.

"James, the son of Alphaeus, has intentions to prevent your friend Mary Magdalen from taking control of the church movement in Jerusalem. He intends to take the position for himself, and I think he will have the help of the one called Simon the Zealot, and perhaps one other person in your group." What lunatic impulse had caused me to come out with this I had no idea. This sounded as if there was some connection between us, as if we were friends or even both members of the church group, and only I knew how unlikely that was.

She looked thoughtful. "That must have taken some courage to speak in such a way, what makes you think he intends this?" Her own voice was a soft as my own. Even religious people can have secrets.

"I can't give you any words or even actions of his that will make you believe me, just take my word for it, I watched him yesterday at Mark's house, when he came close to saying that no woman should be their leader, and again here today. I think the reason he said nothing when they came back from the tomb is that Peter was speaking his words."

That comment touched a similar thought of her own, I could see it in her face.

"Peter is a good and honest man, he would have no part in any plot."

"I believe you, I agree with you. The fact is that he is not only good and honest, he is open and direct - he is a man without guile. I'm sure he would never take part in any plot - just as long as he realised that it was a plot. But I'll tell you that I can make men dance to my tune, and still think it's their own choice, and I'm not the only man alive who can do that."

"Are you suggesting that James has led Peter astray?"

"I'm suggesting that he would like to."

"And who do you believe is helping James, apart from Simon? You said there was someone else."

I took a deep breath, I shouldn't have started down this road, my normal belief that you should never volunteer applied to this situation. I had broken my own commandment by doing just that, and sure enough I was now being led deeper and deeper into causing offence to one or another of the people I wanted help and handouts from. "I can't tell you that - I'm not as sure about them."

She looked at me, her face inscrutable, I couldn't read anything into it. "You think it's Mary Cleopas don't you?" My surprise must have shown, but there was an obvious reply.

"For you to make that guess means that you must already think it yourself."

"No it doesn't, Mary Cleopas is his mother."

"But they have different names, he is James the son of Alphaeus."

"He was her first husband, he died and now she is married to Cleopas who was the brother of Mary's husband Joseph." He eyes indicated Mary the mother of Jesus. "But I'm sure you're wrong, James is very orthodox in his beliefs that's true, and of all the disciples he had the most difficulty in accepting that our Lord's commandment to love your neighbour as yourself meant we should regard absolutely everyone as our neighbour. But he would never plot to overturn Jesus' explicit instruction."

"I should never have mentioned this, it was foolish of me, but now that I've said it will you promise to tell Mary Magdalen?"

"I'm sure she'll share my opinion, but I will tell her."

That duty dealt with, I was free to return to Mark's house and arrange to see my new employer, whatever the future might offer I had now settled any debt that I owed these people. Warning them to watch their backs had a drawn a line between us, no matter where the work with Mark's cousin might lead I knew that it wasn't going to be amongst these people in Jerusalem. It was time to move on from my miraculous escape from death, it was time to turn my back on this religious infighting, it was time for another of my new starts.

Mark's cousin was a man called Barnabas, from Cyprus, and that evening just before the first watch of the night he came to see me. Matthew and Thomas had yet to return and Mark made an excuse to leave us alone together.

Barnabas hadn't washed and was still dirty from work, a thin sheen of dried sweat across his forehead. He had that tannery smell about him that comes from handling freshly cured leather all day. At first he said nothing, but simply walked around me, I half expected him to prod my flank and look at my fetlocks.

"Mark's told me of your past." That was all, no question, just a statement. I bit back any sarcastic retort that might once have emerged, and concentrated on being reasonable.

"Then there's not much I can add, I was once a sinner and probably still am, the difference now is that I want to change. I want to leave all that behind me. I'm a time served tent maker, I would be grateful for employment and would be true to my master."

"But is there any repentance in you for your past life? The Torah tells us that repentance is one of the first requirements of mankind."

"I am ready to go to the Temple and offer whatever sacrifice is called for, as atonement for my wrongdoing." This wasn't the moment for half measures.

He looked at me appraisingly. "The Book of Proverbs tells us that doing charity and justice is more desirable than sacrifice."

"That is exactly how I intend to live."

He stroked his chin and said, "Mmm - I wonder."

I kept my mouth shut, I'd already offered more than I planned to deliver, the first rule of negotiating is just to say exactly what you have to say and then stop talking. Never be embarrassed by awkward silences, just ride them out, with your mouth firmly shut. The first of the negotiators to break this rule will always give something away that they needn't have. I don't know why life works this way, but you can take my word for it that it does. He didn't know about the rule and so, at last, felt he ought to say something.

"Well I suppose I could use another pair of hands." There was a further long pause, and then. "I'm only talking to you at all because Mark claims that he can see some good in you, but if we were working together would I have to sleep every night with one eye open, waiting for you to creep up on me?"

"I give you my oath that will not happen."

He looked unconvinced. "The trouble is that, unlike my cousin Mark and his friends, I'm an observant Jew. You see the Jesus people believe that when someone strikes you across the face you shouldn't strike them back, but simply turn the other cheek so that they can strike you again. However, I'm a lot more traditional. I believe in an eye for eye. So if you ever tried to creep up on me then you'd need to be a lot faster with a knife than the average roadside purse snatcher."

Another of my little maxims is that when everything else has failed, then you can always try the truth. So I tried some with him.

"Barnabas, when I was a criminal it was always to serve my own ends. The problem was that I wasn't as good at it as I needed to be, that's why I got caught. Right now my best prospect is to get an honest job with an honest employer and start all over again. So I won't be creeping up on anyone in the middle of the night - and certainly not you."

"I hope so, because I'm well aware how gullible Mark and his friends can seem to an outsider. You will probably have spent the last two days imagining that you are cleverer than the people helping you, that you could trick your way round them. The fact that you're wrong will sadden most of them and they will pray for you to come to God. I, on the other hand, am more likely to strike you than pray for you."

"I understand you Barnabas, I truly do."

"Perhaps now you're beginning to."

No matter how much I hated him for seeing through me, he was still my best hope for any future that held something other than digging ditches till I died. It looked as if I was about to make a return to the world of honest employment, and wasn't at all sure if I was happy with the idea.

Early the next morning Barnabas took me to his yard, set near the tannery pits outside the east gate from the lower city. Tannery work was forbidden inside the walls, because of the smell of all that stale piss being stirred up every day, and it made sense to put a tent makers yard next to the site of their main supplier. Besides, renting the amount of floor space needed for tent making inside the walls of a crowded city like Jerusalem would cost a fortune.

We had some breakfast while sat together on the low wall that marked the edge of his yard. The early morning sun was shining directly into our faces, in front of us we could see the Bethany road winding its way down the near side of the Kidron Valley, bending this way and that through the stone walled terraces and then up the far side past the Mount of Olives. The heat was not yet oppressive, the morning freshness still lingered in the air, it was the best time of the day. A slight breeze coming out of the valley brought smells of olive, acacia and jasmine that temporarily masked the pungent smell behind us. Once we got started then I knew it wouldn't bother me, but for a while I was grateful for something better.

"You haven't asked me where you'll be working, don't you care?"

I thought for a while. "I suppose that if I haven't asked - then I can't be all that bothered, but you might as well tell me."

"Alright, we have a few days work to finish here and then we'll be heading north, we're going to be working in Jezreel for a few months, certainly through the summer. Do you know where that is?"

"All I know is that it's where they threw Jezebel out of the palace window to be eaten by dogs. That's one of the few history lessons I can remember."

"You can forget about Jezebel, our only interest is that it's a garrison town of the Tenth Legion, it's in southern Galilee, on the main north south road from Syria to Jerusalem and Egypt. The Neptune Cohort that we've been dealing with in Jerusalem have been transferred up there, and we're going to be following them. There's too much business involved to give it up half way through a contract."

I still didn't much care where we went, as long as it was away from Jerusalem and all the flogging and crucifixion and dead preachers, but I'd noticed something that I hadn't expected. "I saw that you had two young apprentices in the yard, and that the whole place was cleaner than any tent maker I've ever seen before."

"You'll need to get used to it, because that's the way I like it and that's the way it's going to stay. This place can make a great deal of money if it's properly organised, and that means keeping the place clean and tidy, knowing where everything is. If we run out of thread half way through the day because somebody forgot to check the night before, then I'll be angry, and that's another thing that wastes time."

"If this place makes a lot of money that's more than my last master ever managed, mind you he never managed to keep it very clean either. I thought all tent yards were dirty, I thought that was just the way things were."

"Not where I'm concerned, this business is run to make money, as much as I can honestly and decently manage."

"So you're a rich man?"

He swung round to look at me, surprise all over him. "Do I look like a rich man?" He held up his calloused hands. "Do these look like a rich man's hands?"

"So where does it all go?" And this time I really was interested in the answer.

"We have already established that I'm an orthodox Jew, and I pay my tithes to the Temple, as I ought, and I trust you do the same. But I also sympathise with Mark's work and the beliefs of his group, I'm not sure if I'm ready to join them yet, but I certainly think they're worth supporting."

"So even though I escaped from the Jesus group, my work will still be paying for them?"

"Certainly not, you'll be paid a fair wage for your work, as we agreed. What business is it of yours where I put my profits?"

"That's fair. What did you think of Jesus, what sort of a man was he?"

"I never met him myself, I was going to hear him speak this week, but . . ."

It wasn't necessary for him to complete the sentence. "I met him, we had a few words while we were waiting to be taken for execution."

That surprised him, he hadn't expected someone like me would have actually spoken to the great preacher. "What did he say? What was he like?"

I took a moment or two to get the words straight in my head. "It was after the four of us had been flogged, and were waiting to be taken up to the street to drag our crosses to the Hill of Skulls, he came over to me and put his hands on my arm and said 'You have been given time to find repentance, now go in peace'."

"He actually said that to you - how did it feel?"

How it felt was an odd question, but a good one. Most people wouldn't ask how such a remark *felt*. But the fact is it had *felt* of something. "Well the strange thing is I don't see how he could have known that I was going to be released - none of us did, but he still said go in peace. And as for how it felt, well I'm not sure." I stared across the valley, squinting slightly in the direct sunshine, Barnabas stared at me, waiting silently for me to go on.

"It sounds stupid to say so and it makes no sense, but the only way I can describe it is to say that it felt as though the sun had shone on me." I even pointed a hand out in front of me, as if he might not have been too sure which sun I was talking about. "The sun - it truly felt as though the sun was shining on me, it warmed up all the front of my body. But we were in the basement below the place of judgement, there was no sun, just soldiers and darkness."

He was still turned sideways, staring at me. "How could you ever dare to sin again, after something like that?" His tone was incredulous.

"I hadn't eaten properly for a week, I'd just been sentenced to death and flogged, nobody's mind can be working properly in those circumstances."

He grunted. "Even you aren't stupid enough to believe that. Now get off your lazy bum and come with me - there's a long day's work to be done."

Then three days later, having said our goodbyes to Mark, Matthew and Thomas; our small band of travelling tent makers and sinners set off for Jezreel, in the footsteps of the Legion. We had a line of ten donkeys and the four of us; Barnabas, myself and the two boys walked alongside. It seemed quite natural for us to band together with other travellers, in the hope that the resultant group would be too large to suffer ambush, from people like me.

CHAPTER EIGHT

The road north was a revelation to me, brought up in the rocky hills of southern Judea, where the prevailing colour of every landscape is some variety of brown or yellow. Where apart from the land along river valleys or near an oasis, any vegetation has to be watered by the hand of man. But as we travelled north through Samaria and into Galilee, we began to move through a countryside I'd never seen before. There were standing fields of wheat, almost ready to be harvested, and even where no crop had been planted there were meadows with wild flowers; everywhere you looked there were trees and greenery. Jerusalem seemed to stand on the dividing line between two worlds

Jezreel is a handsome town, and a busy one. Situated in the foothills of Mount Gilboa it overlooks the wide and fertile Jezreel Valley, which at that time of the year, and seen from that elevation, was a picture of agricultural abundance. The soil round there is too fertile to waste on olives and vines, they can cope well enough in lower quality ground. There were patches of green vegetables and orchards of figs, but covering the biggest area was the yellow shimmer of grain, apparently they call this place the bread basket of Palestine. Winding through the middle of it all could be seen the biggest and busiest road in Galilee, it was a commanding location, which no doubt accounted for the presence of the Legion garrison.

Back home in Kerioth there were no inns worthy of the name, just some dirty sheds by the animal stockades where travellers could huddle up for the night; and what shops there were served strictly local produce to a strictly local population. In contrast Jezreel had several inns that were both clean and extremely busy. Although the town was by no means the largest in the area, the citizens were well dressed and the shops and market stalls were almost the same quality one might find in Jerusalem. Owing to its position on the main north south trade route the produce in the shops was varied and cosmopolitan, and so were the customers.

The surprising thing was not that this display of good living attracted my attention, but that it made me think of how to earn some of this wealth for myself, rather than thinking of how to steal it. Scarcely more than a week with Barnabas and I was already beginning to think like him, I just hoped the effect wasn't irreversible.

Once again we found accommodation for the tent yard near the tanning pits on the downwind side of town, and lodgings for ourselves with a widow near the synagogue. Barnabas had been here before and, unlike me, it seemed that people who'd met him once were happy to do so again. We had the donkeys unpacked, and our materials sorted out and ready for work by noon on the first day. That afternoon he left me working with the two boys while he went off to pay his respects to his contacts at the Legion. He hadn't exaggerated when he said that his ideas of running a business were very different from anything that Jacob and I had ever managed.

The fact that I was surprised by the religious inclinations of the widow, in whose house we were staying, is more a sign of my sluggish mental state than anything else. Despite his own orthodoxy, Barnabas had made no secret of his sympathy with his cousin Mark and his friends in the Jesus movement, so I should perhaps have expected to find myself mixing with more of them.

The lady in question, Esther, was a friend of Barnabas's cousin Mark, and was the local leader of the new church. Barnabas felt that it would be dishonest not to mention my background, which produced the predictable shocked reaction, not everyone wants a convicted killer living under their roof, and I was politely asked to wait outside. As I didn't wish to spend my nights sleeping in a ditch I was greatly relieved when, after a few minutes of earnest conversation, the lady apparently decided that it was her religious duty to help a fallen sinner. Entering such a household it felt as if we'd spent three days trudging the roads, only to end up where we started, in the house of a devout and God fearing woman who saw my prospective repentance as something she could happily pray for.

However, unlike the occasion of my meeting with the women in Jerusalem, this time I wasn't a shocked and bleeding casualty, this time I could stand up for myself. And in fairness to her she made no attempt to convert me or preach at me. She was a good cook and the beds were clean, beyond that I felt no urge to venture.

Esther and Mark both came from the small town of Cana, which was less than a day's journey north of Jezreel. They had been working as serving staff at a wedding, two or three years earlier, at which Jesus, his mother and Mary Magdalen had been guests. Apparently Jesus had performed a miracle, turning water into wine, and it had been sufficiently impressive to convince them of his credentials. Then when Esther's husband had died, she had moved down to Jezreel and used her inheritance to set herself up running a lodging house. Jesus himself had stayed at her house when passing through, which made it an obvious gathering place for his followers, and as a natural progression made Esther the leader of the local group.

She welcomed Barnabas, on the basis that any friend of Mark's was a friend of hers, and I somehow slipped in along with that. I don't recollect any of us mentioning my own background to anyone outside the household, and although my history could hardly be kept a secret, none of us thought it sensible to push it in people's faces. For the moment keeping my head down and labouring quietly sounded like the best idea.

We had little contact in those days with the Jerusalem group, and that suited me perfectly, Jerusalem was nothing but bad memories to me, I was happy to be in Jezreel. At the yard we divided our time between repairing the Legion's existing tents, and making new ones. It was hard work, but the professional level of our organisation and the fact that we had the right staff numbers made it a job that we could all take some pride in. As the weeks wore on and the days grew hotter, even the abundant greenery of Galilee, which had at first so surprised me, began to fade to the duller and more parched shades of summer. The fact the Jezreel was built on a hillside meant that it was not quite so hot as the valley floor below us, and we sometimes caught the occasional breeze coming inland from the sea, even so we usually stopped work for the two or three hours after noon. For the first time in my life I began to feel settled, the daily urge to kick over the traces and break out in some way had begun to recede. I could even imagine the day when people might treat me with respect, at least until they found out more about me.

Barnabas had several times offered to accompany me to the Sabbath synagogue, but I had no trouble in turning him down; politely but firmly. Discovering the world of work was more than enough novelty in my life for the moment, besides which, as a temporary resident in town I wasn't on anybody's list to receive a visit from the Temple guards to discuss my continuing absence.

My own interests lay in more earthly matters, and I became a regular visitor to the nearby taverns. A man needs some place of relaxation after a day's work, and although I've never been a drunkard I do find that wine has the magical ability to soothe aching muscles. Besides which, for several evenings each week Esther's house served as the meeting place for her Jesus group, and I found their determined goodwill quite difficult to cope with. Once they had identified me as a sinner, for by now the news was slowly creeping out, they were unwilling to ignore the possibility of redeeming me. Esther herself, I had no trouble with and although a little pious I could talk to the woman, however, far from helping me out on these occasions she seemed amused by her friend's attempts to save my soul. Hence my unwillingness to spend every evening hour at the house.

The two apprentice boys we employed at the yard had caught some whiff of my background, probably from piecing together overheard comments, and seemed to be quite thrilled by it. Being young and impressionable, and lacking any of the details they were pleased to be working next to a major criminal, and one who had so narrowly escaped a gruesome death. It was always the astonishing escape that caught people's attention, rather than the reasons for the original conviction. This reputation then somehow spread in a corrupted form to the local taverns. I was not unhappy, and did nothing to correct the more foolish rumours of my exploits. It gave me a certain status and a certain swagger. It was only late at night that the dead children came back, to let me know they were still waiting for me, but no one else knew about them, just me.

All things considered I had found a place for myself in life and was beginning to settle into quite a comfortable routine. But these things never last, and not long after Pentecost everything changed. And remember what I tell you: change is usually bad, in fact change is almost always bad.

We received a visit from Barnabas's cousin Mark, who had sheltered me in Jerusalem. You could say that he brought us news of their continuing work, but it sounded more like a breathless battlefield report. As was usually the way with the Jesus people, Mark observed no confidentiality, but gave us his news while sat at the table eating with Esther, Barnabas and myself.

His account told of Jesus appearing not only to the women by the tomb, and to some of the disciples at the Sea of Galilee, but now to the others in Jerusalem. He had instructed them to preach his message wherever people gathered, both to Jews and Gentiles. In the following weeks there had been mass baptisms and it was said that there were now more than three thousand followers in Jerusalem alone.

There was a light in Mark's eyes as he spoke. "We've achieved an astonishing momentum, but we have to keep up the pressure, we can't hesitate now. Already, with the thousands so far baptised we can fill the Temple Square; it's such a sight - you have to come and see it. We're close to the point where they'll have to acknowledge our right to worship in our own way. It's simply amazing, in such a short time."

I could see Barnabas getting caught up in Mark's enthusiasm, some of it even washed over me.

"With Peter leading us on the streets, and the steadying hand of James as our leader we can begin to . . ."

"James as your leader?" I said quietly interrupting him. I put my knife down on the table and looked at Barnabas. I would have said, I warned you this would happen, but it was plain from his discomfort that he remembered my words. "I was beginning to wonder why you hadn't mentioned Mary his mother, or Mary Magdalen."

Esther watched the interplay without commenting, I would tell her later. No one had anything to add to my own remark and so I waved my hand, vaguely indicating that he should carry on. "Take no notice of me, I'm just an outsider."

"It seemed best that way." He said softly, his voice muted by guilt. However, even my dampening presence couldn't keep the man down for long, and he was soon back in full flow; recounting how Jesus had finally left them all, ascending to heaven at Pentecost accompanied by a roaring wind and tongues of fire. These people certainly knew how to do the job properly.

His report on current events safely delivered, Mark then came to the heart of the matter. He said that it was now time for Barnabas to put aside his earlier doubts and join in what he described as this glorious new beginning.

"This is the biggest adventure you'll ever see in your entire life, no one has ever seen anything like it before. We can move mountains, in fact we're going to move mountains, and we want you to join us - what do you say?"

The Zealots had no monopoly on zeal, Mark's face was shining with the stuff. I almost joined up myself to avoid disappointing the man. He was smart enough to know he'd said enough and leaned back in his seat to wait for a response, some acknowledgement that a round trip of six hard days on a dusty road might prove worthwhile.

The three of us looked at Barnabas, but he was oblivious and stared straight ahead. Whatever he was looking at, it wasn't in this room. He was clearly wrestling with his decision, but there was nothing I could say that would help. All I was sure of was that this idea of him heading back to Jerusalem would put me out of work, if he went then our entire contract with the Legion in Jezreel would go with him. These things were done on a personal basis, the Legion's agreement was with him as the master tent maker, not his criminal assistant. Mark had spoken of there being more than three thousand followers in Jerusalem now, surely they could do without an extra one. I looked at the table to avoid my face revealing my thoughts.

Eventually it was Esther who leaned forward to put her hand on Barnabas's hand. "You've always known in your heart that this moment would come, haven't you?"

He looked at her, clear eyed and resolute. "Yes, and I'm ready for it, thank you for all your help over the last months."

I thought that was all very sweet and all very well, but did it mean he was going or staying? Did I still have a job, or not? I stared at him, waiting for the answer. He turned to me.

"This means that you'll be a lot busier now, but I think you're ready to cope."

"So you're staying here?"

He looked puzzled. "No, of course I'm not staying here, my duty is in Jerusalem, I should have seen that earlier. I shall be leaving with Mark tomorrow at dawn."

"So how exactly is that going to make me any busier?"

He looked even more puzzled, and spoke slowly. "Because I can't be in two places at once - so you'll be doing part of my work as well as your own, that's why."

"You want me to carry on with the Legion contract?"

"Well who else is going to do it?"

"But that will mean me negotiating with the Legion - and handling the cash."

"Do you have a problem with either of those?"

"The last time I dealt directly with the Legion I was rude to an officer and got a kicking, and the last time I handled a lot of cash I stole it, if you remember, I'm a thief."

This time it was Esther who spoke. "Are you? Are you a thief? You've been living under my roof for the last three months and you haven't stolen anything yet. Should I start to lock up my valuables?"

I didn't know what to say to that, and for a moment I said nothing, Barnabas filled the silence. "We both know what you used to be, but we also know what was said to you in that basement in Jerusalem: you've been given time to find repentance. God knows I've been slow with my decision, and you're even slower than me, but you can't be so stupid as to ignore a gift like that - can you?"

I swallowed, this was all going too fast for my liking. "Just because I might not be a thief any more, doesn't mean I've turned into one of your lot."

Esther leaned forward to speak softly. "But you will do, when you've had enough of being tormented by The Children, whoever they might be."

I felt faint, and denied everything. "I don't know what you're talking about."

She leaned back in her chair and looked at me, her tone wasn't cruel but it was very direct. "I've listened to you talking in your sleep at least once a week since you got here. Would you like me to tell you some of the things I've heard?"

I shook my head, unwilling to take this conversation any further.

That afternoon Barnabas took me with him to the Fretensis barracks, where the Neptune Cohort of the Tenth Legion was based. The Centurion responsible for tent maintenance, Sextus Flavius, was a businesslike man with not enough time on his hands to waste any of it giving me a hard time. He seemed to have a good relationship with Barnabas, and after only ten minutes of talking was happy to accept me as the new point of contact for repairs and replacements. We clasped hands briefly, and before we'd left his office he was already talking to his next visitor, about grain supplies.

We spent the rest of the afternoon at the yard, talking to the two boys about their own new responsibilities and the fact that from now on they would have me as their day to day master. Our last call was with the Temple clerk who held our cash deposits, introducing me as no longer just the assistant, but from now on as the man to deal with. Here, for the first time we faced some slight resistance, this man had heard of my past and raised his eyebrows expressively at the news of my new responsibilities. Barnabas told me to take a walk around the square for ten minutes, and when I returned the clerk was more accommodating: not quite enough to smile at me, but at least I was accepted. In the space of one afternoon I had been turned into what could pass for an upright citizen. Surprisingly, I found that I liked the idea, even though my new prominence would mean I would have to start attending synagogue more regularly.

The next morning at dawn Esther and I said goodbye to Mark and Barnabas, as they went to join a south bound group of travellers already assembled at the nearby inn, and I went to the tent yard. By lunchtime on that first day it felt as if things had always been this way.

Once a week I sent him an account of our work at the yard, a tally of income received and expended, and a figure for cash deposited. And in exchange he sent me a report of what he and the other Jesus followers were doing in Jerusalem, these I shared with Esther and the other members of her group. After a month I asked for, and received, his agreement to promote one of the apprentice boys to be a cutter and hired another boy. In town the people openly referred to me as Jesus Barabbas, the tent maker. I was hooked as firm as any fish, I'd tasted responsibility and found that I handled it well. I was twenty six years old and had finally turned into a man.

CHAPTER NINE

At this time in my life two separate threads begin to vie for supremacy. Superficially, I was now the tent maker, that was my business and my life, it was how I was defined. But below the surface there was another life pushing itself forward in fits and starts, prompted by my weekly letters from Barnabas. He was now a fully convinced follower of Jesus, and told of the growing persecution suffered by his friends in Jerusalem; the Temple Council were becoming more and more desperate to put a stop to the mass conversions of orthodox Jews to the Jesus movement. Their public meetings were regularly disrupted and broken up by hired thugs, all the leading disciples had been arrested and interrogated, sometimes brutally. Attempts had been made to have them charged with blasphemy, but even the use of bribed witnesses had been insufficient to convince a court.

There was a mounting sense of hysteria, which even by the overheated standards of public life in Jerusalem was becoming a threat to public order. According to Barnabas, the situation was so delicately balanced that the last time soldiers had been sent out to arrest disciples, they had been instructed to do it quietly and politely, so as to avoid provoking a riot. The High Priest had demanded they should stop preaching Jesus' doctrine of salvation, and the inclusion of Gentiles into this offshoot of Judaism. The disciples' standard reply to this had been to say that they obeyed the laws of God before the laws of man. It looked like a deadlock, and it was deadlock that couldn't last.

A growing number of Jesus' followers were now trying to avoid this confrontation by spreading out from Jerusalem, across Samaria, Judea and Galilee. Which from the authorities' point of view simply made the problem worse, by spreading an infection which had previously been contained. Even here, as far north as Jezreel, we were seeing a trickle of displaced people on the road.

The tone of Barnabas's letters, far from being desperate or frightened, was almost elated, he felt they were having a real impact. The memory of Jesus' own trial, which I had stood and watched, had made them all the more determined to avoid being bullied into silence by legal threats and false witnesses.

Beyond sending me friendly greetings from Joanna and Mary Magdalen, he showed very little interest in personal matters, and made no pretence of taking any interest in tent making. I was glad to be out of harm's way, they might resist threats of trials, imprisonment and death in the belief that they were about God's business, but I wasn't so sure. What I did know was that I was alive and their man was dead; I didn't even mind if their man came back from the dead, just as long as I stayed alive. This was one storm that could blow over without any involvement from Jesus Barabbas.

The Legion Centurion, Sextus Flavius, was a decent enough sort and had recently taken to offering me the occasional mug of wine when I called to discuss the next weeks schedule, or to collect an outstanding bill. Each time it happened I had to make a determined effort not to smile stupidly at the fact that I was sat drinking with a Centurion, when I should have been nailed up by one.

Sextus Flavius and I even discussed the growth in the Jesus' group popularity. He was a twenty five year veteran and had served throughout North Africa and

Asia Minor, there weren't many types of religion he hadn't seen. Baal, Mithras, Jupiter and even on one occasion a large goat: he'd seen them all being worshipped somewhere or other. As far as this one was concerned, he regarded it as a purely local squabble: the High Priest and the Temple versus the Jesus group. He didn't mind which lot won, as long as they didn't interfere with the payment of tax and cause him and his men any trouble. Without giving the matter too much thought, I assumed that this would probably be a fair summary of the official Roman position. I could remember how utterly unconcerned Pilate was with any charges of blasphemy, all he cared about was the maintenance of public order.

As a newly observant and synagogue attending businessman, I heard each week the official view of the confrontation in Jerusalem. Our senior Rabbi was in no doubt at all, we must be very careful to avoid the snares and traps of false religions, designed to tempt us from the narrow way. Moses had taught us and the Prophets had warned us, and it was not up to us to rewrite the Torah. Jesus was never mentioned by name, it didn't seem necessary, simply that the Law and the Prophets were there for our support and guidance, as they always had been. I don't know what the women upstairs in the synagogue were doing, but most of the men downstairs looked at each other and nodded agreement at this statement of the official line.

While Barnabas had been with us, even though not then a fully subscribing member of the movement, Esther had instinctively deferred to him as being a friend and confidant of the Jerusalem inner circle, and that was certainly how I saw him. However, since his departure she had begun to take on a much more active role for herself. The local group needed a focus and a leader, and Esther was it. She not only held regular prayer meetings at the house, but was the leader of a group of people who made it their business to visit the sick and provide food to the poor. Without the presence of Barnabas, the well connected figure from Jerusalem, she grew in stature and confidence herself. In fact she was so self confident that she had even stopped trying to persuade me to join in with her meetings. As far as I was concerned she was content to accept an extra cash payment from me every week as the full discharge of my religious duties. This arrangement suited us both and I still usually managed to find myself at the tavern during her evening meetings.

Throughout the summer my letters to Barnabas told of the profitability of our business with the Tenth, and of our growing sales of saddles and panniers to the passing trade on the main road. His decision to move the business to Jezreel was being justified on a daily basis. The business profits passing back to him, through the network of Temple fund transfers, must have been a significant boost to the Jerusalem group, and more than once it crossed my mind to deduct a handling fee. It was only the fact that his letters frequently mentioned the Jerusalem group's shortage of money, that caused my hesitation in that area. If they were that desperate for funds, he might notice when I started taking a cut.

I'm not a stupid man, and even as my letters reported these successes, I was aware that I was not just running his business but effectively living his life. If I wasn't going to skim the profits then the only other thing I could do to benefit from the arrangement was to enjoy myself, and I tried to do just that. Even the frequency of my nights spent tormented by visions of The Children waiting to lead me to hell, their eyes accusing, the wounds in their heads still bleeding, had grown less. Sometimes I could go for a week and not be visited.

As Barnabas's letters continued to recount the success of their preaching, the letters which Esther received from Joanna told a slightly different story. The original instruction left by Jesus, that his closest companion Mary Magdalen should assume control of the church in Jerusalem had, as I foretold, been overturned. Formal leadership of the group was now in the hands of James, with the most active street preacher being Peter. It seemed the group of women that I had met were no longer involved in any part of the organisation.

Some people might be puzzled by this, Esther certainly was, but not me; I know how these things work. The first task of any successful plotter is to destroy everything about their predecessor, simply replacing that person is not the end of the matter, victory on its own is never enough, somebody has to be seen to lose.

This isn't the rule of Jesus Barabbas, it's the rule of life, just look at what happens when one King supplants another; seizing the throne is only the first step, next the old king's memory must be defiled, his relatives must die and his monuments be torn down. So when James replaced Mary as their leader there was never any possibility of her remaining in place as a valued member of the community, one way or another she had to disappear - to make his takeover complete. I am myself surprised that other people find so simple a point surprising.

It was the fourth week after the Day of Atonement, and the remorseless glare of high summer had faded. The heat of the day still warmed your bones, but there was no longer any need to seek shelter at noon. I had finished early that day and was going back to the house for my meal, before taking a walk down to one of my usual taverns. As I approached the house I could hear a lively and excited hubbub of female voices and assumed it to be one of our neighbours; Esther's visitors were friendly enough, but usually a little too serious for excited chatter.

However, when I reached the door it turned out that it was indeed our house receiving visitors. After the brightness of the day, I was momentarily blinded by the dark interior, which is why it came as a surprise to be hugged by an unknown female.

"Jesus Barabbas, how lovely to see you again, what an astonishing change there's been in you since our last meeting." I knew the voice and squinted to see the face.

"Joanna, what an unexpected joy." And I meant it. Since acquiring some small degree of maturity I sometimes found myself saying things that were neither cynical nor untrue.

As my eyes accustomed themselves to the interior gloom I saw Mary Magdalen and two other young women that I didn't know. Then with a blink of surprise saw that one of them was holding a swaddled baby. As the girl with the baby looked to be no more than a serving girl, I automatically assumed that it wasn't hers, but concentrated on completing my greetings before making the obvious enquiry.

In the days following the crucifixion - and that was the term now used with special emphasis on the words, an element of reverence, as if it were a singular event. Crucifixions themselves might occur on a regular basis, but there was only one we regularly referred to. As I was saying: in the days following the crucifixion, Mary Magdalen had seemed to me to be a rather preoccupied and remote figure, which in the circumstance was natural enough. She had certainly been kind to me, but it had felt more like a general benevolence to all humanity than anything personal to me. Which could have been why I had preferred to pass my warning about James through the more approachable Joanna, even though in retrospect it had been a waste of time.

They had arrived only an hour before myself, having taken six days to make the journey from Jerusalem in slow easy stages, and for a while there was the busy hum of news being exchanged and questions asked. Eventually it seemed appropriate for me to ask my own question.

"Whose baby is it?"

Mary smiled. "All children are a gift from God, and this one is no different. We all love her equally."

Anyone with even a hint of tact would have understood that they had just been told to mind their own business, but as neither tent makers nor bandits are noted for their tact, I pressed on. "Your sentiments do you credit Mary Magdalen, but who is the mother?"

"The mother is the hand maid of God, Jesus Barabbas, some things are not given for all men to know." She wasn't smiling now, I had pushed her into an area that was too serious for smiling. "With the present situation in Jerusalem, any idle speculation over parentage could be dangerous."

"Is that why you're heading north - to escape persecution?"

"It seems the most prudent thing to do."

As the exchange of news resumed around us, I started to work things out in my head, and it didn't take a great deal of effort. Assuming that the mother was amongst those present, and that it wasn't either of the serving girls, then the mother had to be either Mary Magdalen or Joanna. The child didn't look any more than a couple of months old, and reckoning that the journey had started as soon possible after the sixty six day purification period required for a girl; then working backwards from there, the mother would have been about three months pregnant at the time of the

113

crucifixion. Another woman could possibly have guessed at that stage, but the average man wouldn't and certainly not me.

"I'm sorry to have intruded Mary, but can I ask you what happened over Jesus' instruction that you should take the leadership of your followers in Jerusalem?"

She looked at me for a moment before replying, perhaps wondering if it was any of my business. The others waited with me to hear her reply. They all obviously knew what had happened, but were probably interested to hear how it was going to be explained to an outsider.

"Joanna told me of your warning, and I'm sure you meant well by it. But not everything that is meant to happen does so, and even the things that do happen might not do so immediately."

"You're right to dismiss my enquiry, I'm not a follower of your way and these things are none of my business. I simply wished to see if my understanding of the characters involved had been correct."

This time she didn't smile, she laughed, and it was a warm and earthy laugh; the laugh of a country girl. "Jesus Barabbas, there was never any chance of mistaking you for a follower - you have absolutely no sense of humility. You should practise sometimes."

Esther nodded her head in agreement, as if I'd ever given the woman grounds for complaint.

"But your question's a fair one, James was elected to the leadership of our group, and I'm sure that he will do his best to live up to that honour. Those of us who don't lead must follow, and I promise you that I am quite content in that role, all of us here will do everything we can to support James."

That was fine as far as it went, but it still left one question. "And his mother, I think her name was Mary Cleopas, where does she stand in this readjustment of your leadership? Does she support her son, or does she think that you should have that role?"

"You're anxious to find disagreement where there is none. Mary Cleopas lives in her husband's house now, and that is as it should be. And as for who she supports, she is at one with the rest of us, she supports our continued work in spreading the word of Jesus."

We both knew that this was no answer at all, and that pretending there was no conflict was never going to be the best way to resolve it. But it was also the case that I had pushed myself too far forwards, if I said much more they'd expect me to join in with the next prayer meeting.

The travellers stayed with us and rested for two days, before continuing their journey. They were two very happy days, because although I was, by my own choice, still an outsider I found them to be very lively company and there was a lot of laughter. One slight surprise occurred immediately following their departure, when Esther made what she seemed to think was an obvious remark.

"I think you coped very well with Mary's visit, self control is an important virtue."

"Self control about what?"

"About not giving in to the temptation to tell Mary how you feel about her."

It took me a moment to phrase my answer to this observation of my inner thoughts. "Are my feelings so obvious?" Esther didn't bother replying, instead she simply smiled in that annoying way that some women have. "You don't think she noticed do you?" I asked.

"No I'm sure she didn't." Was her answer, with only a touch of insincerity.

Even so, my abiding memory of that time is the sense of foreboding they all had about events in Jerusalem. The Temple authorities and the Council had

115

no intention of allowing the new church group to acquire any more converts. They might have sat back and waited if the disciples had kept themselves to themselves, but that wasn't happening. Peter and the others, who now included Barnabas in a very prominent role, were preaching the word of Jesus as loudly and widely as they could, almost aggressively so. It was as if they were looking for a confrontation, and the religious authorities were eager to accept the challenge. And if the child was, as I suspected, Mary Magdalen's then I couldn't be the only one who was leaping to a conclusion about who the father was. As a safe home for the new born child and her mother, almost anywhere in world would be preferable to Jerusalem. Of the possible people wishing them ill, I had some trouble choosing which I distrusted most; the priests, Pontius Pilate or Herod, I wouldn't care to trust my life, or my dog, to any one of them.

On the morning of their departure, Esther and I walked with them to the square, where they were joining the next north bound group. Joanna was talking to Esther, one of the serving girls had the baby and Mary Magdalen walked alongside me.

"I'm not sure you understand the danger you're in, the fact that most of the trouble is in Jerusalem, doesn't mean it won't spread." She said.

"Rioting in Jerusalem is a way of life, just because it's affecting your friends this time makes it seem more important than it is."

"That's exactly my point, this isn't just another of Pilate's general crackdowns in response to some provocation by the Zealots, this time it's specifically our own people who are being attacked; or as you call them: my friends. And the people carrying out the attacks are other Jews, not the Romans. It would be easier to deal with them, but if we're being attacked by our own people that doesn't leave many places to hide."

"But I still say that it's a Jerusalem problem, you'll be safe up here, Esther will find somewhere for you to stay."

She shook her head. "Jesus Barabbas you should stick to your tents, because you don't seem able to grasp what's going on. Unless Peter and the others agree to give up spreading the word of Jesus, then the Council will keep on arresting them and imprisoning them, until they do. There have already been arrests in Jericho, and it won't be long before they reach you here."

"Then why doesn't Peter leave it for a while until things die down? He can go back to preaching next year, when it's quieter."

Mary stopped walking and turned to look at me in astonishment. "How can you even ask such a thing? There can be no question of waiting, or the Lord's death will have been in vain."

I shrugged, when confronting that level of fanaticism there wasn't much place for logic. No mention was made of a final destination, and I didn't pursue the matter. The main part of the caravan they were joining was bound for Damascus, but even if they carried on that far Damascus itself was one of the biggest crossroads in the world, they could go anywhere from there.

It was clear that they regarded talk of parentage and destination as equally dangerous, as if they feared pursuers might soon be asking questions about them. I thought they were probably taking themselves and their danger a little too seriously, but if that's how they felt then good luck to them.

When I finally got home from work that night the house seemed quieter and duller without our visitors, Esther's local friends were as worthy and devout as ever, but undeniably less fun, and the women less attractive than Joanna and Mary. I didn't stand a chance with either of them, I was about as unclean as it's possible to be, the simple fact that they talked to me at all was surprising. But a man can dream.

CHAPTER TEN

Autumn gave way to winter, and the work continued without pause, I had even taken on another member of staff. There were now four people working for me while I, in turn, was working for Barnabas. It was a strange situation but one I was prepared to rub along with, he had taken a chance on me when in his position I certainly wouldn't have. This indicated, even to me, that I owed him something. The money I was passing back to Jerusalem must have made a significant contribution to running the group and it felt good to think that my work was supporting a civil uprising. My life might be more sober and honest now than it ever had been, but at least I was paying for somebody else to get into trouble, which I childishly found to be very satisfying.

I had begun see a young widow in town on a regular basis, Hannah, for that was her name, had two small children and worked with her mother in the bakery on the corner. To be honest it was more an arrangement of convenience than a source of passion, we were both unattached and wished not to be. I don't think that either she or her mother had any idea about my past and I was in no hurry to enlighten them; they were were both orthodox mainstream Jews and unlikely to have taken such a pragmatic view of my life as Barnabas.

Esther had always exercised a degree of reticence about her group of Jesus followers, approaching only those possible converts she had some reason to believe might be sympathetic. This was in direct distinction to what was happening in Jerusalem, with Peter, Mark, Matthew and the others standing up in the Temple or the market place and telling the crowds they would all go to hell if they didn't follow the word of Jesus. It wasn't difficult to see why the priests were annoyed and wanted them silenced, a man should be discreet about these things. Esther's approach to revealing her views was a bit like my approach to telling people of my past. It wasn't exactly a secret, but neither of us rushed to accost strangers with the details.

"There is nothing shameful about our beliefs, quite the opposite," she explained, "it's just that for the time being we feel it better to approach those who might be interested directly - rather than trying to interest everybody all at once."

"In other words you'd rather I didn't mention it to anyone?"

She was uneasy to have her views put so starkly. "There's no question of keeping quiet about our beliefs, we just feel that we can spread the word best through our good works in the community, rather than confronting people and antagonising them needlessly."

"That could be a long job, and it's not what Peter and the others are doing. They're confronting everybody - they're standing on street corners telling anyone who'll listen that they can save their souls by believing in Jesus." As I said this I was aware that she was too much of an easy target, and that I should pick on people my own size. Our conversations on the subject often seemed to leave her uneasy, she was the only strong figure in her group and it looked as if she was stuck with moving at the speed of the most nervous member. It was probably more sensible to think of her as just my landlady.

Hannah had picked up clues from me about Esther and her friends and simply thought of them as slightly peculiar, a group of people who were picking an argument on a subject that didn't need arguing about.

"What exactly is it they believe?"

"It's something to do with the crucified preacher, Jesus, they say that you have to trust in him, and he will come back to life again to be the King of the Jews."

"Is that what he said?"

"Well it's not what he said to me, he told me that I had been given time to find repentance, and that I should go in peace."

"Well that sounds nice enough, I suppose." And with that Hannah's mind moved on to more interesting topics, such as whether she needed to do any washing that afternoon. Talking to Hannah could give someone an elevated view of their own intelligence.

Her understanding of life was even more direct than mine. You were born a Jew, you lived as a Jew, you observed the Law - or most of it, you worshipped in the Temple and when your time came you eventually died a Jew. It wasn't something to argue about, it was just the way life was. The fact that I was lodged with the leader of a group who were trying to rearrange these basic rules was in itself enough to raise eyebrows. The one point in my favour was that I had noticeably failed to join Esther's group of Jesus followers, this allowed me to be seen as an eccentric rather than a troublemaker.

From that information she went on to assume that I was as unquestioningly orthodox as her, and so when circumstances permitted she was happy to offer me comfort on cold nights, and I got all the bread I could eat. The possibility that I might not care very much for either her or Esther's religious views didn't seem to have occurred to her.

You may gather from this catalogue of everyday normality that, apart from me working all hours, nothing very much was happening in Jezreel, and you would be right. But it's always the way that you only see what you've got when you lose it. So it was with me until the Festival of Lights that year. Not having much regard for the symbolism and the candle lighting I have always thought of Hanukkah as no more than a marker for the start of the coldest months of the year, it's when you know that winter has officially begun.

I was at the yard laying out two new papilios, that's the standard infantry tent the Legions use. I had managed to increase production significantly by increasing the floor space at the yard in order to make up the tents in pairs, one next to the other. I then paid a bonus at the end of each week to whichever team had made the most progress on their particular tent that week. I hadn't quite doubled production, but we soon could. I had told Barnabas about this in one of my weekly letters, but in his reply the following week he hadn't taken any notice and simply told me more about his latest preaching in the Temple.

It had occurred to me, more than once, that I could probably make more money as businessman than as a highway robber. It's a strange world.

As I was saying; I was at the yard, laying out two new tents, when these two men turned up. At first I thought they had come to talk about tents, it's what people do in a tent yard, but they weren't very talkative. They were dressed like overseers, not common workmen, and their attitude was distinctly superior. Although they were Jewish, I wondered if they were from the Legion's quartermaster's office, some of their staff were locally recruited.

"Good day masters, what can I do for you." I said pleasantly, thinking they might want to place an order.

One of them completely ignored me, but the other stepped towards me. "Are you Jesus Barabbas, the convicted murderer and paid agent of Barnabas the Cypriot?"

The men had stopped working to watch. Not liking his tone didn't stop me from feeling suddenly cold. This was a man very sure of himself, he had back up of some kind. I didn't know what my problem was - but I was sure that knocking him down wouldn't cure it.

"I am Jesus Barabbas, tent maker, and you are?"

"We're your new masters - read this." He thrust a scroll at me, but as I put out my hand to take it, he suddenly drew it back and turned to look at his friend. "Can convicted murderers read?" He asked, as if genuinely puzzled.

"This one can." I said and snatched the scroll. It was in high Hebrew, some sort of priestly declaration, you would need to be a Rabbi to understand it all, but I understood enough. It was issued in the name of Caiaphas the High Priest, and was to the effect that the holder was engaged on the official business of The Council in Jerusalem and that all persons should offer every assistance to them consistent with The Law.

"This says nothing about you being my new master." I said almost throwing it back at him. "It says that I should offer you my assistance, perhaps you had difficulty reading that part. Now do you want me to assist you with my foot up your arse?" I wrenched the heavy hide trimming knife from my belt and stepped forward, my left hand partly raised in front of me, the fingers spread wide to grasp clothing. The knife in my right hand was held out to my side, that arm slightly backwards, exactly the way you go into a fight if you intend to kill someone. I might be a tent maker now, but you only had to scratch me to reach the old ways.

The two of them stepped back, putting their hands to their sword hilts, they recognised trouble. This time the other one spoke, only it was more of a sneer. "Your friend Barnabas is in prison, he will appear in court in the next few days on a charge of blasphemy and will then be stoned to death. Which is what they should have done to you."

"Get out, get out of here now. If you have Temple business to conduct then go to the synagogue and conduct it there. This is a tent maker's yard not a religious meeting place."

"Our master's a tent maker and he'll be setting up his business here, if you're lucky he'll only take half your yard. We'll be back next week, and then you'll either cooperate or join your friend in prison - that's a promise."

Then without another word they walked calmly out. They had just dealt with me, and my display of bravado had made no difference to anything. But who their tent making master might be I had no idea.

When I got home that night I found Esther talking to two of the male members of her group, they looked worried. For once she included me in her discussion.

"It's all over town, there's a team coming up from Jerusalem on Council business, they're supposed to be rooting out any followers of Jesus."

I shrugged. "What can they do? You pay your Temple taxes, you go to the synagogue, just keep your head down and things will soon quieten down again."

"You don't understand, they're arresting anyone known to have spread the word of Jesus. Which means that if anyone tells them about me, they'll arrest me and take me before the Council on a charge of blasphemy."

"I don't see the problem, you've kept things so quiet - hardly anyone knows about you. It'll be alright, you haven't been making a fuss, they're hardly likely to bother with you. If it's any help I promise not to inform on you." I gave a brief and bitter laugh. "Anyway I've got a real problem to sort out, I've just had a visit from some crooks who are trying to take over the tent yard, and they apparently have the High Priest's authority to do it."

She looked unexpectedly shocked. "Do you mean that they showed you a scroll from Caiaphas, instructing all persons to give whatever assistance they required?"

"Yes, I kicked them out, but that's not the end of it - they'll be back and I don't know what I can do to stop them."

"It's the same people, they've been going round town wanting information about anyone holding prayer meetings in the name of Jesus."

"You could understand them being interested in seeking out malcontents or subversives, but why would somebody like that be interested in taking over a tent maker's yard?"

The two men who had been with Esther when I arrived were trying to encourage her to join them on trip they were about to start. "But I have no reason to visit Nazareth." She was saying, with a puzzled look.

"It doesn't matter where we go," one replied, "the point is that we won't be here. This persecution can't last for ever, just keep moving for a few days - to make it more difficult for them to find you, and after a while they'll lose interest. Then we can carry on as before."

"No, it's my duty as the head of the church in Jezreel to be here where our people can find me, if I run and hide then they'll have won without even touching me." Listening to this I thought her reference to *The Church in Jezreel* was rather overstating the situation of a small group of frightened people meeting for semi secret prayer meetings four nights a week.

One of the men made a more useful point. "There's no shame in staying alive, even if it's only for the sake of your friends." But she wouldn't be moved.

"I've been too cautious until now, we were told not to hide our light, yet that's exactly what I've been doing. It's time I made my position clear; on behalf of our whole group."

I found her position difficult to understand, points of principal have always baffled me. You should simply look for the greater good for yourself in any set of circumstances and go with that. Points of principle usually involve doing the very opposite.

They were unable to make any progress and had to leave it at that, leaving me with the knowledge that while I was worried for my job, Esther for her friends were worried for their lives. It seemed a little one sided, but as I said we all have to look out for our own interests in this world, no one else will do it for us.

That night when I called round to see Hannah at the bakery, I found her taking an unexpected interest in the visitors from the High Priest, it wasn't normally her sort of area. It turned out her mother was a staunch defender of the status quo, and had been questioning her daughter about my own sympathies.

Hannah was a pleasant and very convenient young woman, and even her children were bearable, on occasion, but you wouldn't call her clever. "It's alright, my mother would never do anything to hurt you, she knows that we have an understanding." She accompanied this with a meaningful look, which I chose to ignore.

"She's always going on about threats to the Mosaic Law, and the sanctity of the Torah, but she would never cooperate with someone she thought was trying to steal your business."

And for the time being that was as far as I could take matters with Hannah. For the next few days town was buzzing with stories of the Commission from Jerusalem, as the two men called themselves, making threatening noises about who they might drag off in chains, for preaching false doctrine. But nothing actually happened, Esther stayed at home and I kept on working, it was all talk at first.

On the second day of the following week the talking stopped and the action started. I received not two visitors at the tent yard, but five of them. The first two that I'd already met, with two supposed workmen who looked more like vagabonds and a small well dressed man who said his name was Saul. Having spent most of my own life as a nasty piece of work, I can recognise the feature when I see it in others, and he was one.

"You," he pointed at me, "come here." making our respective positions crystal clear. It was like a dog pissing on trees to mark its territory, he'd just pissed on me, and now I was his. I looked around, my own staff were huddled together looking frightened, they weren't going to be much help. But then they were tent makers, which is what they were supposed to be, not fighting men. His staff were all ready for trouble, and it looked like they'd could handle themselves. I've proved that I can fight, and I don't mind killing, but this wasn't the day and this wasn't the place. But one day Saul, I promised myself, one day it will be the day. Then I did what I'd been told and went over to him.

"Jesus Barabbas, by the order of the High Priest I, Saul of Tarsus, am commandeering half of this yard and two of your men, you may continue to work in the other half, for as long as you do nothing that interferes with my work or offends my principals. My assistants," he gestured to the two men I'd already met, "will give you any necessary instructions. You will obey them as if they came direct from me." And with that he simply turned and walked off.

"Wait." I called after him, trying to retain some small vestige of dignity. "I might once have been a criminal, but I'm an honest tax paying citizen now, don't I at least merit some sort of explanation?"

He paused in his stride, and turned back to face me. "Never forget that you merit only what I choose to give you. But if you're so interested then I'll tell you. My job is to seek out heretics wherever they may be hiding, and then drag them out into the light of day to answer to the Council. I am now expanding the area of my search to Galilee, and for that purpose I am establishing a business here to pay for my staff. As well as being a servant of the Council I am also a tent maker, which is why I chose to give you the honour of being my assistant."

I couldn't think of any clever answer to that and so just stood there, but now he'd started on me he felt the urge to go further and took a couple of paces back towards me.

"Jesus Barabbas, that was one of the names used by your so called King of the Jews, wasn't it?"

"I can't help that, nobody asked me about it. Anyway he wasn't *my* King of the Jews."

"Is that so, and yet you work for Barnabas, one of his strongest supporters." He stared at me for a while, apparently musing at this connection. "Are you a heretic Jesus Barabbas? Or are you simply a friend of heretics?"

"I'm just a plain working man who goes to synagogue every Sabbath and pays his taxes, I'm no heretic."

This time he laughed, but unlike Mary Magdalen's it wasn't a pleasant laugh. He came even closer and spoke more quietly. "Understand this Jesus Barabbas, a heretic is anyone that I say is a heretic, and the High Priest agrees with me."

He looked so fanatical, you could almost imagine him believing this sort of deluded rubbish. As he resumed his unhurried and extremely self confident departure I wondered if I'd better start to believe it as well.

I looked on helplessly as his men cleared the space they wanted and began to unload the mules they'd brought with them. This brought my increased production crashing down to earth, I no longer had the space, and he'd taken half my men, it was going to be a problem to keep up with the Legion contract.

CHAPTER ELEVEN

I would like to say that I agonised over what to do with the last weeks profits, the coins were wrapped in my belt, and waiting to be paid to the synagogue clerk for transfer to Jerusalem. But the truth is that I didn't so much agonise, that's not my style, as vaguely wonder what I ought to do.

Saul's message was clear, he was going to root out heretics, by which he meant any followers of Jesus, and if he caught me sending money to Jerusalem he might think that was all the evidence he needed. The least I could expect was a flogging, and the worst would be to have my existing sentence of crucifixion reinstated. Could they do that? I didn't know. The only certainty was that crossing this man Saul was a stupid idea. He was the sort of man that you gave way to, as many times as you had to, and just hoped that he got bored and moved on. This is a very weak position - but also a very realistic one.

I went back to the house, what I needed to do was to write to Barnabas explaining that Saul had confiscated the money, and that I would try to save and hide whatever I could of our future profits, but that things didn't look too promising. That way he might be half expecting it when he found there was nothing in the pot. I honestly felt that I'd fulfilled my side of the bargain, before Saul arrived I had sent almost every penny he was owed, but now the danger was just too great. No one but a fool carries on when facing a brutal operator like Saul, this wasn't my fight and I wasn't about to make it mine. The Roman view began to look increasingly reasonable; if some parts of the local population were determined to kill each other, then let them get on with it, just as long as the survivors pay their taxes. You could understand their reluctance to join in before they had to.

Esther was alone when I got back to the house, looking pale and nervous. "I've been to the synagogue," she said, "the Rabbi told me that this man Saul wants to question me, apparently someone has informed him that I am involved in the Lord's work."

"Then you should do what your friends told told you last night; leave town, hide somewhere."

"That would be to desert my people, I have to be here to support them." She looked frightened but determined. The fright I could understand, it was the determination that was going to be a problem.

"If you leave town for a week or two, you might have deserted your people for a while, but you can always come back when Saul has moved on. Whereas if you get yourself killed, then you've deserted them for ever." She couldn't think of any answer to that so she just pressed her lips together in a thin line and shook her head. This was ridiculous.

"Look there's not much more than forty or fifty of you all told, and the two who were here last night said they, and some of the others, were leaving town for a while; all you have to do is go with them."

"If I run away now, then I'll run away the next time. Some of us have to stand our ground, and then one day there'll be enough of us to make a difference." The woman was possessed, I'd never seen her like this before.

"Are you mad? There'll never be enough of you if you're all dead. I've met this man Saul and he's a complete fanatic. He won't be impressed by you standing your ground, he'll just have you dragged off to

Jerusalem in chains and you'll never be seen again. That won't prove anything or help anyone."

"It's all I can do."

I sighed, she was impervious to reason. "Who told them about you, did they say?"

"No, but I'm sure it wasn't you."

I closed my eyes and rocked backwards and forwards in despair. "Of course it wasn't me, nobody was offering a reward for you. If they had, then I would probably have turned you in. That's what they said about that other man from Kerioth, Judas."

"You knew Judas?"

"We're from the same small town, we were neighbouring families, we were both stamped out with the same iron. The disciples say that he took money to betray your master - so why shouldn't I take money to betray you? The only problem is that nobody offered me any."

"You think that we turned our backs on Judas don't you?"

"I was there at Mark's house when the disciples talked about it, there was a struggle brewing between those who supported Mary Magdalen becoming your leader or James the son of Alphaeus. In order to prevent the argument turning nasty and splitting the group, Simon Peter unified them around their dislike of Judas. Some of them thought that Judas had been obeying Jesus' instructions, but he persuaded them to expel Judas from the group regardless, without any further contact."

"If that's true then it would have been wrong to abandon someone who needed their help, or even in his case to make amends."

"On the contrary I think Peter did exactly the right thing: he sacrificed one man in order to keep your group together. Or would you rather your movement had died on the cross with Jesus?"

My hectoring tone of voice seemed to have brought out a more determined response on her part. "The fact that you're skilled in argument doesn't necessarily make you right. The disciples are only human, they were faced with the greatest crisis imaginable, they did what they could."

"And that's exactly what you should do now."

She simply shook her head again and carried on. "Since you were there when these things were first discussed I'll tell you something you might not know. You mentioned an argument between the supporters of Mary Magdalen and James. You even tried to ask Mary about it when she was here."

"And she never answered me."

"Perhaps she thought it was not a subject for unbelievers, but she told me what happened. It's true that our Lord's instruction was for Mary Magdalen to become the first among the disciples, and this never happened. But I don't think it was quite the rejection you seem to imagine. Mary agreed to the change because she thought the most pressing need for the remaining disciples was to spread the word in the Temple and on the streets of Jerusalem, which could only be done by men. Her feeling was that if the men were called on to do this, then they should be led by a man. Her withdrawal was to preserve the very unity that you spoke of yourself."

"If you'd said that she had withdrawn because she was pregnant I could have believed you; anything else you just said was no more than an argument for Peter becoming leader. From what I read every week in Barnabas's letters, James should never have been considered. You might not like to admit it, but there's something seriously wrong with your leadership."

"I'm sure you mean well, and in time will come to understand things better."

She was closing the argument down, she didn't want to hear any more uncomfortable facts. "You shouldn't be so sure that I mean well, I don't, and neither did James. Now are you going to leave town and avoid Saul, or would you rather risk your life and the future of your group for a gesture?"

"There's a big difference between a gesture and an act of faith."

I had just about reached the limits of rational argument, if she was going to disappear into acts of faith, then I couldn't follow her. There was one possible point still to make.

"You think that I'm well intentioned - well you're wrong and this is the proof." I unwrapped my belt, took out Barnabas's money and slapped it onto the table in front of her. "This is the money which I should have handed over to the synagogue clerk this evening, to be sent to Jerusalem. But I didn't, I stole it, because I was afraid that it could tie me in with your lot. That's all you need to know about me."

She said nothing, but looked at me calmly, waiting for the rest.

"There is no more, there's nothing else to say. Take the money, and save me from sin. Use it to pay for your journey. I no longer care about the money - just get out of here."

"I will have to be dragged out."

"Then I wash my hands of you, whatever happens now is on your own head." With that I turned and walked out.

For a while I wandered the darkening streets, but then, in want of company, thought I might find some consolation for Esther's obstinacy with Hannah. I made my way to the bakery, if nothing else the place always smelled good. The children were in bed, which made for a more peaceful atmosphere than usual and Hannah, in her placid bovine way, was pleased to see me. I hadn't eaten, and so she warmed some mutton stew for me.

After I'd finished eating I started drinking, and during all of it I was moaning about my various problems. Something, I'm not sure what, stopped me from talking about my conversation with Esther. It probably just struck me as unlikely that Hannah would have much to offer on such a subject. But I did go on about the injustice of Saul and his men taking over half my yard.

"They can't do that." She said, indignant on my behalf. "You can take them to court and demand restitution under the law."

I explained things slowly and simply. "The trouble is that the only courts to deal with this are Rabbinical, that means they're run by priests. And that then means that Saul's authority from the High Priest will outweigh anything I could possibly say."

"Oh." She was a pleasant young woman, and a good mother to her children, but that was as far as it went. By this time it was Hannah's bedtime, and being too fed up with life to make any further effort, I went with her. It wasn't my normal practice to spend the night there, but the large size of the building and the early hour of their morning start meant that my occasional presence got lost in the general comings and goings of the business.

Her two boys were somehow able to sleep through the clatter and bang of the bakehouse's pre dawn start, but I usually gave up the struggle and helped out with stoking the oven or some other menial task, until they stopped for their first break.

That morning we had only just sat down to our breakfast, it being about dawn, when Hannah's mother

136

arrived. A short bossy woman, the sort who always seemed to know better than you what you should be doing with your life, and happy to tell you. Her approval of me was conditioned by two things; first that I had money and second, that she knew nothing of my past. If either of those two changed then so would her approval. The synagogue committees she sat on would never tolerate one of their members mixing with a rapist and murderer - and quite right too.

We greeted each other politely, she didn't care what her daughter and I got up to as long as the surface formalities were observed and marriage resulted. If she could have read my thoughts she would probably have killed me. I didn't mention Saul, no doubt she would tell me that I should be honoured by the presence of this interloper. However, I didn't need to raise the subject, she did it herself.

"I'm pleased to find you here Jesus Barabbas, I assume that now that woman Esther has been dealt with then you two will announce your betrothal, and you can move in here officially. Of course we were pleased to see that you never made any . . ."

I was astonished, and silenced her by simply talking over her. "What d'you mean - Esther has been dealt with?"

She stopped, her face expressing genuine surprise. "When I was telling that man from Jerusalem about her, Saul, that was his name, he said they would go round there last night and arrest her. I assumed that was why you were here."

My chair scraped along the floor as I pushed myself angrily back and rose to my feet. "Why exactly were you telling Saul anything about Esther?"

She was immediately defensive. "I was doing no more than telling him what you'd told Hannah - about Esther being the leader of a group of heretics."

I swung my accusing glare at Hannah, who shrank visibly back in her chair to get further away from me. "Anything I said to you about Esther was in confidence, you promised me - you faithfully promised me."

She started snivelling, the favourite defence of the feeble minded. "Don't shout at me, I didn't mean any harm." She whimpered. Then her mother stood up to join in, she wasn't much taller standing up than sitting down, but she was making a point.

"You leave my daughter alone, she doesn't need your permission to speak to her own mother."

I jabbed an accusing finger in their general direction. "If Esther's come to any harm because of either of you, then I'll make you regret it if it's the last thing I do." I had already started to leave the room when the mother started to screech something about never having liked me. I was too angry to think of any coherent or sensible response and found myself sweeping up a small stool from the floor, turning round and throwing it at her. I should have remembered that you must never rush that sort of thing and so hadn't aimed properly. Instead of knocking her head off, it had just smashed against the far wall without, unfortunately, having damaged her on its way. There was a roomful of shocked faces behind me as I stormed out of the house.

It was now plain to me that I should never have abandoned Esther last night, she was stupid and obstinate and had ignored my best advice, but I should have stayed. I didn't have any idea what that would have accomplished, I hadn't been a lot of use when they turned up at the yard - but there was still a guilty feeling that I should have been there.

The streets that I strode through were filled with the normal bustle of a town getting ready for another day's business, but I registered none of it, I was too sick with the prospect of what I'd find.

There was a small crowd of people gathered round the door of Esther's house, they were trying to see something that was fastened there, it looked like a notice. A man at the front was reading it out for the benefit of those who couldn't read, his finger moved along the lines to show which bit he was at. I pushed my way through, I lived here and had no intention of joining a queue.

As I elbowed my way through the onlookers some of them recognised me. "It's him, it's Jesus Barabbas." Everyone turned to look at me, transferring their attention from the man reading the notice. People began to clap me on the back and smile at me, it was as if I'd done something popular, something to please the crowd.

"Well done, it was high time somebody sorted them out." And from another side: "Good work, you deserve every penny of it." And from someone at the back: "Good for you."

Ignoring all of them I pushed my way even more violently to the door. There was a notice nailed there, a proclamation. I tore it down, this was my notice, not anybody else's.

'Citizens of Jezreel. The heretic Esther of Cana has been arrested for blasphemy against Moses and God and for the spreading of false doctrine in the name of Jesus of Nazareth the executed criminal and the false Christ. As a reward for his great assistance in tracking down this dangerous woman and her associates the Elders of the Synagogue have awarded Jesus Barabbas the tent maker thirty pieces of silver. In the name of Saul of Tarsus, Commissioner of the High Priest. '

I turned to look at the crowd, my back to the door, surrounding me was a sea of smiling faces all looking at me. There wasn't a single thing I could say that would convince anyone of my innocence. I had been paid the traditional wage of a traitor and everyone knew it. Saul wasn't just more powerful than me, he was also cleverer than me, much, much cleverer.

But then, beyond the throng around me there was another figure, partly hidden in a doorway, positioned to make a quick escape. Even at that distance I knew it to be one of Esther's group, she had called him her Deacon, he pointed his hand at me and mouthed a word. There was too much noise around me for his voice to be heard, but after he'd repeated it a few times I recognised the shape his mouth was forming. The word was 'Judas, Judas, Judas'.

CHAPTER TWELVE

I slammed the door shut behind me and looked around, the house had the cold dead feel of an empty property: there was nobody here. The place was in good order, there was no disarray, nothing had been turned over and searched. They hadn't needed to search, they'd already had all the information they needed. Esther was known to enough people throughout our community for it to have been certain that somebody would have talked, even without the malicious folly of Hannah and her mother, Saul would have found her. She really should have left.

I sat at the table wondering if there was anything that could be done to help her, but even as the thought occurred the answer came with it - no. I'd been hearing about the results of Saul and his men looking for heretics in the last few days. Doors broken down in suspect's houses, people dragged from their beds in the night, children left without parents. None of this came close to touching me, they weren't my broken doors or my abandoned children. Life can be a bruising business, I'd found that out for myself, and now these people were making the same discovery. Looking after my own safety was going to be all I could manage, which meant that I should stick to tending my own garden - not theirs.

Sure enough, there on the table in front of me was a brown leather pouch, the top tied with a drawstring; I didn't need to open it to know its contents, thirty pieces of silver. That sight helped me to recover my sense of proportion. Saul probably imagined that I would throw the coins back in his face, but that would only be worth doing if it would make a difference to anything; as I might have mentioned I don't go in for points of principle. Nothing I could do would change the fact that I'd been branded a traitor, even if it was only a traitor to the Jesus group, in which case I might as well keep the money.

Hannah and her mother had annoyed me, and missing her mother's head with that stool had annoyed me even more, but then life is full of small annoyances. The main result in my own life from this morning's performance was that I would now have to look elsewhere for free bread and a willing woman. I told myself that I should try to moderate my emotions about other people's problems.

From what I'd seen of Saul in the last twenty four hours there were no grounds for optimism or hope, he had come to Jezreel specifically to trace and arrest the local Jesus group and enforce Jerusalem's ideas of orthodoxy on the local population, and that was exactly what he was doing.

Judaism has always been a faith able to encompass a wide variety of opinion, but even Judaism has its boundaries. The behaviour of the crowd around my door made it plain that most of them agreed with Saul, splinter groups and breakaway movements weren't welcome at a time like this. The Zealots understood this simple fact and built their movement around it. Their appeal to the crowd was that we should all stand together against the Romans, and against any Jews who helped the Romans and it made a lot of sense. It even appealed to me, and I'm no more political than I am religious.

But despite my determined rationality there was something else, something less rational and even less welcome, and that was my view of Esther's behaviour. I had given her good advice and she had failed to take it, so whatever happened was her own look out, she should have done what I said. I had no reason to feel guilty. Any earlier doubts I might have had on that subject were no more than passing fancies, it was time to get a grip. Unfortunately I wasn't able to close things down at that and walk away, her actions hadn't just been stupid, they had also been brave. It's rather like music, I can't play an instrument or sing very well but I like to listen to others doing it. So it is with bravery, I don't possess any myself but on the rare occasions I see it, I do admire it in others. I've always had a fondness for minority movements, the people who are howled down by the mob, the same mob who would have jeered at me hanging on the cross.

Whatever the rights or wrongs of her dead leader, or even her risen from the dead leader, or his frightened and squabbling disciples, Esther's steadfast certainty was the sort of thing that someone weaker than me could be attracted to. I shook my head and wondered if this was the moment to kill Saul, before he turned his hostile intentions in my direction.

The man was duplicitous and ruthless, exactly what I had always been, but he was better at it than me; and he had a Cause whereas I had only ever had myself. With his presence so firmly planted in town and in my own business I was going to have to choose my direction, standing at the crossroads wasn't good enough. If I wasn't going to kill him, then I would have to work with him. The man had humiliated me in my own yard and in front of my own men, so it wasn't an appealing prospect, but then neither was going back to my old life as a fugitive on the road. They'd caught me once and would probably do so again, which was something that didn't bear thinking about.

With the situation at the tent yard in such a state of turmoil, I should have been giving that my full attention, but there was one more thing I needed to do in town. By the time I'd changed into my work clothes and left the house, the crowd of onlookers had dispersed and the accusing figure in the doorway was gone. I walked through the market to the synagogue, if there was any word of Esther's current condition it would be found there.

Saul had brought with him a small squad of auxiliary troops, presumably to transport any prisoners back to Jerusalem, two of them were sat by the well outside the synagogue's front porch. They would be a good place to start, so I introduced myself as Jesus Barabbas, tent maker and paid informant.

"There's fourteen of them," said one of the troops, "six women and eight men, They were flogged last night, but didn't say anything useful. Two of our boys are with them now, the usual routine is to have them make a voluntary statement before we take them away, along the lines of how they were always mistaken and bitterly regret their past sins. You know the sort of stuff."

I nodded my understanding. These were locally recruited auxiliaries and had no direct connection to the Legion. "Do you know if this lot are going to say that?"

"I would think so, most of them do. Those boys can be very persuasive."

"What's likely to happen to them in Jerusalem?"

The two men looked at each other doubtfully and shrugged. "Difficult to say, the way things are. This lot are causing all sorts of ructions at the moment, Pilate must be rubbing his hands together, whenever it's Jew fighting Jew it makes his life a lot easier. They'll be up before the Council for sure."

"And then?"

"Well there haven't been any stonings yet, but it's only a matter of time, people say that Caiaphas is ready for some show of strength to frighten the rest."

I thanked them and left it at that. My walk out to the tent yard was a jumble of competing thoughts, trying to weigh up each side of the argument. My need to make a choice was imminent, once I arrived at the yard there would be no more time for thought, I would have to act.

Barnabas would have to be informed that half his premises had been expropriated, with the consequent damage to the business, there wouldn't be much he could do about it, even so he would have to be told. But then what was I supposed to say about the reports he would undoubtedly receive from the remnants of the local Jesus group? They would have told him that I was a traitor and that I had taken Saul's money. I had sat and listened to Peter and the others discussing what they should do about Judas. Their comments about leaving the final judgement to God had struck me as ambiguous, had they meant that they would kill Judas in order that God should have the earliest opportunity of judging him? They were desperate enough to cling at any wild straws.

Avoiding trouble by siding with the Jesus group looked like being a problem, that pointing finger from Esther's Deacon was a fair summary of what they would think of me: Judas, Judas, Judas.

I walked into the yard, expecting to see Saul's two assistants, instead to my surprise I met Saul himself, it looked as if he'd been waiting for me.

"Jesus Barabbas, good day to you, I thank you for your help last night. Hannah's mother said that you would wish me to be informed of the happenings at your house."

This was a master tactician at work. He hadn't only been thinking his own thoughts, he had also been thinking mine. He knew that his display of strength yesterday had humiliated me, and he also knew that I could jump either way this morning. With those opening words he had made clear that he was offering me an olive branch, not just continued freedom and employment, but also a relationship that would enable me to save face. The heavy knife was still in my belt, and although fiery and determined, he was only a small man; none of his assistants were to be seen, it was just the two of us. I looked at him and imagined disposing of his body, it wouldn't be difficult, my own men were sufficiently loyal to me. For a moment he was at my mercy, perhaps my thoughts were visible on my face for there was none of yesterday's arrogance on his. Yet still, satisfying myself by killing him would just be to strike one head off the Hydra. If he disappeared then Caiaphas would simply send a replacement, and another, and another. At some stage there would have to be flight or agreement.

I stepped forward and pointed my finger at him. "If you think you can come in here and steal my Legion contract, you can think again. If we're sharing this yard then you'll have to find your own work. Is that clear?"

He didn't smile at this disguised capitulation, he merely inclined his head in agreement. "Naturally, we shall procure all our own orders and cause no interference to yours. My only requirement is that we should share the labour force to both our advantage, so that when one is busy he may have more men, and vice versa."

He was lying, and he knew that I knew he was lying, if ever it suited him he would ruin both me and my business, and yet it was nicely done. We were both pretending that I was still the master of my own affairs. I stepped forward and we clasped hands, supposedly to seal a bargain that neither of us regarded as anything more than temporary. I had never mentioned Esther, instead I had just climbed into bed with a viper and, as might be expected, my bowels had turned to water.

The disappearance of some of the more active members of the local Jesus group effectively ended their activities, or at least such activities as I ever heard of. Esther's older brother turned up to claim the house, complete with his wife, married daughter, her husband and three children. There wouldn't have been any room for me, even if they'd wanted me, which they didn't. I took an upper room at the tavern I most frequently drank at, which is what I should have done in the first place.

To my great surprise Saul's tent making business was almost as successful as my own, he proved to be a competent and time served tent maker himself, but rarely spent more than half of any working week with us. Most of his time was spent on Temple business, using Jezreel as his headquarters to scour the surrounding district, sniffing out heresy and blasphemy wherever it was to be found. His aggressive methods caused fear and resentment in some, but overall you couldn't claim he was unpopular, a great many of the population thought that he was doing no more than enforcing the law. I looked the other way, partly out of cowardice and partly because I didn't wish to dwell on what had happened to Esther. She was in the past and a man shouldn't dwell in the past.

Sextus Flavius had kept true to our agreement, and hadn't split his order for the Legion tents between Saul and myself. In fact, improbable though our relationship might sound, he and I had always got along very well together, and our meetings now always included a flagon of wine and time spent putting the world to rights. This had kept our side of the business in full employment, leaving Saul's men to concentrate on caravan work and the steady turnover of travellers needing saddle repairs and the like.

Saul's deputy, Samuel, one of the original two who had visited us, was still a thoroughly unpleasant creature - but in view of my arrangement with his master, not quite as unpleasant as he once had been. But then Samuel was never the one to watch, he was no more than another of Saul's pet dogs and like all the rest of us he barked on demand. The one thing you ought never do when dealing with Saul was to take your eye off him, he was a fanatic and like all true fanatics the chances were that he was more dangerous when pretending to be nice than when showing his true colours.

Shortly after Esther and the other prisoners were taken back to Jerusalem to stand trial, Saul himself followed. Jezreel wasn't big enough or important enough to detain a man like that for long. He had set up a listening post with staff in place, complete with a profit making business to pay their wages, it was an efficient use of resources. His men would send him regular reports of events in southern Galilee and, should circumstances require it, he would return to sort out any further heretics. In the meantime he was free to pursue the larger battle still raging on the streets of Jerusalem

For the space of six weeks Barnabas made no contact with me, despite my letters to him continuing as normal. Even without his correspondence I was still getting regular news from Jerusalem, we were on the main north south road and there were travellers at the inn every night talking about the disturbances. Far from dying away, the disciples in Jerusalem were becoming ever more active, they would never defeat the Temple Council, let alone Herod or the Romans, but against all expectations they were growing in numbers. The fact that the High Priest was sending out men like Saul to hunt down the Jesus followers meant that he was worried, and if they were strong enough to worry him then it was worth gambling some of my money on them. The main strategy would remain my alliance with Saul, if nothing else it was earning money, but in the background I needed to keep my options open with the disciples. A man never knows when he'll need friends.

For this reason I had explained to Barnabas how Saul had tried to smear my name with the accusation that I had betrayed Esther, I didn't go into details but asked him to wait until he'd spoken to me before coming to judgement. I also told him that I could no longer send his money back as a transfer between synagogues, for fear of the authorities intercepting it, and so was holding it on his behalf. However, it seemed from his lack of reply that he had already made up his mind about me and wasn't interested in my excuses. I had apparently been cut adrift from their movement, not any great loss in itself you might say, considering my association with Saul. The thing is, I always like to have a get out plan, in case my first scheme goes wrong, and this lot were a growing presence on the streets. It would be a shame to lose touch with them.

Then one day one of the boys at the tent yard happened to mention casually that he'd heard my friend Mark from Jerusalem was back in town, and staying at the house of Zachary the wine merchant.

"How long has he been here, d'you know?" I asked, trying to sound casual.

"Since yesterday, my sister told me, she lives across the street." I shrugged as if it didn't matter and carried on with my work, but it mattered. If Mark was in town without talking to me it confirmed that I'd been cut off, the disciples no longer trusted me. They'd washed their hands of me. I might not have bothered otherwise, but the feeling that they'd decided to abandon me, rather than the other way round wasn't the way I liked things to work. I determined to put things right, and knew exactly how to play this. I rushed back to the yard, where I had Barnabas's money hidden in the shed we used for storing the cured hides. This would prove my friendship.

I went to the house and knocked at the door, a young woman answered. "Yes sir."

"I'm here to speak with Mark."

"I don't know of any such person, this is the house of Zachary."

She stood in the doorway, one hand on the door to stop me pushing past her. "I am a friend of John Mark, and I know he's here, please tell him that Jesus Barabbas waits outside."

"I know you Jesus Barabbas, you were once a friend of Esther and are now a friend of Saul and do his bidding." She stood staring at me, it was my move. If I was the traitor she made me out to be, then she was putting herself in danger by listing my shortcomings so openly. That meant that she was another of the Jesus followers, they seemed to have no concept of their own safety.

"Please, just ask Mark to speak to me, either here or some other place of his choosing."

This time Mark came to stand beside her, he stared at me for a moment and then gestured her to let me enter. I followed them into the room, there were a group of men and women sitting round a table, one of them was Esther's Deacon, the one who had called me Judas. The atmosphere was colder than midwinter.

"I've brought Barnabas's money."

"Does that include the thirty pieces of silver?" Asked the Deacon.

"No, I spent that. I didn't ask for it and did nothing to earn it, it was left on the table in my house. What do you suggest I should have done with it, thrown it down the well?"

"Saul just gave you thirty pieces of silver, for no reason?"

"Oh he had a reason all right, Esther was a friend of mine and he wanted to make it look as if I'd sold her, which is why he put that notice on Esther's door, thanking me for my cooperation. Have you ever seen a notice like that before?" A collection of sullen faces stared silently at me.

"Well have you?"

This time three or four of them shook their heads, which was a small improvement.

"The money and the notice were intended to deceive the easily led, and they certainly deceived you. In case you'd forgotten Barnabas owns the biggest tent yard in the area and I run it in his absence, Saul is another tent maker and he wanted to force me to cooperate with him."

This time it was Mark who spoke, and he wasn't nearly so hostile as the Deacon. "How would that make you cooperate?"

"By separating me from my friends, and leaving him as my only ally. Every man needs friends and he made sure that you lot would be standing in doorways, pointing your fingers at me and shouting Judas." I locked eyes with the Deacon, who was still angry and unwilling to let the matter drop so easily.

"That man is pure evil, he is hounding God fearing people to their graves, and you have chosen to lie down with him."

"Unlike you, I live in the real world and I needed to take a real decision. I could either cooperate with him, or openly confront him - there was no middle ground. I chose to cooperate with Saul to avoid him taking over Barnabas's trade completely. Because if I hadn't agreed

151

to work with him that's what he would have done, and I couldn't have stopped him. This way at least you still have the income to support your work in Jerusalem. How would you have supported that work?"

Some of my stuff is so good that I even impress myself. The Deacon was a long way from happy, but unless I was fooling myself there was now a hint of uncertainty in his face. I needed to drive home my advantage.

"If you want to find out who reported Esther to Saul you should speak to Hannah the baker and her mother. You won't have any trouble finding them, they sit next to your wives in the synagogue every Sabbath."

From the uneasy glances that were being exchanged this information was no surprise to some of those present, they just hadn't wanted to hear it from me, it had been easier to blame the convicted criminal than listen to him.

"Mark, I can understand that Barnabas might not have wanted to write to me, having heard false reports of my actions, but as God is my witness I never betrayed Esther." That part was the absolute truth; I had just one more thing to say.

"I came here to give you Barnabas's share of the tent money, and now I've done that I'm going. If you want me for anything Mark, I have a room at the Sign of the Trident on Fore Street." Then in line with my long held views on negotiations: say just what you must and then shut up, I shut up and walked out. It might or might not be enough to get me back in with them, but I find that it's always worth trying to have a bet on both sides, and that had been my best effort.

CHAPTER THIRTEEN

On the evening of my confrontation at the house of Zachary the wine merchant, I received a visit from Mark at my lodgings at the inn. He was more conciliatory than his colleagues, even if that wasn't saying much.

"The reason you haven't heard from Barnabas is that he's been in prison, but they failed to convict him and he'd just been released before I left. He sends his best wishes to you, and thanks you for being so prompt with the tent profits - we're permanently short of money and that's been a big help."

I felt a great sense of relief, greater than was strictly justified by the relative unimportance of the Jesus group's opinion. It must have been the case that I'd come to appreciate having Barnabas as a friend, and if that is what he was, then he was my first. I'd had acquaintances and I'd had followers, but I'd never had a friend before; I just hadn't realised that fact until now. It made me unusually open with my feelings.

"I don't mind what the Deacon and his friends believe, but you and Barnabas, as well as Mary and Joanna all trusted me, and I haven't betrayed you. I begged Esther to go into hiding for as long as Saul was in town, it would only have been for a week or so, but she wouldn't. She kept on saying that her place was to remain as a visible symbol of the group's presence. It was dangerous and stupid, and now she's been taken. Does anyone know what's happened to her?"

Barnabas shook his head. "The Sanhedrin don't have the authority to condemn people to death, but we all know it happens. Prisoners are officially listed as having been released, but then are never seen again."

Now that I'd given my display of aggressive innocence to his people this afternoon, showing myself as the victim, I felt the urge to be helpful. I don't think it had anything to do with me being a good person, it was more likely the appreciation, now that Esther had disappeared, of just how friendless I was without Mark and Barnabas. "How would you have acted in my place?" I asked him.

"I don't know, but I can see that you're torn between the rigorous efficiency of Saul and the possible gain that association would bring, and some vague desire to retain our friendship. You might think that you've made your big decision - but you haven't, you're still wavering about what really matters, you're still undecided."

We were silent for a while, each looking at the other, I didn't know where else to take this but he seemed to.

"You're resisting any faith in Jesus, the true Messiah, and I'm going to do nothing to drag you to him. You'll have to take that decision on your own for it to mean anything. But it might interest you to know that I said openly that I thought you would steal Barnabas's money, and looks as if I was wrong. I found it as difficult to trust you, as you do to trust Jesus." He smiled. "Perhaps we were both wrong."

"Can I do anything to help you?"

"Yes, you can keep your eyes and ears open to see what information you can pick up about Saul's plans, we need as much notice as possible of where his next purge could be. Esther might not have listened to your advice, but I think she would have listened if it had come from me. If I'd known in advance what Saul was planning then I would have suggested that she take whatever steps were necessary to avoid him."

"I probably won't hear much at the tent yard, all we talk about is business - tent business."

"Then offer to help him, in any way you can. The fact of the matter is that as far as our local community is concerned you're an outcast, despite hearing your explanation today it would be difficult for them to dislike you any more than they already do. And from Saul's point of view he knows that you're damaged goods, you've been sentenced to death once and only escaped by what looked like a miracle. He might feel that he can use you."

"Don't underestimate him, he's an extremely clever man."

"I'm sure he is and we should tailor our approach to allow for that. If half of what you say to me is the truth, then perhaps half of what you say to him is true. The point is that anyone else I asked to get close to him wouldn't be telling any truth at all. For once in your life you would be the most honest of the possible candidates."

"Is that all you think of me, that only half of what I say is true?"

"That's a higher figure than it used to be. But more importantly, if you think about it, the information someone close to Saul could provide us with could not only save lives, it could protect our growing network."

"If I were to help Saul in a way that would persuade him to confide in me, then I might be partly responsible for your followers being unjustly imprisoned or flogged, or even killed, is that what you want me to do?"

He thought about it for a moment before replying, and then said: "The ends should never justify the means, but sometimes we have to be pragmatic. It's not about what I want you to do, it's what you want for yourself. Jesus said that you'd been given time to find repentance - you alone, of all the people on earth had been given that gift. Yet for the last year you might as well have spent your days playing with yourself. Is that what you want to do with your life?"

It felt as if I was back in court, standing before Pilate with my hands tied and realising that I'd run out of arguments. I shook my head, defeated. "No that's not what I want."

"Then listen to these names and memorise them, these are the people that you can leave messages with, and those messages will reach me wherever I am." He then gave me a list names, places and towns, and had me repeat them back to him several times over, until he was satisfied.

"When you speak to Saul, the most important thing you need to remember is that he is a completely orthodox and highly educated Pharisee, he studied under Gamaliel and could have been a priest or a lawyer. The more complicated your lie the more directly he'll see through it, you must tell him only what you can say with complete conviction. Remember what you said yourself : he is a very clever and able man. You can only tell him what you believe to be true; you aren't convincing enough to lie to someone like that without it being obvious."

"Then it's going to be difficult to spy on him, without me telling him what I'm doing."

"Not necessarily. Are you proud of having been a thief, a rapist and a murderer?"

I could feel the anger boiling up in me. "You and Saul might both be a lot cleverer than me, but that doesn't mean you can talk down to me. So don't try it."

"You didn't answer my question; are you proud of what you were?"

"Of course I'm not."

"Do you wish you hadn't killed your master? Do you wish that you hadn't been a highway robber?"

"Wishing won't change anything, I did what I did."

"But if you could go back in time and change things, so that your young cousins weren't crucified in your place, would you do that?"

I stared blankly at the wall of my room, unwilling to meet his eye, not much caring about the rich travellers I'd killed, or even my cousins, but seeing instead the two small children whose deaths I had ordered to save my own face, and who still visited me in the night.

Eventually Mark spoke again. "Thinking about it isn't enough, you have to say it."

The words were dragged from me, but they came. "Yes - I wish that I could go back and change things."

"Then that is your first step towards atonement, your next step is to live an honest life and perform godly acts."

"And how exactly does that help me to spy on Saul?"

"On its own it might not, but if you were to try and listen to what I'm telling you, that might." His patience was showing signs of fraying, so with great effort I kept quiet.

"You will tell Saul, in all honesty, that you wish to work towards your atonement by performing godly acts, and to this end you wish to assist him him his work. He is a man very much convinced of his own virtues, and if he sees in you an honest desire for atonement then that should be sufficient. There's no need for you to mention that the acts you have in mind are designed to protect and keep safe the servants of the risen Lord."

I was astonished. "That's almost as dishonest as my own behaviour."

"Not at all, each individual part of what you tell him will be the truth, you will simply not feel it necessary to burden him with every detail."

"My earlier question still remains: what if in the course of my duties I am to cause harm to those he seeks to persecute?"

"No great cause is ever without its problems, and where necessary you should consider not only your own atonement, but also the service of the greater good."

I had previously thought of myself as ruthless, I was wrong, when compared to either Saul or Mark I was no more than a country boy come to town. God save us all from religion.

*****

Events moved faster than I'd anticipated, my conversation with Mark had been the week before Pentecost and at that time there had been no sign of Saul coming back to Jezreel. Then in the days following Pentecost we found out why. The markets and inns were filled with reports from Jerusalem about the Sanhedrin having broken with all tradition, and possibly even the law, by condemning a man to death; though some reports made it sound more like an enraged mob at work.

It seemed that a Greek Jew called Stephen, an associate of the disciples, had been taken before the Sanhedrin on a charge of blasphemy, and far from apologising or trying to deny the charge, had attacked his accusers. I was told by two people who claimed to have been there, that his performance before the Council had been completely unrepentant, even defiant. He acknowledged no wrongdoing and demanded that his accusers tell him which of their forefathers had not persecuted and killed the prophets. This was clearly not the response of a penitent man, and there had been uproar in the chamber.

At this point the different accounts varied slightly; some said that the Sanhedrin had formally sentenced him to death, and others that the onlookers had just dragged him out. In either case the result was the same, he had ended up outside the Damascus Gate, the very spot where I should have been crucified, and there had been stoned to death.

This was interesting for two reasons, first because it would surely be seen as opening the floodgates. There had been a sense of impotence in the Sanhedrin's dealings with the Jesus people. They were desperate to stop their activities but couldn't manage to convince the Romans to take an interest, and without Roman interest they were restricted to interrogating them, flogging them and briefly imprisoning them; all of which the prisoners accepted quite cheerfully. But as long as the Jewish authorities stayed within the law they were unable to impose the death penalty - the only thing that might have worked. This very problem had been discussed in the synagogues in Jezreel, with a general public feeling that this somehow wasn't good enough. But with this recent execution or murder, whichever it was, all that had changed. When you've had one slice off a loaf, it's a lot easier to take another. If Esther had still been alive in some dungeon before Stephen's death, then I reckoned she wouldn't be for much longer, there was gale about to sweep through the Jesus followers.

The second point which made this case interesting was the identity of the ringleader of the mob which had carried out the stoning: Saul. He really was serious about his work, and for a highly educated young man, who'd had the best teaching the Temple could offer, he didn't mind getting his hands dirty. I've clubbed people to death and I've stabbed them to death, but I've never stoned anyone - that's cold blooded, that's just dirty.

During the strange period between my being a simple tent maker and becoming a spy in the enemy camp, I received a visit from Joanna. This time she was travelling with just her personal servants, there was no sign of Mary Magdalen, or the baby. She simply knocked at the door of my room at the inn one evening. For the first time, and to my surprise, we embraced. It was the warm and natural embrace of two friends, friends who haven't seen each other for a while. I poured her some wine and asked what brought her to my door.

"I have to return to Jerusalem, there's so much fear amongst our people since the death of Stephen, the disciples need as much help as possible."

"What help can you be that won't put you into the same position as them?"

"My rank as the widow of Herod Antipas's chamberlain gives me access to places and people that none of the others can reach. I can move freely through the most severe of Saul's purges, his people would never dare touch me."

I must have been favoured with some tact for once, because I never asked about Mary or the baby, thinking that if she wanted me to know she would tell me. Instead we chatted companiably for a while and then she left me for her own lodgings, once more with a friendly embrace.

It was only after she had left me that I worked out what had been happening, her journey to Jerusalem, and the reasons she gave for it, were undoubtedly genuine: but her real reason for visiting me had never been raised. I was sure that she had come to express her unspoken gratitude for my agreement to accept Mark's commission. It gave me a great deal of pleasure to think that I was now regarded as 'one of them', not in a religious sense of course, but at least as a trusted friend. It felt good.

I found myself becoming increasingly nervous at meeting Saul again, my last dealings with him had been about tents, an area where I was in command of my subject. But the next time would find me at risk of being exposed as a liar, and Stephen's fate made for uncomfortable thoughts about what happened to his enemies.

The actual meeting, when it came, was undramatic. I arrived at the yard one morning shortly after dawn, and found that he was already there. Needless to say the talk did not immediately turn to stoning people.

He greeted me with the clasped hand of friendship, after all we were pretending to be partners, so why not? He asked for my help in fulfilling a rush order his men had got for mule panniers for one of the caravans going up to Tyre. Naturally I was pleased to be of service and lent him the use of one of my men for the week. After which there was a pause in the conversation, and having little skill with subtlety I drove to the heart of the matter.

"Tell me what happened in Jerusalem, the inns have been filled with all sorts of stories about the man Stephen." I reckoned that not raising the subject would be more suspicious than doing so. It seemed he agreed, as his answer was perfectly natural.

"He was an unrepentant heretic, he stood before his judges and claimed that he could see God waiting to welcome him in Heaven, it was a disgraceful performance. If ever a man deserved death he certainly did. To give you some idea of his arrogance, his last words were to request that God should forgive the rest of us." He shook his head as if disbelieving the memory.

"I didn't think the Sanhedrin were allowed to condemn people to death."

"Not normally, but in the cases like this where public blasphemy has caused such enormous outrage, then I think they have little alternative."

"Won't the Romans object?"

"The Romans are delighted that the Sanhedrin have finally found their backbone and started to impose some order on the streets. There'll be no complaints from them." Then he looked at me, slightly puzzled. "I didn't know you were interested in religious matters."

I shrugged. "I'm constantly surprised that with my background the Rabbi so much as lets me into the synagogue each Sabbath. Surprised and grateful I suppose. Even people like me can change eventually."

"I'm pleased to hear it; I take it you received my purse of the silver?"

I needed to stand up for myself, rolling over in front of someone as aggressive as Saul will never get you anywhere. "I feel you intended to do me a disservice by that note on my door and the purse of silver, but you didn't succeed. I had made Esther's views well known to everyone I met, even to Hannah the baker and that pompous mother of hers. It was hardly a surprise when you finally joined all the rest of us and managed to work out what was happening."

He raised his eyebrows, this wasn't the approach he'd imagined. "You had no shame in living under the roof of a heretic?"

"Why should I? I drink at the fountain next to a Samaritan, or would someone like you rather go thirsty?"

He laughed, and it sounded genuine, so I gave it one more turn of the screw. "As I'm under an obligation of Atonement, if you want my help you need only ask for it, leaving proclamations nailed to my door really isn't necessary." Then I left it at that, and turned the conversation back to tents. He had all the information he needed and if he wanted me, then he would have to come to me, and that way he might believe it.

It took him another week before he did, and like me he had little time either for subtlety or a cautious approach.

"You said that you were under an obligation of Atonement, are you serious in that statement?"

"Completely serious. I've discussed this with a close friend and have made my confession of wrongdoing, and now wish to behave with humility and perform godly works. If you have any service that I can perform for you of that type, then please say so. You're an educated man, you must be more familiar with the requirements than me."

"The interpretation of godly works is much debated by teachers, would you be willing to accept my direction in this matter?"

I struggled to maintain a humble composure, I needed at all times to remember the danger this man posed, his pleasant conduct towards me today couldn't conceal his fanaticism. I gave the necessary answer. "In matters of tent making I would argue any point of yours that I disagreed with, but in matters of the Law you are clearly my superior."

He seemed satisfied with that, but how good I was at reading his mind was an open question, and a costly one if I got the answer wrong.

"You're a strange man Jesus Barabbas, you don't seem to know it but you have the finger of God on you in some way, whether for good or ill I'm nor sure. Perhaps you could be useful, there's a constant need for trusted helpers and I've already seen that you're a good worker." There was another of those pauses, which seemed to litter our conversations, then he came to the point. "You should make arrangements for your senior man to manage the business in your absence, in the same way that Samuel does for me. Then when circumstances require it I may call for your assistance."

CHAPTER FOURTEEN

My travels with Saul were many things, but chief amongst those things was the fact that I was constantly tired and dusty. Where most men take food and drink for their sustenance, Saul's main fuel was anger and outrage. He was angry that the Jews, God's chosen people, should be fooled into believing that the promised Messiah could be someone who had been executed as a criminal; and he was outraged at the doctrine of bodily resurrection. This level of constantly simmering anger made him a difficult man to please.

From a distance you might have thought him calm and under control, as I had; but standing close to the man you were more likely to think yourself close to that mountain in Italy, that has so recently as I dictate these words, destroyed all around itself. He really could be that frightening, not in the sense of his worldly power, but rather in the sense of his ever ready willingness to explode. If this man could ever harness the power of his emotions, his impact would be devastating.

Following the death of Stephen the slow dispersal of Jesus' followers from Jerusalem became a rush, as people known to be of that persuasion decided not to wait for Saul's men to beat down their doors in the night. Their fear was well founded, even a casual association with the teachings of the man I had simply called the preacher was enough to justify your arrest and probably a flogging, if nothing worse. The earlier and slower dispersion of these disciples had already begun the establishment of small church groups in a wide variety of towns, and it was to these small beginnings that many of the new wave of fugitives turned. The effect was felt primarily in Judea and Samaria, the two provinces closest to Jerusalem, but the results of the dispersal were now being felt as far afield as Damascus and Antioch, both of which were said to have communities of Jesus' followers. If the Sanhedrin had any sense they would have turned all their efforts to confining the disciples to Jerusalem, allowing this sort of indiscriminate persecution merely made their problem worse. If you can't control this sort of thing in one place, then you have no chance of controlling it in ten places at once.

Most of my information came from travellers talking at the inn, since the death of Jesus as a relatively unknown country healer, his name was now the routine subject of everyday conversation. The man was much more famous dead than he ever had been alive. You could understand the Council getting nervous, this sort of fame was almost a challenge to the Temple's ability to say what it was to be Jewish. Apparently the new movement was producing a different version of Judaism, and one that didn't seem to need the Temple. I'd be lashing out if I was them.

Saul had come round to see me in my room at the inn, to sort out that week's financial settlement between the different parts of our mixed business. Since discovering the pleasures of making a lot of money legally, as opposed to not very much illegally, I had become something of an enthusiast for proper book-keeping and had the impression that Saul had always been that way inclined. We had agreed our division of the profits and split the take into our two separate piles but for once, instead of then taking his leave, Saul accepted my offer of a jar of wine. I wasn't sure if this was a sign that he was coming to trust me, or if he simply felt like having a jar of wine, it was sometimes difficult to tell with him.

"Do you ever think back to your time as a thief and highway man, to some particular action that you regret?" He asked, and I wondered if this was the beginning of an interrogation about how sincere my supposed repentance was.

"I regret all of it." I said carefully. He would have to direct the way this conversation went, I was volunteering nothing.

"No, I can't see that level of equality. When I look back at my life, certain actions and people stand out - some good, some bad. Doesn't everyone see things that way?" It sounded like a genuine question, from someone interested in an answer. So I gave him one.

"From the sound of you, there's some particular action that you regret, some particular person that you treated unfairly, and you wonder what to do about it." I would see him in hell before I talked about the two dead children who visited my nights. But his situation might be similar to my own.

He lifted his head to stare at me directly. "You could tell that from what I just said?"

"That and your brooding attitude. I think that mixed in with all your strenuous work for the Lord, there's something *you* regret, something that you wish you could change."

He sighed. "You're right. There was something about the heretic Stephen, who I told you about last week, something about his unrelenting defiance that surprised me. His appearance before the Sanhedrin was an astonishing performance, he said they were circumcised only in their bodies and not in their hearts." I must have looked surprised, it was a good insult to level at an orthodox Jew, I would have to remember it. He mistook my expression for disbelief.

"No, he really said that, and more. He demanded that they answer not just for their own actions, but also for the actions and sins of their forefathers. They didn't know how to answer him."

"But you had witnesses to his blasphemy, didn't you?"

"Yes of course, I always make sure there are witnesses. A careful prosecutor will never allow there to be any doubt about the verdict. As it turned out I didn't need them, with all that business of him standing up in court and saying that he could see God. But for a while he almost turned the tables."

I could imagine him being unhappy, he wasn't a man accustomed to coming second best in any contest. Even so there was some aspect of Stephen's death that bothered him, in any other man I would have called it guilt or remorse, but neither of those emotions seemed to fit the man.

In the weeks following my recruitment as his assistant I had run errands for him in Caesarea, in Nazareth and in Jerusalem. On that last trip I had used the opportunity to visit Mark and Barnabas and make my report to them in person. They were in good spirits but growing tired from the constant pressure, Saul's men harried them at their every public appearance. Paid hecklers tried to disrupt their meetings and there were regular summons to appear before the Council and the Temple's Committee of Public Decency. There had previously been almost two hundred so called disciples in Jerusalem and upwards of three thousand active followers, but most of them had left. Some had wanted to leave and some had been told by their senior brethren that they ought to go. The result was that there was now only a small group, mostly of original apostles and close associates, left in Jerusalem, it was easier to keep track of what was happening to each of them and to organise a defence for their repeated court appearances.

When I'd first met Barnabas he had been a sympathetic bystander, it had taken the death of Jesus to convert him to a believer, an event which had left me unmoved. Everyone else seemed to have an opinion on the man, either good or bad, it was beginning to look as if there was something wrong with me for not joining them.

Being unable to make the enquiry with the one person most likely to know the answer, Saul, I used my time in Jerusalem to see if there was any news of Esther and the others arrested with her in Jezreel. I was unable to make any progress, the prisons were overflowing with Jesus' followers. They had been dragged in from miles around, some of their names were known and some not, and some were no more than people falsely accused to work off old scores. The position was chaotic and after two days I'd run out of time and had to admit defeat, the fact was she had disappeared into a pit of Saul's making and was unlikely to be seen again. I had been reluctant when Mark manoeuvred me into becoming his spy, but the more I saw of this harassment, the more I inclined to his point of view. I have only ever killed anyone for money, doing it like this, for a religious disagreement, is a sort of sickness.

I was at Mark's house, with him and Barnabas, when James came round, he was accompanied by Andrew and Peter. I stood as they entered, if not actually engaged in robbing them, I'm quite polite to most people. I greeted them in a friendly fashion, but in return was openly ignored.

Instead, the three visitors carefully avoided even looking at me, which was difficult as I was standing in front of them, while James addressed himself to Mark.

"I'm surprised to see you sharing your house with a profane person, by inviting such uncleanliness into your home you bring a taint upon yourself."

There was a moment of uncomfortable silence as Mark digested this rebuke. "I see no profanity in anyone here." He said, being less willing than myself to engage in an argument. But even this soft answer wasn't sufficient, and James gestured in my direction.

"Anyone who is not with us is against us, and this man is an unbeliever. It is written that we must reject that which is unclean - lest we ourselves become defiled."

That made James's opinion of me fairly clear, it was somewhat similar to mine of him. Mark remained polite in face of this implacable stance.

"I'm sorry if I have offended you my brother, but this man is working on my behalf and at my instruction, for the benefit of all of us. And in so doing is putting himself into serious danger."

"If he wished to be in danger for the Lord's sake, he would acknowledge his sin and join us in the market places to proclaim God's holy word. That would be to work with us openly, and not to hide in dark places."

If one were to assume my good faith, a considerable leap I agree, that would have been a travesty of my position, but then I suspect he already knew that. Although they said nothing themselves, that very silence and their pose, standing shoulder to shoulder with James, made plain Andrew and Peter's agreement with him. However, as my business with Mark and Barnabas was complete it seemed like a good idea to relieve Mark of the duty of defending me any further. I turned and clasped Mark's hand, and then Barnabas's, thereby intensifying their uncleanliness, and bade them both goodbye.

On my way out I was unable to resist the foolish urge to pat James on the arm and wish him goodbye as well. He didn't flinch, but I felt his entire body stiffen at the contact. Making my way down the street I was filled with the thought that I would never want to be a part of any church run by that man.

My own and Saul's business in Jerusalem completed, I joined a lightly burdened, and thus fast moving, north bound group at dawn the next day for the three day journey back to Jezreel. I had worn out as many pairs of sandals in the last six weeks as I had in the previous six months.

The rest of that year continued in our new way of working, for four or five weeks at a time I would be nothing but a tent maker: working in the yard, visiting my suppliers and visiting my customers in the Legion. The normal round of a successful businessman. Whenever I heard any talk that might be of interest to Mark I would visit one of our agreed contacts and leave a written note, usually accompanied by a purse of coins from the business. I had no way of discovering if any of my reports were of any use, let alone if they kept anyone from captivity or death, but I imagine that's the way of it for a spy. You ferret out whatever information you can and pass it on to your contact, it's a case of working in the dark and hoping for the best.

Then after a while in the yard, there would come another flurry of activity helping Saul, usually by carrying instructions to his various agents in the towns of southern Galilee. Occasionally I was sufficiently trusted to deliver reprimands to his subordinates, and impose requirements for certain actions to be undertaken more vigorously. The man was like his own small whirlwind of energy. To many of those agents this gave me the appearance of a man on the inside, a man they could trust and with whom they could discuss their work. This in turn provided further information for my next report, it had become a self generating cycle. Even the tents continued to make money, although I was pleased to note that it wasn't as much as when I had been the full time manager.

My personal relationship with Saul was a strange plant, it grew crookedly, and in odd directions but it did seem to grow. At the yard, all our dealings were on the surface, and conducted in front of the others, the forced takeover of half my working space, and the pooling of our manpower had, against my expectations, been beneficial to trade. There was never any slack time for the workforce, if one of us was temporarily short of work then we would switch the men onto helping complete the other one's orders, and of course be paid for it.

It was out of hours, when he would sometimes visit me in my room at the inn, supposedly to talk about me carrying out his errands, but as often as not simply to talk. The first time had been when he had hinted at some slight unease over the stoning of Stephen, a possible sense that he might not be quite the pure and undefiled instrument of God that he liked to pretend. I had always known that purity was not a human condition, the more frequently anyone tells you they're doing God's work, the more frequently you should count the spoons. He didn't mention Stephen again, but he didn't mention Stephen in the same way that I didn't mention the dead children. These things weren't mentioned because they were always there, they never went away, and neither of us wanted anyone else to realise that. He might be a clever man, but that dazzled him and blinded him to the abilities of others.

Instead, we talked about the importance of ensuring the unity of the Jewish people, the danger of allowing any split to weaken our position when dealing with the Romans. We talked about the importance of rooting out false doctrine, and the importance of my personal works of atonement. In short we talked about anything you could think of; anything except the possibility that he might entertain the slightest doubt about the rightness his work. His certainty would have fooled most people, it even came close to fooling me.

It was coming up to Rosh Hashanah again, and winter was beginning to take a firmer grip, when I realised that Saul had become especially focussed on events in Syria. In the same way that the original persecutions in Jerusalem had encouraged the emigration of Jesus' disciples to the outlying areas, so the subsequent success of his efforts in Samaria and Galilee had forced them even further afield. This had led to his latest obsession, that the large Jewish communities in Antioch and Damascus had become infected with the Jesus disease. It had become a regular topic of conversation, with him wondering aloud what could be done to deal with the problem. His presence was required in Jerusalem on such a regular basis, that travelling to Syria as well was out of the question. Even a fast journey from Jerusalem to Damascus would take six days, and Antioch was three days further than that.

It finally came to him that the obvious solution was to send his menial jack of all trades, me, to assess the situation in Damascus for him. He was sufficiently concerned that my mission should go well, that as well as paying my expenses, which was routine, he would also supply two servants to accompany me. I assured him that he who travels light travels fastest, and said I would go alone. The last thing I needed was to have his hired hands watching my every move.

The thing that bothered me about this assignment was that it didn't look as if there would be anywhere for me to hide. My earlier errands for Saul had all involved me performing some particular task, carrying a message or ensuring that some other person had done what they'd been told. The trip to Damascus offered no such easy compliance. He would expect me to provide a detailed report on the state of the Jesus movement in Damascus and the names of the people involved, it wasn't clear how that could be falsified in a way that wouldn't be readily apparent. I scribbled a note to Mark, asking for guidance and dropped it off at the stall of my contact, a butcher in the flesh market. I told him to make sure it went as quickly as possible. He shrugged and spread his hands. "These things take as long as they take." He said unhelpfully.

Unfortunately, *as long as it takes,* took too long and a week later, before any reply had reached me, I was obliged to set off. Saul was unusually intense, even for him, as he wished me a safe journey.

"You must understand that these people might appear to you as devout Jews, attending synagogue and observing the law, but there's a darker side. You can't follow their teachings without destroying the foundations of our faith, it isn't possible."

I clasped his hand and looked him straight in the eye. "You have my word that I'll make every effort to find them." The possibility of thereby finding Mary Magdalen made that a certainty, she might be too good for me, but for the time being I would settle for just being in her company and using my imagination. That's one of the good things about depravity, about being at the bottom of the moral heap, you can acknowledge your baser instincts - you needn't cloak them in nobility.

I had joined one of the horse mounted convoys, the fastest there are It's an expensive way to travel, but I was spending Saul's money, and he'd got it from the Temple - so who cares? The only problem was my lack of experience on horseback, most of my journeys were on foot, leading a mule. So although it felt unusually grand to be surveying the countryside from this lordly height, it was also very uncomfortable and at each stop on the way I found myself walking bow legged for a while.

I made my way north through the pleasantly rolling countryside of Galilee, grateful to be travelling in the cool months of winter, and worrying about how I could satisfy Saul's requirements for information, without condemning more people to suffer Esther's fate. And all the while the only thing to take my mind off this weighty problem was my increasingly sore arse.

CHAPTER FIFTEEN

There are two possible roads from southern Galilee to Damascus, and we were using the eastern route, crossing the Jordan south of the Sea of Galilee, and heading up through the Roman city of Gadara. Some of the travellers, better versed than myself in such matters, were concerned about the simmering border dispute in this area between Herod Antipas and Aretas, the Arabian ruler at Petra.

The caravan master waved the concern aside. "Neither of them'll do anything to touch us - we're the cow they want to milk. They both want Damascus and the caravan routes in and out of there, the last thing that either of them will do is to interrupt the trade."

"Is there no danger of border fighting?" Asked another.

"Not really, Herod would be mad to attack Aretas on his own, so until he gets the Legion down from Antioch to help him, it's going to be a stand off. The last I heard he was petitioning Tiberius in Rome to sort things out, but God alone knows how long that could take."

The subject was discussed to and fro, and I listened to the various strands going on around me, but didn't join in; this was all new territory to me and I knew nothing about the politics of it. It was as much as I could do to organise my own affairs without disaster, never mind organising international relations.

On the morning of the third day, shortly after we had left our overnight accommodation, the caravan master stopped us on the brow of a hill and gathered us round him. Satisfied that we could all hear him he pointed to a long ridge of snow capped mountains away to the left of our route, paralleling the line of our travel and stretching out of sight to the north.

"That my friends is the famous Mount Hermon and the range that the Greeks call the Antilibanus, there's snow on those peaks even in the height of summer." The politer ones amongst us not already familiar with this revelation made suitably impressed noises, although frankly my interest in mountains is small, and in snow, even smaller.

"And that," he said sweeping his arm round in a grand gesture to point directly ahead of us, "is Damascus, the oldest city in the world."

This time I actually was interested and peered in the relevant direction. There I saw a broad patch of brilliant green, indicating a successful and massive irrigation system, and at its centre a collection of shining white blocks and shapes, surrounded by a wall. This time we all made suitably impressed noises, even I suspect those who had seen it several times before.

Having given us a few moments to admire the view he spurred us onwards. "There's still a long way to go, and we need to be there before nightfall."

My contract with the caravan formally ended with our arrival at the tetrapylon in the heart of Damascus, the meeting place of the four main roads into the city, and from the sound of things a home to every language in the known world. I left the horse with some relief, they might be fast but three days sat on the back of one would take another three days to recover from. With my saddle bag over my shoulder I made my way through the crowds and along Straight Street, looking for the sign of the Golden Hart, the inn that Saul had recommended. Straight Street itself was the broadest and most opulent street I had ever encountered, far grander than anything in Jerusalem, and ran right through the heart of the city, with shaded colonnades along both sides. The inn was easy to spot, its sign hanging out above the stalls of the street traders, and having spotted it, I walked past. The fact that Saul had suggested the place was adequate reason to find my own accommodation. True, he was supposed to be cleverer than me, but that didn't mean that I had to be stupid, if he wanted me watched then his watchers could earn their money.

I settled myself into a large and anonymous inn between the main market and the Temple of Jupiter, as I agreed the rate with the innkeeper it was clear that I was just one of a hundred people he would speak to that day. The easiest place to lose yourself is always in a crowd. Having eaten at the inn I took a late evening stroll round the edges of the market and began to appreciate the difficulty of my task, Damascus wasn't just the oldest city in the world, but after Rome, it was also probably one of the biggest and busiest.

I was told at the inn that there were eight synagogues in the city, but I had no intention of wasting time with the small fry. The next morning I presented my letter of authority to the senior priest at the main synagogue, which is how Saul would have played it.

The High Priest of Greater Syria, as he styled himself, a tall man with a severe expression and a magnificent black headdress agreed to receive me. He waved me to a chair beside his desk, without raising his eyes from a document he was studying, and which he continued to study. Though not especially hot, it was a bright sunny day and in the length of time he kept me waiting I was able to observe the sunlight from the window move the shadow of a candle holder slowly across the floor. A prouder man than me might have been offended, but I just watched the slow progress of the shadow and assumed that he engaged in this sort of display as a compensation for not getting enough sex at home. At last he laid his document aside and looked at my scroll, the one requesting his assistance in my 'vital work', and then he looked at me: his expression less than enthusiastic.

"What exactly is it that you expect from me? This isn't Jerusalem you know, or Jericho, or some other Judean collection of mud huts." He waved the scroll around dismissively. "You're in Damascus now, we have our own hierarchy and we run our own affairs."

"Perhaps so sir, but nonetheless the Sanhedrin have always had final authority in matters of the law, in all Jewish communities even in the Diaspora. Heresy and blasphemy are their direct responsibility, and that's why I'm here."

"I don't need any instruction from you in the Sanhedrin's more absurd claims, and no matter how far reaching they imagine their powers to be, you can take my word for it - their authority stops where Syrian territory starts." He looked at me, satisfied the matter had been dealt with.

"I understand your opinion perfectly sir. However, when Herod receives the assistance he seeks from Rome in his dispute with Aretas, which he surely will in the coming months, then with a Legion to back him up you may very well find that his boundaries suddenly incorporate Damascus. In which case the small matter of having assisted me could confer a significant advantage to yourself."

As I might have mentioned earlier, I have a good memory, and the casual chat between the merchants while we were on the road had lodged itself in my head.

He pursed his lips and nodded to himself, the point had struck home. "Saul has the reputation of a hot head, and we don't need any of his rabble rousing round here, or riots like they're having in Jerusalem. Can you assure me that these things will be handled discretely?"

"You have my solemn assurance of that sir." He didn't look completely convinced, but he'd decided in my favour, by a narrow margin.

He handed me back my scroll, lifted a small brass bell and gently shook it, a young man in a black robe came in so quickly that he must have been waiting outside the door. "Take this gentleman to speak to Simeon, and say that he has my authority."

I rose and bowed briefly to express my gratitude. "Thank you sir."

Simeon was not naturally inclined to be any more welcoming than the high priest, but under direct instruction from his superior was prepared to assist me, in as much as he had to.

"We have very few of that sort of person in Damascus. One hears stories, naturally, but this is hardly fertile soil for the followers of a Galilean country preacher. Our local population are a good deal more sophisticated than the simple farmers you might be accustomed to dealing with."

I found myself mildly stung into defending the people I was supposed to be pursuing. "Our reports speak of a sizeable group of Jesus' followers in this area. Some of them may well be fleeing the persecution in Judea, but we understand most of them to be local - no doubt, as you say sophisticated, but still local."

He raised his eyebrows at this disagreement. "Where exactly did you say that *you* came from?"

"I didn't, but I'm originally from Kerioth in southern Judea, perhaps you've heard of it?"

He looked surprised, and almost offended at the suggestion. "I wouldn't have thought so." He said, and then began to sort through a pile of scrolls on a side table. "Yes, here we are. Reports from individual synagogues on those citizens believed to be of doubtful integrity. This should be what you're looking for."

The two of us spent the next hour looking through the last three month's worth of rabbinical gossip: who was sleeping with whom, who was not paying his suppliers, who was regularly missing Sabbath services; but absolutely no mention of any followers of Jesus. Yet Esther had told me that there was a strong Jesus community in Damascus, they couldn't all have disappeared.

"Are you sure their presence would be reported?"

"Naturally, we would take a very stern view of that sort of belief spreading through the Jewish community, it would have to be firmly dealt with."

"How exactly would you deal with it?"

"Well in the first instance the synagogue involved would be issued with a notice instructing them to bar such persons from attending until they had expressed contrition."

"And if that didn't work, if there were still more of these believers in the congregation?"

He thought for a moment. "Then we have the power to impose financial sanctions on any synagogue failing to comply with the High Priest's instructions, that will bring them back into line quite smartly."

He had made it certain that any priest reporting the presence of Jesus' followers in his congregation would be subject to a lot of time wasting trouble and possibly a fine, and was now using the lack of such reports to prove they didn't exist. The man was an idiot and shouldn't have been let out of the house without a helper. I looked at him to make sure he wasn't making fun of me, but he wasn't, he actually believed what he was saying.

I stood up. "Simeon, you've been a great help in my enquiries, and on behalf of Saul and the Sanhedrin I would like to express my great appreciation. Thank you."

For the first time, he stopped looking peevish and smiled at me. "I'm pleased to have been of assistance, and only sorry that you seem to have wasted your journey here. Even so I'm sure you'll enjoy your time in our city, you must try to find time to look at the rug market, it's world famous and well worth a visit." And on that curious note we parted.

This was perfect, I couldn't have planned it better. I now had the statements of the local High Priest and his assistant, backed up by reports from individual synagogues to confirm that there were no followers of Jesus in Damascus. Or at least not in sufficient quantities to be worth bothering with. That should cover my report to Saul, there wasn't much chance of him coming here on the strength of that. The most surprising thing of all was that, as someone uninvolved with either party, I found myself pleased at being able to obstruct Saul's pursuit. These people weren't supposed to mean anything to me, it must just have been my pleasure at fooling the unstoppable Saul.

None of which made any difference to my own desire to find them, and in finding them perhaps find Mary Magdalen. I walked back down the street and bought myself some fried fish with a piece of bread wrapped round the end to hold it by, it was extremely hot and very tasty. How to find a small group of people, who didn't want to be found, in one of the biggest cities in the world? I spent the afternoon browsing some of the huge variety of stalls and shops, in the vague hope that inspiration would strike me, it didn't. In the end I went to the baths and spent an hour in the hot water, if nothing else it cured some of the aches produced by three days on horseback.

A good night's sleep in a better bed than I was recently used to was a welcome event, but not any more helpful. My only hope was to see if any of Esther's friends from Jezreel, or her home town of Cana had made there way up here, that could be my way in. I started the next morning in the Beth Aaron synagogue, one of the smaller ones that I'd ignored yesterday. I spoke to the Cantor, and as I could think of no story more convincing than the truth simply explained that I was from Jezreel and had been a friend of Esther of Cana, were any of her other friends in this area?

His answer was immediate and definite. "I don't know anyone from that area." In fact his answer was so immediate and definite it was almost as if he'd expected it. He was noticeably incurious about my origins or my name, and if it weren't for the fact that I couldn't imagine a Cantor lying in a synagogue, I might have mistrusted him. I thanked him and moved on.

My next stop was the Mount Zion synagogue, and this time I was able to speak with a Rabbi, but it made no difference. "I'm sorry that I can't help you, but I don't know any such people." It took me almost the whole day to cover all available synagogues, in some there was no one presently available and I had to return later, but eventually I had spoken to them all. There was apparently nobody from Jezreel or Cana in Damascus.

One explanation was that word had spread from my meeting with the High Priest yesterday that I was here on behalf of Saul, and I was being lied to in order to hide any of Jesus' followers. Or perhaps there really wasn't anyone here from southern Galilee.

I made my way back through the market, towards the inn, trying to work out an alternative approach. It had been a tiring day and I was frustrated at my lack of progress, but I should still have been more alert. I was seized from behind and lifted from the ground, the point of a knife wedged in my back. Other people must have seen, but none intervened, and I found myself being pushed faced first against a wall in a nearby alley. It was rough handling and it hurt every bit as much as it was supposed to.

"Jesus Barabbas," a coarse voice said in my ear, "we know who you are, you're a Judas and a traitor. You will have left Damascus by tomorrow morning or we'll come for you again, and next time we shall want your blood."

I had relaxed as they manhandled me, having surprised me to begin with, they had the edge. Their words made it clear that their next move would be to let go of my arms, either to simply leave me with their warning echoing in my ears, or to step back and club me, to reinforce the point. Whichever way, the grip on my arms would slacken. They should have realised that I'd been pulling this sort of trick myself too often to be surprised by it. I made no struggle, they thought I was shocked and frightened.

The grip on my arms slackened and then released. I used both hand to push myself backwards off the wall and towards them, jerking my head back as I went. And as I went, a club smashed into the wall where my head had been. Considering the violence with which I'd thrown my head back, it's lucky that I actually hit something, otherwise I could have done my neck a serious injury. Instead, happily, the injury was done to one of the men behind me, with whose face the back of my head collided.

I wrenched the dagger from my belt and, with the first one already falling, turned my attention to the man with the club. He was an amateur and still trying to work out why his club had hit the wall rather than me, this sort of work needs practice to be any good at it - just like most jobs.

I grabbed the front of his tunic and swung him back against the piece of wall I had just vacated, and then stuck the point of my dagger into his throat. I slid the point far enough into his flesh for him to understand that struggling would be dangerous. He froze and stared sullenly back at me.

"Judas." He spat, repeating his original insult.

I sighed. "Look you're obviously not very good at this sort of thing, and that's to your credit, clubbing people in alleys isn't the sort of thing a man ought to be good at." The man on the floor groaned and began to stir, so I kicked his head and turned back to the man against the wall.

"The fact that you think I'm a traitor means that you must have spoken to some of the Jesus group from Jezreel, the problem you have is that I'm not a traitor - well not to you anyway. I didn't betray Esther and her people, that was just a story put about by Saul. Now I don't care if you believe me or not, but for what it's worth Saul thinks I'm here on mission for him, but I'm actually here to help you."

I paused to let him call me Judas again, but he didn't bother, so I continued.

"I have no intention of leaving Damascus before I've done what I came for, and that is to speak to someone from your group, one of your leaders. So you go back and tell them that I have a room at the Green Palm near the market, they're to get a message to me telling me when and where to meet them. I will come without guards or soldiers, just me, on my own. If they're worried about their identities becoming known they can even wear sacks over their heads for all I care. Have you got that?"

He nodded, reluctantly, but he nodded.

"Right, I'm going now, so you take your friend home and do something about his nose, it looks like it's broken." I didn't bother looking back as I walked away, he wasn't that much of a threat.

The really interesting thing about that meeting was how rapidly Peter's opportunistic accusation against Judas had turned into an accepted fact. The very word Judas now meant traitor, it might not have been fair but mud sticks. As the man himself had said to me: 'It was never supposed to end this way'.

CHAPTER SIXTEEN

I was sat alone in my room later that evening when there was a knock on my door. I opened it, ready for trouble and instead found Mary Magdalen, accompanied by a plainly dressed older woman. They both greeted me politely, and waited to be invited in. For a moment I stood there, astonished, and unable to make any rational response. I had wanted to find her, there was no doubt of that, in fact I had longed to see her again. The point about this longing was that there was no obvious explanation for it.

It was easy enough to say that her charm and personality drew me towards her; but that wasn't the answer. Nor was it something as straightforward as sexual attraction, that sort of thing I recognised and could deal with. As an explanation it sounds ridiculous, in fact it is ridiculous, but when Jesus spoke to me after the trial, I saw nothing beyond his eyes looking into mine and felt he had seen my soul. Talking to Mary gave me a similar feeling, she had achieved some level of being I had yet to reach. That was the attraction.

She stepped forward to embrace me, which broke the spell and I welcomed them both in.

"This is Lydia, she is one of the two elders of our community in Damascus, despite what I told her about you she was still interested to meet you." This last was said without any trace of a smile on either of their faces, so I took it at face value

"I'm sorry about the two boys earlier, I hadn't explained how things were, it never occurred to me that they would be so foolish. Were you hurt?"

189

I shook my head. "No I'm fine, though they're a little bruised, but how are you?" I almost asked how the baby was, but the presence of the other woman constrained me.

"I'm well, thank you. I received word from Mark, only today, that you were playing the role of Saul's helper, is this safe?"

"A lot safer than your position, and a hundred times safer than the disciples in Jerusalem. Since Stephen's death there have been several further stonings, I'm seriously worried about Mark and Barnabas."

"We all are, but this is a stage we must go through. Have you decided yet where your own loyalties lie?"

"The only certainties about my position are that I dislike and distrust Saul, and that I would never betray you, beyond that I'm no better than I ever have been."

"I can see how much you'd resist being pushed, and that you'll only move at your own speed - but this isn't an issue where you can stand in the middle, you have to join one side or the other. I'm not surprised our Lord felt he needed to give you time to find repentance - you're probably the slowest person I've ever met."

I could think of no useful comment to that and so made none, meanwhile her companion, Lydia, added her own views.

"Mary assures us that you are to be trusted, however, it's difficult for us when someone bearing the authority of that self appointed persecutor Saul arrives in our city, and begins to ask searching questions about us and our whereabouts."

"I had little option, having agreed with Mark that I should volunteer to act as Saul's assistant, I was then obliged to go where he sent me. The alternative would have been for him to come himself, or send some other emissary less sympathetic than myself."

"You're too late to stop that, it's already happened. There's someone else from Jerusalem asking questions in the synagogues, trying to pass themselves off as one of us."

That gave me a cold feeling. I should have realised that Saul would never have trusted me to work on my own in a matter of such importance; whatever I said in my report about Damascus would be cross checked against his other agent. I would have to do something about it; if I was going to be any use to Mary's friends, then mine would have to be the only report to reach Saul.

"Who is this person, where can I find them?"

Mary put her hand on mine. "Our work cannot be done with a dagger, which is why those boys who attacked you were so wrong."

I hated lying to Mary, but it was her that was wrong, there are some jobs that can only be done with a dagger. "I accept that." I said, looking her straight in the eye. "I would simply like to see who it is, in case it's someone I know."

"We cannot be the ones to bring death to the streets of Damascus, our way is the way of peace."

"You have my word, Mary, that I will do nothing to bring death to the streets of Damascus. I accept that your philosophy is to turn the other cheek to your attackers."

Lydia nodded her approval at this acknowledgement of correct procedures, while Mary looked at me through slightly narrowed eyes.

"I sent word to Mark, asking for guidance on what to put in my report to Saul, but his reply hadn't reached me before I had to set out. What I need from you is some suggestion of what I could say that might sound convincing and yet would cause you the least trouble.

Could you prepare something for me to write, and then meet me back here tomorrow evening?"

Now I'd moved the subject away from my own actions, they both felt more comfortable agreeing with me, and we parted on that basis.

Once more alone in my room I unwrapped my pen and ink and scraped clean a small square of vellum to write my message. I then wrapped and sealed it before carefully addressing it to: *The servant of Saul who would seek out heresy.* Then wrapping a cloak around myself I made my way to the sign of the Golden Hart on Straight Street, if this was Saul's preferred inn then I reckoned the owner would know who to give it to.

The next day, at mid morning, I stood talking to a stall holder about his brassware, and agreeing with his views on the proposed increase in stall rents. It was a slow conversation but he didn't seem to have any other customers, and more importantly, from where I was standing I could see everyone who approached the stall of Hiram the leather worker on the far side of the street.

As my brassware selling friend and I chatted, drank some hot water and lemon juice and generally merged into the background, I saw my target appear. He was a man of my own middling height, with no particularly noticeable features, exactly the sort of person who could go anywhere and not be noticed. What gave him away was the fact that he was supposed to be meeting someone, his eyes darted all round the area, trying to spot another man on his own, me.

Having cross questioned the innocent stall holder, he eventually gave up and turned to leave. I made my unhurried way behind him. I was satisfied that he was my man and I had no desire to spend time on the street cross questioning him, the faster this was dealt with the better. As he turned into the alley that would lead him back to the Golden Hart there was just time for one quick question.

"Do you have my money?" I called out. He stopped and turned, one hand under his tunic. I limped up to him, the old tricks are often the best. "My note said to bring the money, do you have it?" I asked in a complaining voice as I drew closer, my back hunched over and my right foot dragging sideways in the dirt.

"Do you have the names you promised?" He was slightly nervous, looking beyond me to see if I had any more able bodied friends who could be threat.

"Here they are." I said, pulling my own dagger faster than he pulled his.

I would have run, empty handed, if anyone had appeared as he fell, but there was no one. I knelt down to take back my own note and his purse, and then pausing only long enough to wipe my dagger clean on his tunic, hurried on my way. I had forgotten the blood tingling thrill of becoming an animal again, of striking your prey so much faster than they could ever strike you. But as I turned the corner to mingle blamelessly and undetectably with the crowds on Straight Street there was another reaction. It was Saul's reaction to the death of Stephen, and my reaction to the night time visits of the dead children. Was it was guilt, or was it regret, or is there a difference?

I shook my head at the impossibility of whichever emotion it was. There had been a problem and I had dealt with it, permanently.

That night my two visitors returned, not the dead children, but Mary and Lydia. This time Lydia was slightly more relaxed, having seen last night, that despite my background and association with Saul, Mary treated me as a normal person. I poured them both some cordial and prepared to discuss their views on my report to Saul.

"We haven't been able to discover any more information about Saul's other agent in the city." Said Lydia. "We just know that there's a man who doesn't belong here, asking questions."

"That's alright," I said, "the man in question has left town, and won't be coming back. Which means that whatever I say in my report, on your activities in Damascus, there won't be an alternative version."

"How do you know the man has left town?" This time it was Mary, she had sat forward in her seat, and her tone was sharply questioning.

I was slightly taken aback, the neutrality of my comment had been intended to close that subject, not open it up. "I've just heard that he's left town." I said lamely.

"HOW DARE YOU?" Mary had risen to her feet, the better to confront me; she'd worked it out.

Her voice was controlled but furious, a pointing forefinger jabbing in my direction. "How dare you do this in our name, in the name of the risen Lord?"

The attack had taken me by surprise, but with a sick feeling in my stomach I could see where she was going, but Lydia was confused. "How dare he what?" She asked Mary, but Mary was still intent on pursuing me.

"You're a clever man Jesus Barabbas, you found him when we couldn't - didn't you?"

There was no possibility of avoiding the question. "Yes, I found him."

"And then what did you do to him?"

I was silent, I couldn't say the words.

"What did you do to him?" She repeated, stepping closer and speaking more forcefully.

I looked at the floor, unable to meet her eye. "I killed him."

Lydia gasped. "You killed him, when you had agreed last night there would be no bloodshed?"

"You betrayed everything we stand for, is that what you did to Esther?" Mary asked, her voice colder than the snow on the mountain tops.

I closed my eyes, Judas's words came back to me; 'It was never supposed to end like this'. "I would never have betrayed Esther deliberately, but I did gossip about her, and the gossip gave her away." If I had spoken any more quietly, they wouldn't have heard me.

"With this murder you have tarnished the names of hundreds of good men and women in this city. Are you actively evil, or just stupid?"

I could feel all my life catching up with me, a wave of hopelessness came up out of nowhere and washed over me. I sank back in my chair and put my head in my hands. "All I wanted to do was to help my friends." I said, almost to myself.

"You're not our friend Jesus Barabbas, we don't have time for friends, you're either a believer or a non believer. Anything else, including you, is irrelevant. Which side are you on?"

The truth about my cleverness was; that like beauty it was only skin deep. The trick I had used to discover Saul's other man in Damascus was more a proof of his lack of caution than my brilliance. Then I thought back to meeting Jesus, the real one, in that dark and foul basement in Jerusalem. That man was no more a simple country preacher than I was, I had been touched by God and had felt it right through my body, yet even then I'd tried to ignore the fact. And it was me who'd said that Saul couldn't see the obvious - no wonder everyone was calling me stupid.

Then I remembered one of the other things that Judas, in the depths of his despair, had said at the crucifixion: 'That man is the Messiah, the one the prophets spoke of'. How many clues does one man need?

Mary had been touched by the same thing, but where I had rejected it, she had welcomed it with open arms. My determination not to see what was right in front of me should win a prize from somebody, just as long as I didn't kill everyone in sight first.

I took a deep breath and looked up at her. "I'm ready, what should I do."

From that point, at least for a while, life became simpler, there were basic and obvious things to do and we did them.

That afternoon, Mary with Lydia and her companion Ananias took me to an upstairs room, in a house set in the city walls. There in the presence of a small group of other converts, referred to as fellow disciples, I was baptised in the name of Jesus, in water and the spirit. We all then shared a meal together, which seemed to be a natural part of the process. One of the women was carrying a small baby, and Mary held it herself for a while, but then so did most of the other women. I didn't ask - if she wanted me to know she'd tell me.

After we had finished the meal, Mary asked me if I was truly sorry for my sins, and when I said that I was, she broke a piece of bread and gave it to me saying that it was in remembrance of the body of Christ. Then she gave me a glass of wine, in remembrance of the blood of Christ. She then put both her hands on my head and said that my sins had been forgiven.

How such a completely impossible thing could be the truth was beyond me, then and now, but I was simply and deeply grateful for it to be so. I don't know what my facial expression was, probably dazed. Mary took one look at me and then caught hold of my hands, saying that I felt this way because I was in what she called a state of grace. Then she laughed and said that I shouldn't worry, because in my case it wasn't likely to last very long.

CHAPTER SEVENTEEN

Four days later I was back at the tent yard in Jezreel, and found Saul there, paying one of his now infrequent visits. I unpacked the scroll on which I'd written my report and handed it to him. He made no attempt to unroll it and merely looked at me questioningly, he wanted to watch my face as I delivered it.

"You were right about them being in Damascus, I managed to track down a large group of them. Their leaders are an elderly couple, a man called Ashur and his wife Mardina, and with their extended family and friends it came to more than twenty people, I've listed where they can be found in the scroll."

"Those are strange names."

"They're Assyrian Jews, from the north east. But that's Damascus for you; it's like the tower of Babel. Jerusalem might be cosmopolitan, but it can't compare with Damascus. It's an astonishing place."

"And they're permanent residents in the city, not just fleeing from Jerusalem?"

"They seem to have been there for years, they're all tin smiths and have a large shop near the citadel. I was walking round the place and talking to them, just days ago. It's all in the report."

He considered my words, with pursed lips and narrowed eyes. "It's possible I might have been mistaken about you Jesus Barabbas, for a while I was concerned that you might have some sympathy for these people, that you might have doubts about my work. The fact that you lodged with the woman Esther raised a question about your orthodoxy. It had occurred to me that you might claim to have found nothing in the hope of deceiving me."

"The trouble with you Saul is that you see enemies round every corner. Why d'you find it so difficult to see the blindingly obvious? I lodged with Esther because her beds were clean, her rent was fair and her cooking good. What exactly do *you* look for in your lodgings?"

He shrugged my question aside as no more than the lightweight nonsense you might expect from me, but I wasn't ready to give up. Avoiding an obvious subject is much more suspicious than tackling it head on. "Since we're speaking of Esther, where is she now? Will she be coming back?"

He looked shifty, which was unusual for him, his enormous self confidence could carry him through most situations without a tremor. I was sure that I'd guessed correctly the last time we'd spoken, the man had doubts about his work, or at least about the way he was doing it. That accounted for his eagerness to pursue heretics more vigorously than anyone else; he was trying to convince himself. "She was an old woman, the strain of the questioning must have been too great, she died in prison."

As he spoke, I knew he was lying, but in exactly what way was unclear. Had her death been even more unpleasant than he was admitting? I couldn't see through the lie, but if I clenched my fists any more tightly my fingers would snap.

The brave people in this life aren't the ones who have no option; they're just unlucky. Nor are they the ones who feel no fear, they're just not very intelligent, which isn't the same thing at all. The really brave are those who start off by being afraid and who could step to one side, but then the steel enters their soul and they stand their ground and do the thing anyway. That's bravery, and that's what Esther had done. Mary might have been correct in saying that my state of grace wouldn't last for long.

As I listened to Saul mouthing his poisonous nonsense I wondered how on earth I had ever found it possible to imagine a genuine working partnership with him. I would have been much better employed killing *him*, instead of his agent in Damascus. This restriction of theirs on killing people seemed to be a major drawback in becoming a follower of Jesus, and there didn't seem to be any easy way round it.

I determined to stay neutral, it was my best hope of learning something. "If you already know these people are heretics, what exactly is it that you question them about?"

That might have a step too far, and he looked at me sharply. "You said that in your desire to seek atonement you would accept my direction in these matters, have you changed your mind?"

I laughed out loud and gestured to the scroll he held. "That tells you all you need to know about my loyalties. If you doubt me, you should send a second man to check that I've done it properly, but I'll bet he doesn't get as much information as me." Well not from the alleyway I'd left him in he wouldn't, but it hardly seemed worth mentioning that.

He nodded his grudging acceptance of a fair point, and our talk turned to tents.

Lydia had provided me with the full and accurate details of an old established Damascus family of tin smiths and recent converts to Jesus, every single detail I'd supplied to Saul was correct. The only possible problem was the so far unmentioned fact that they were about to depart, bag and baggage, family and friends, to settle in Harmath in Assyria; where they intended to live, work and spread the gospel of Jesus. Harmath, being another five days journey north of Damascus was well beyond even Saul's reach. All Saul's men would find would be an empty nest, I would just have to hope he took it well.

For the next two days I was occupied showing my face at the Legion barracks, around our various suppliers and with the accounts clerk at the synagogue. You can get away with being an absentee landlord, but it's not so easy to be an absentee tent maker. Saul seemed more withdrawn than usual, and it wasn't just with me. If anything he was now more open and easy with me than he was with his own people, more than once I heard him speaking to his former right hand man, Samuel, in terms that would have caused some men to walk out. The only thing I could think of was that he was mentally preparing himself for another of his major campaigns, and finding it difficult. The man was like a tightly drawn bow string, if not released soon he might snap, with unpleasant consequences for anyone nearby. My way forward wasn't obvious.

But then in the midst of my dealings with Saul, the Lord turned his face and smiled upon me, or however Mark might have put it. I saw the man at the meat market, he was talking to another man, and at first I only knew that I knew him. I hung back for a moment, unsure of how I should greet him; was he an old acquaintance from Kerioth, as Judas had been at the crucifixion? Or was he . . . and then with a gut clenching rush of cold sweat I knew him, and thanked God that I'd held back.

He was Jairus, the leader of the Zealots, the man who'd sold me and my two young cousins to the Romans to be crucified; after first taking care to steal all our money. I'd stopped dead and was staring at him, that was no good. I began to saunter amongst the stalls, my head angled slightly away, but my eyes fixed firmly on him. He was giving an instruction to the other man, who was clearly his junior, the other man said yes to what he'd just been told. Jairus nodded his dismissal and turned to walk away, the other man went in the opposite direction. I followed Jairus, but carefully, the last time we met he'd beaten me. I felt like a fisherman with a very big fish on a very thin line - move softly and take care - don't snap the line.

I hung so far back that I almost lost him, but any closer and he would have seen me, then a squad of legionaries came down the street in the opposite direction. It wouldn't have occurred to me to attach any significance to this, soldiers are not uncommon in a garrison town and we all have to rub along together. But Jairus turned his back to look at a display of vegetables, and kept on looking until the troops had passed. That didn't demonstrate his interest in cabbages, it demonstrated that he was no longer working for the legion.

Since that awful night in Debir, when I'd lain bound at his feet as he sold me, I'd always consoled myself with the possibility that one day, just maybe, one day I might have the chance to return the favour. Well today was the day.

I followed him to a large house on Gilead Square, where the door was opened to him by someone who seemed to be a friend. That was all I needed, I sauntered casually on until I'd turned the corner, and then I ran, and I carried on running until I reached the Tenth Legion barracks. Sextus Flavius was pleased to see me, we enjoyed our conversations together, but I didn't normally arrive out of breath and sweating.

"Are the Legion engaged in any sort of cooperation with the Zealots?" I demanded, not caring for pleasantries.

He was as surprised at the apparent stupidity of the question as much as at my condition and tone of voice.

"Of course not, there's a major action taking place against them in Judea at the moment."

"Then that could account for the presence of their leader here, rather than there."

It took two or three minutes to describe the situation, another two or three minutes to fall in a sixteen man squad, and not much longer to get back to Gilead Square. Some of the men went round the back of the house and the rest of them went through the front door, as if it weren't there. There was a great deal of banging and shouting for a while, and then it went quiet.

As Jairus and four other men were led from the house he turned his face my way - his gaze drifted blankly across me without recognition, but who cares - I'd won. And whether they crucified him, sent him to the mines or sent him to the galleys, I didn't care about that either - I'd still won.

Sextus insisted on offering me a half share of the reward money he was going to get, but for the first time ever I turned down hard cash. You can never tell in this life, I'd already got enough money, and one day I might need a favour from a friendly centurion.

After the excitement of settling an old score, life returned to the longer slower game of my relationship with Saul. I had assumed that after his usual visit of three of four days in Jezreel, to ensure his own side of the business was prospering, he would once more disappear on Temple affairs. Which meant that in order to provide Mark with any useful warning of forthcoming trouble, if Saul failed to volunteer his next destination; I would have to probe for it.

Unfortunately, this time I didn't need to ask, he wanted to take me into his confidence.

"You're not the sort of person that I would normally wish to work with, Jesus Barabbas, but you seem to have proved yourself reliable so far. Although I didn't discuss the matter with you I did in fact have another man in Damascus, my servant Eliezer. He is, or was, a reliable man and should have returned by now, and yet I've heard nothing. No sign of him and no message, it's most unlike him, the possibility exists that his head has been turned by the very people he was supposed to be pursuing. It's happened before."

That was a revelation, Saul's own men becoming followers. The idea that I might have killed another convert was unfortunate, but surely Lydia would have known about him - then she would really have been annoyed. I dismissed the thought as he spoke further.

"I shall be mounting a major campaign in the next few weeks to root out this continuing heresy, but first we must go to Jerusalem to make final arrangements with the Council. Then with a small team of helpers we can make a start, and this time you can join us." He smiled at me, imagining that I would be pleased with this honour.

I smiled back at him. "I'm very grateful for the honour, where shall we be going?"

"Damascus, where else? You have identified the ring leaders, and you can take us to them. Then if expertly questioned they will lead us to others. Once you have a sufficient number of them, there will always be some who talk. You'll see."

I realised then that my baptism as a follower of Jesus could have been premature. The idea that this deranged little son of a whore would ever be allowed to arrange that Mary Magdalen and Lydia be flogged and tortured was so absurd that I didn't even consider it.

"That's excellent news, I look forward to being at your side wherever you go. You can rely on me."

"We shall leave for Jerusalem tomorrow at dawn, until then." He clasped my arm briefly and turned to leave. I stood for a moment, I was familiar with the idea of prayer, but not well practised at it. I had no idea how these things worked, or if God would even hear me, but I thought it so clearly that I might as well have been speaking out loud, I might almost have been shouting it.

"Lord I know I'm not supposed to, and I know there'll be a price to pay in this life or the next, but you made me what I am, you put me in this position and you know exactly what I'm going to do next." Then not knowing what else to say to God, I too walked away, still muttering angrily and wondering if Mary Magdalen would shout at me as much about this one. The only good thing was that the dead children hadn't been back for me in the night recently.

This time Jerusalem meant something different to me, it meant the active centre of our church, of my church. Our entrance to the city was through the Damascus Gate, and to reach it we had to walk directly past the Hill of Skulls, the site of the crucifixion; the place where I should have died. At one time I would have regarded this as a place where things ended, including the lives of my two cousins. Now the opposite was true, I saw it as a place of new beginnings, my cousins had been told that 'Today you will see glory', a remark I had once dismissed but now took seriously. Even the crowded twisting streets of the city looked like places of opportunity, and I wondered how many of those crowds were new converts, like me. Even the journey down here with Saul had been more relaxed, he probably thought that any change in the atmosphere between us was due to my acceptance of the role as his respectful assistant. In reality, it was more due to my satisfaction at having removed his second man in Damascus without arousing suspicion. The dreaded persecutor Saul might not be quite as invincible as once imagined.

One thing remained unchanged: my opinion of James the son of Alphaeus, I didn't like him. Despite being unusually well qualified for the attribute, it had taken me a long time to come to humility, and he seemed to be taking even longer. In the face of continuing reports of Peter's tireless work on the streets, and his success as an evangelist, my initial reservations about him had vanished; but James remained a problem for me. Mary had explained that the church was made up of ordinary men and women, that we were all fallible and must simply do our best. Lydia had said that whatever fault we saw in others we should always remember that they might be able to see even greater fault in us. None of these things I argued with, all these things I agreed with, and yet, and yet . . . As I said, for so many reasons, my baptism might have been premature.

Saul had lodgings with friends from his days as a student of Gamaliel, they were mainly priests, but even if it had have been the sort of establishment I could have fitted into, I wouldn't have been invited. In Saul's eyes I was an employee not a colleague. I told him that I would stay with my own friends and join him the following day.

I found a room at a pilgrim's lodging house near the Temple, deposited my travelling roll with the owner and then sent word to Saul, saying where he could contact me if he wished. Having done my duty I went to lose myself in the crowds that always seemed to fill the Court of the Gentiles, the Temple's huge colonnaded outer courtyard, a noisy mix of country people come to the city, and city people come to fleece them.

The shaded archways along each of the four sides of the outer courtyard, completely surrounding the central part of the Temple, were filled with stalls and traders. There were the obvious money changers, ready to convert any currency into Temple Shekels, this was reckoned to be less defiled than Roman coinage and was needed to purchase your sacrifice. The standard rate was four Denarii to one Shekel, which equalled a working man's pay for four days, it was little wonder there was resentment. Close by them were the stalls which actually sold the sacrificial doves and lambs, noisy and smelly. Then there were the men selling mementoes, small lamps and candle sticks and the like, all marked with the Temple symbol, this gave you something to take back to your village to show where you'd been. Even more numerous than any of them were the food stalls; the smell of the roasting meat struggling uneasily with the smell of shit from the live animals. It was a chaotic scene, but the best place in the city to lose anyone trying to see where you went. I made my way slowly and haphazardly through the crowds for a while, before sliding discreetly through a convenient exit and heading for my real destination.

The reunion with Mark and Barnabas was truly a joy, it was like being greeted by long lost brothers, it was like a homecoming. It came as a surprise to realise that their joy at my conversion had nothing to do with adding another person to their growing congregation, but was motivated by nothing more than their delight at what it meant for me. This was a level of altruism that I would have to practise, most of my attitudes came from my earlier life and probably always would. If I'd ever even considered the subject, goodness had never been more than a vague aspiration for me.

Although neither Mark nor Barnabas had been amongst the original twelve of Jesus' apostles, they were both at the very heart of the mission in Jerusalem. Even following the exodus of so many of the new believers, the preaching in the Temple and the market places was continuing unchecked, as were the arrests.

There had been eight separate stonings since that of Stephen, but each one of them had been of relatively recent converts, none of them had been high profile leaders of the movement.

The Sanhedrin were playing a cat and mouse game, determined to maintain their attack on Jesus' followers, yet unwilling to risk the public outrage that would come from the execution of their leaders. Nor had their attempts to build a convincing case for sedition achieved anything like the certainty required to persuade the Romans to take it on. Pilate knew he'd been fooled in the case of Jesus and had allowed himself to be pressured by the Sanhedrin's panic. Although he couldn't have cared less about the death of a Galilean peasant, he was very much concerned at the idea that some collection of Jewish priests were pulling the same trick twice. People needed to see that he took his own decisions, so whatever problems the Jews were having, they would have to find their own solution this time.

To my surprise this personal reprieve was seen by the apostles as a failure, rather than an escape. They were willing to push their message as loudly and as publically as possible, no matter what the consequences to themselves. There was still an unspoken, but real, sense of guilt at their behaviour during and immediately after the crucifixion, when they had scattered and hidden themselves. Now each of the deaths of the less prominent disciples seemed to goad them to fresh efforts, as if they had somehow failed in not managing to get themselves killed. It was the reckless folly of a group of drunks, who haven't yet worked out just how much it's going to hurt when they take a tumble. It was intoxicating just to be with them, and I was even ready to put aside my lifelong reluctance to volunteer and join them on the streets; until Mark pointed out that I wasn't even supposed to be seen with them - let alone arrested with them.

I asked after Mary, Jesus' mother, and was told that, because of the disturbances, she was living with friends just a few miles outside the city. The fact that no further details were offered seemed a clear enough hint that any idea I might have had about visiting her were probably a waste of time.

One of the first things Mark said was to reassure me about the trip to Damascus. "You can relax about getting word to Lydia and Mary, we've already sent word, with two separate messengers. So by the time you arrive they will have taken whatever steps are necessary to keep themselves safe."

That was careless of me, I should have asked him about that. I was so sure that Saul would never make it to Damascus that I wasn't bothered about what might happen there. The trouble was that I was the only one who knew about the accident that he was going to meet on the way north. I had yet to work out the precise nature of this accident, all I knew for now was that it was going to be fatal - all the best accidents are. All hell would break loose when Mary found out, but there was nothing to be done about that. However, here and now I had to pretend to be concerned.

"Does that mean they'll keep out of his way altogether, and not put up some show of bravado like Esther?"

"My message has made it clear to Lydia that her duty is to keep herself and Ananias safe while Saul is with them. We don't need any more martyrs, that's our role here." His tone was perfectly matter of fact, he meant every word of it, and I wondered how I would cope when my time came. But that's a thing you can never know, until it happens.

"And Mary, what about her?"

Mark laughed. "I sent her my love, and said that I prayed for her every day, but the idea that I could give her instructions is foolish. She will do whatever she thinks is best, if I were there with her I would ask for her advice, rather than giving her mine."

I was like a child picking at a scab, I knew I should leave it alone, but couldn't help myself. "She should have stayed in Jerusalem and taken charge, just as she was always supposed to, shouldn't she?"

He was less able than me to hide behind a facade of dishonesty, which left the truth written all across his face. He looked miserable and guilty. "Peter's a good man, there's nobody better than him on the streets - we'd be lost without his example and determination. He's only just come back from Samaria with John, they were helping Philip to deal with a false prophet claiming to work in Jesus' name."

He paused, so I prompted him. "We're not talking about Samaria, we're talking about Jerusalem. Peter's a good man - *but*."

"But he's no politician. Peter deals in plain truths and certainties, his faith is stronger than any of us."

"Which left the way open for a man who is a politician."

"Perhaps we needed a politician to be our leader, perhaps that's the way forward."

"Perhaps we needed Mary Magdalen, which is what Jesus said in the first place."

He looked helpless. "What's happened has happened. In the end it was all done with Mary's agreement."

Our meeting, which had been so happy was now reduced to an uncomfortable silence by my refusal to accept the simple fact that James was their leader, and if the apostles all accepted it, then why shouldn't I?

"I'm sorry. You're the ones risking your lives every day on the streets, it's your choice - not mine. I'm no more than Saul's arse licker and bag carrier. I should have kept my mouth shut."

He shook his head. "Now that you're one of us, you have every right to speak out. The truth is that I also would have preferred Mary to lead us, but Peter accepted James's assumption of the role and he was the senior one amongst us. Judas would have known what to do, perhaps if he'd still been alive he might have argued the point; who knows?"

Mary had been right I needed to practise a little more humility, I asked him to tell me about Peter's time in Samaria.

CHAPTER EIGHTEEN

Despite the fact that the desire to preach Jesus' teachings on the streets occupied most of the apostle's time, an interesting viewpoint on the relationship between their characters emerged on the day before Saul and I departed. I was at Peter's house in the old town, with Sara his wife who, despite never having met me before, once she had established who I was had welcomed me as a friend. It was a little after noon and we had been sitting and talking for an hour, I was telling her about my time in Damascus and describing the various characters involved. On the basis that she was likely to hear about it anyway, I even told about how my killing of Saul's man had led to my conversion and baptism, when Peter himself came home. He had some writings he wanted Sara to copy, in order to fasten notices around the city to encourage attendance at their meetings.

He greeted me with a hug, the man was as open and honest as Mark had said, and insisted that I repeat most of what I'd already told Sara. "We've heard stories about events in Syria but only at third or fourth hand, how many are there? Where do they meet?"

"My best estimate would be about three or four hundred active converts, arranged in about eight different groups, or churches. The one I was with was the largest, and was led by a woman called Lydia with a man called Ananias; it was them who baptised me. Then after we'd had a meal together, Mary Magdalen gave me bread and wine in remembrance of Christ."

He then wanted to know how Mary was keeping, and the child? I looked at him, waiting for some more detail of the child, but none was forthcoming, he simply looked back at me and waited for my answer. Well that was fair: I wasn't telling him my secret, which more or less evened the score.

I was in the middle of answering his question when James and Simon came in, they were hurried and harassed and came to a dead stop when they saw me. For a moment they stared silently, but not for long. "You - what business have you in this house?" James' voice was that of man addressing an unwelcome intruder.

It was less his question that I found interesting, than Sara and Peter's reactions. Sara was horrified at this rudeness to her own guest and Peter was visibly embarrassed. However, it was the weak embarrassment of a man who knows that he should protest, but also knows that he won't. This from a man who openly defied the massed ranks of the Priests and Sadducees without turning a hair, it was inexplicable. Sara looked at him helplessly, she seemed to expect some response as well, but none was made. James ignored them both, he was confident of his ability to behave in this fashion, and continued to stare at me.

"I entered this house as a guest of the master and mistress of the place, and I was telling them of my time in Damascus." I said politely but firmly and then stared back at him, baptism imposed no requirement of tolerating this sort of nonsense that I'd heard of.

"Did you also tell them of your work for Saul, that creature from hell now striding the earth?"

"They are well aware of the role I play in attempting to help prevent . . ."

But James wasn't interested in any reply, he had too much righteous indignation to pour over me. "No man can serve two masters, and you aren't even trying. Did you tell them that you informed your master Saul about our brothers from Shiloh lodging in the city? Information you learned yesterday at Mark's house."

"I agree that I heard talk of those people yesterday, but you have my word that I made no mention of that to Saul. I would never do such a thing."

"Unless it was for another thirty pieces of silver."

"That was unfair and you know it. If we don't practise the forgiveness of repented sins then what do we do? I've changed, and if anyone here wants proof of that then consider the fact that I'm still talking to you, and haven't knocked you down. That's how much I've changed."

"Then can you explain to me how the Council guards knew where to find them. They were all arrested at first light this morning, they're still being flogged and questioned now. Nobody beyond our own small group even knew they were in Jerusalem. We've used that house for visiting brothers for the last three months, without any trouble. Yet within less than a day of you hearing about it, the house is raided by the Council and everyone seized."

Even in the heat of the moment I thought it typical of him that he didn't want me to give my explanation to *them*, but to rather to *him*.

I shook my head. "I can't explain why it happened, I can only promise that it had nothing to do with me. And furthermore, I'd remind you that I've already given Mark advance warning of three major raids on our brothers and sisters in Samaria. Why would I do that if I wanted to betray either you or them? I could have saved myself the trouble."

"It isn't up to me to follow the twists and turns of Satan. I said you were profane the first time I ever saw you, and I was right. Your story of this supposed baptism by some woman in Damascus is no more than another of your lies."

I was beginning to run short of reasonable behaviour. "Some woman." I shouted. "That wasn't some woman. I was baptised by Lydia, the leader of our church in Syria, and then shared the body and blood of Christ with Mary Magdalen; the very companion that our Lord wished to take over the leadership of the church in Jerusalem. A position you now seem to have taken for yourself." The fact that I hadn't got a proper explanation of these events from Mary didn't mean that I was going to let him go free without roughing him up, at least a little.

Before James could reply, Peter came to his feet. "These are hasty words Jesus Barabbas, we have enough enemies in the Sanhedrin without finding them in our own house. In the spirit of unity brother I think it would be better if you withdrew."

I stood my ground for a moment, breathing heavily, that man's arrogance needed curbing by someone. But then I thought of the promises I'd made Mary, and I thought of the act I was already planning to carry out on Saul, and I reckoned that was probably enough for the time being. How Peter justified his actions was his affair not mine.

I looked at Sara, still sitting shocked at the table. "Thank you for your hospitality Sara." Then, with the briefest nod to Peter I turned and left. It was time for me to keep my appointment with Saul, I had arranged to meet him in mid afternoon, at about the ninth hour. He'd told me to look for him in one of the ante chambers to the Hall of Hewn Stone by the north wall of the Temple, a location known by all as the meeting place of the Great Sanhedrin.

As I write these words in my old age, with Chloe by my side to help me, I recognise that this whole world I'm now describing has gone for ever. Titus and his Legions levelled the Second Temple that I knew so

214

well. The Temple where Jesus studied and taught, where he overturned the tables of the money changers - all gone. The gold has been melted down and taken to Rome, the sacred scrolls destroyed, the priests killed. All that now remains are the piles of broken rubble and the hot dry wind blowing dust around the ruins. With the fall of the Temple the Sanhedrin lost not only its home, but also its very reason for existence. Without a Jewish state and a state religion, there is no longer any need of a regulatory body to oversee the law; the law is dead, along with the priests. Will there ever be another Temple or another Sanhedrin? I have no idea, and anyone who tells you otherwise is either a fool or a liar.

But I'm getting ahead of myself, at the time I'm describing the Great Sanhedrin, or the Council as it was usually known, was at the centre of our law and customs, everyone knew of their doings and their judgments. It says a great deal for the followers of Jesus that within a year and a half of his execution the Sanhedrin was devoting most of its time and energy to the vicious but futile pursuit of this once insignificant sect. It was their actions almost as much as Peter's that were responsible for creating such an interest in the movement.

I found Saul, waiting in a large and beautifully decorated outer room, all marble columns and Greek statuary, to go before the assembled Council. He was standing alone and looked uncharacteristically nervous. He even looked pleased to see me, a sure sign that he wasn't himself today.

"Will I be required to speak?" I asked, thereby admitting that I found the grandeur of the surroundings intimidating.

"Not unless they wish to question you, with your background that's always a possibility. They have prior knowledge of my other assistants, they've all been with me on earlier missions."

I looked at the other people in the waiting room: lawyers, priests and rich merchants. I might have taken huge steps towards respectability since working for Barnabas, but I was nowhere near this level. Although Saul himself was a Pharisee, as were the majority of the Council members, you would have needed a very great degree of self assurance not to be impressed by the surroundings.

"I thought you were a member of the Sanhedrin, why do you have to appear before them?"

"I am a member, but in all cases where a member has personal involvement they have to withdraw from the discussion, then if they're required to participate in some way, they do so as a member of the public."

"Has this been the same routine for all your missions?"

"No, this one's special. In strictly legal terms, when it comes to non religious civil law, the Sanhedrin's authority only covers Judea, but all Jewish congregations anywhere in the world are expected to heed its authority when it comes to the interpretation of Mosaic law."

"As I understand things, an observant Jew can turn practically anything into a matter of legal interpretation."

He smiled. "Precisely, you're beginning to catch on. What makes this case so special is the fact that, for the first time, I shall be working in Damascus, and you saw for yourself just how touchy they were about a perfectly straightforward request for information. The Syrians seem to think they're above the law, which is why I need to have my own warrant from the Council, permitting me to arrest and seize the guilty, drawn up so carefully."

A chamberlain in a black robe approached. "Saul of Tarsus." He said formally. "If you would be kind enough to come with me sir, the Council are ready for you now."

The main chamber was even grander than the ante room, as is only proper, and we were led to stand in the middle of the room. Around us ran a huge horseshoe shaped table, along three of the four walls, with the seventy Council members seated behind it. They were all facing inwards towards Saul and I, but not all of them were looking at us. Several were in separate conversations with aides and priests, some clustered around behind them, and some stood in the well of the room leaning over the front of the table. Saul stood waiting, silently and politely, and I stood, even more silently and politely, two paces behind him.

The President of the Council, sitting in the central position on a larger chair than the rest, tapped the table with a small mallet. "Brethren, I call your attention to our well beloved brother Saul of Tarsus. Greetings Saul, I trust we find you in good health?"

"I am as well as I hope you are, your Excellency." The other conversations dotted round the table were swiftly concluded, and all eyes were focussed on my companion. They began to question him about the various regions in which he had recently been active, in each case he provided a summary of the situation. Apart from the President, who I assumed to be Caiaphas the High Priest, each Council member came to his feet before speaking. The proceedings were as formally impressive as I'd expected, the only surprise was just how boring it all was. Thankfully nobody took the slightest interest in me and I struggled to stay awake as they took it in turns to drone on about the need for *swift action*, or in the words of another *decisive action*, or as yet another put it *resolute and determined action*. The common factor in all cases being *action*, with the equally common requirement that it was Saul that was going to take it.

At last it seemed that all interested parties had had their say, the scribes had completed two copies of Saul's warrant of authority and Caiaphas had signed them. Paul held one scroll, and I held the other, we both bowed to the assembly and then took our leave. We'd been standing there so long I was surprised and relieved to find that my legs still worked.

Back in the ante room, there were two priests waiting to speak to Saul, and my presence didn't seem to be necessary, I held out my copy of the warrant to him, but he didn't take it. "You keep hold of it, the reason we have two copies is in case one is damaged or lost, just make very sure you don't do either - misuse of a Sanhedrin warrant is a capital offence."

He had turned away and was talking to the priests, but I thought that I'd spent quite long enough standing silently behind him. "Is there anything else you want me for?"

He briefly gave me his distracted attention once more. "No, no, there's nothing else. Meet me tomorrow morning in the fourth watch, before dawn. I'll be at the Arab stables just inside the Damascus gate with the rest of the party. We shall leave as soon as they open the gate." Then he turned away again, I was dismissed.

The day was almost gone, but it was still too early to go back to the lodging house for the night so I made my way back to Mark's house, at least I had friends there.

Mark was out but I shared an evening meal with Barnabas and two young disciples who'd been helping with a baptism ceremony that afternoon. We had been together for the best part of an hour when one of the young men mentioned that he'd been told about some prisoners from Jezreel being held in one of the city prisons.

"That's where you're from isn't it?" He asked. It's not to my credit that my first reaction was less than interested. The surviving prisoners from Jezreel had to be somewhere, and it was no great surprise they were in Jerusalem; that was exactly where Saul had said he'd send them. The only one of them known to me was already dead.

"Yes, that's right." I said. "D'you know anything about them, any of their names?" I thought that I could at least pass word to their families that they'd survived this long. It might be some comfort.

"I heard there are only two of them left, a man called Abel and their leader, a woman called Esther."

"Esther - from Jezreel - are you sure?" I was almost shouting at the poor boy.

He was startled by this sudden change in my level of interest. "Yes, I'm sure. The man told me that a woman called Esther, who was the leader of the church in Jezreel and had been arrested by Saul, was in the praetorian prison. That was this afternoon he told me, he'd only just come from the prison."

"The praetorian prison is the one that I was in at the Antonia fortress isn't it?"

"No, there are two praetorian prisons. The one you were in is at the Antonia, but it's for men only. Esther is at the praetorian women's prison at Herod's Palace in the upper city. But why? They'll never let you in to see her, the best you could hope for would be to bribe a guard to give her a message."

I was silent, I couldn't work out what I should do with this information, it seemed that I ought to do something - but what? Esther's bravery had been an example to anyone who heard her story, and I was telling everyone I met. The trouble was that her chances of getting out of there alive were extremely slim. She wasn't just a rank and file church member, she was a community leader, and one who had publically defied Saul's instructions. When Saul had told me she was dead, he might just have meant that she was as good as dead.

The more I thought about it the more I thought that this was one of those times when you should take no notice of what a person wanted to happen, you should save them from themselves. Esther would more than likely be happy to die a martyr's death, but I thought there had been plenty of martyrs recently. In fact Jerusalem had seen enough martyrs to last them for quite a while, the difficulty lay in preventing it from happening.

"Couldn't you use your influence with Saul to have her released?" Asked Barnabas.

I shook my head. "He would hate to have to admit that he lied to me, it would make him seem weak, as if he valued my opinion. The fact that I so much as raised the subject would guarantee her death."

"Would the Sanhedrin's warrant of authority help to have her released?" Asked the young man who had provided the information.

"No, even if I could use it to bluff the guards into releasing her, it would only be temporary, as soon as the prison governor heard about it he would send word to Saul demanding to know what was going on. Then at that moment they'd have men scouring the city till they found her, and when they did she would be treated like any other fleeing felon and executed."

"And you with her." Added Barnabas helpfully.

The four of us subsided into a glum silence, they'd all heard me describing her bravery and knew how I felt about her. If it hadn't been for my failed attempt to keep her safe in the first place I might not have taken it so personally; and if it hadn't been for my careless gossip that alerted Saul, I might not have felt so guilty. It must have been this combination of factors which made me unable to accept that I was at a dead end, and that inability led to the realisation that there might be a way.

"If the prison governor can't find Saul, then he won't get the answer that there's something wrong, and if he doesn't raise the alarm immediately then I don't think he'll raise it at all. If he leaves it until the following day, or the following week to admit that one of his prisoners is missing, it will sound like it's his fault."

"Why wouldn't he be able to find Saul? Even I know where to find Saul."

"Because at dawn tomorrow Saul will be on his way to Damascus, and it will be at least three weeks before he's back in Jerusalem."

"Which means that if you wait until after midnight . . "

"Exactly."

The two young men who were Barnabas's assistants were eager to help, and I was equally eager that they shouldn't. "The last time I encouraged two young men to help me in a piece of stupid criminality they ended up nailed to crosses - while I walked free."

Barnabas disagreed. "That was completely different; then, you were trying to help yourself, this time you'll be serving God."

"I don't think James would agree with you."

Barnabas shrugged, unable to argue, but unwilling to join in so openly with the criticism of a fellow apostle. It seemed that we had decided the matter.

In a city as complex as Jerusalem, even in the dark hours after midnight there are some honest men about. All that's needed to avoid the attention of the watch is some appearance of purpose, and I had that. I strode through the upper city intent on important official business, two men at arms matching my pace and striding with me, one at each shoulder, both carrying lanterns. From my bearing and my swagger you could tell that I wasn't the sort of man to welcome damn fool questions from inquisitive night watchmen.

The praetorian prison at Herod's palace is set beside and below the western wall, hewn into the city bedrock by centuries of sweating slaves. Even in the cool of the night I could still pick up the stench of the prisoners, I don't know if you can smell despair but you could certainly smell everything else about them. There would probably have been an entrance from with the palace courtyard, but there was also one directly to the street. The door was old and blackened, as if someone had tried to burn it down, and failed. It looked only marginally less solid than the surrounding stonework. I took out my sword and hammered the hilt as hard as I could against the ironbound planks.

"Open up - open the door damn you."

I was in a hurry and didn't care who knew it. Any attempt at discretion in these circumstances would look extremely suspicious, so I hammered again. Despite the certainty of my informant the door had yielded so little to my onslaught that I wondered if it really was the right door, or even if it was a door at all. Behind me I could hear shutters opening as concerned citizens wondered who was waking them in the middle of the night. I signalled one of the boys to take up the hammering, my right arm was getting tired and I might need it later.

At last, a small portion of a human face, a part with an eye set in it, appeared at the iron grille in the middle of the door. Without bothering to wait for his obvious enquiry, I spoke myself.

"In the name of Caiaphas and the Great Sanhedrin I demand immediate admission, open the door." As I spoke I brandished my scroll in the air.

"Wait." Was all he said, and the face disappeared. There was silence and I wondered how long a self important official actually would wait before starting to hammer on the door again.

Another section of face, with another eye, came to the grille. "What d'you want?"

"I'm here to take one of your prisoners for further questioning - open the door."

"Which prisoner?"

"Esther of Jezreel, one of the Jesus gang. I have the Sanhedrin's warrant here."

"Esther? Why d'you want Esther?"

My anger was entirely unfeigned. "Don't you dare to question me, my orders are to collect the woman and deliver her forthwith to Saul of Tarsus, on behalf of the Great Sanhedrin. Now open the door before I drag you out through the keyhole."

The second section of face disappeared and we heard a succession of metallic grinding noises, then the door swung outwards. There were three of them, facing three of us, all of us had our swords drawn. The middle gaoler looked up and down the street and seeing no one else sheathed his sword, then he stepped forward and held out his hand for the scroll. I sheathed my own sword and passed him my stamped sealed and signed authority. One of his companions held up a lantern and he read the contents, you could tell from the way his eyes moved and his mouth didn't that he was a practised reader. Reaching the end he rolled it neatly and handed it back to me.

"You can't be too careful, it's my life if I get it wrong." Then he turned to one of his men. "Fetch the woman Esther, and get a move on."

The five of us stood there, in a half embarrassed shuffling silence, acknowledging that this time in the morning was no occasion for small talk. We'd already covered the basics and that was plenty.

We heard her coming before we saw her, she was moving slowly, as you might expect from a middle aged woman who has been flogged, beaten and brutalised in God knows how many different ways. As she came through the door I stepped back slightly, I nodded my thanks to the gaoler and then speaking gruffly gave the boys their orders.

"Take hold of her and follow me." Without waiting I turned my back on them and set off down the street, the last thing I wanted was for her to identify me and start asking questions; questions that I didn't want to answer - well not in front of the gaoler.

We had gone some way down the street and turned a corner before I paused, they were struggling to keep up. I took off my cloak and went to wrap it round her.

"Jesus Barabbas!" Was all she said, and then fainted dead away. I caught her as she fell and was astonished at how light she was. One of the two boys put down his lantern on the cobbles and then threw up the contents of his stomach against the house wall. His friend followed suit, at this rate I was going to need a cart to get them all home.

CHAPTER NINETEEN

I arrived at the stables by the Damascus Gate at a slow saunter, determined to demonstrate that I wasn't hurrying. Though I had in fact been sprinting all the way to the last corner, at which point I'd stopped to catch my breath and wipe the sweat off my brow, before casually walking the last few yards. I'm sufficiently small minded for it to be important to me that I should not be seen to be bothered.

The Arab stables were a rich man's establishment, that much was obvious even before dawn. As well as the rows of beautifully groomed horses, there were uniformed servants, there were enough lanterns to see clearly by and there were hot drinks to keep off the chill. This is how the wealthy travel, or in Saul's case, how people who are spending public money travel. My arrival time, after completing my overnight wanderings, was just in time to avoid the need to make excuses.

In the night I'd thought it would be necessary to rouse Peter and Sara, to look after Esther, but Peter was already leaving the house when I arrived, and after a brief greeting left me with Sara. She had the open frankness that so many of these people had, and after settling Esther in front of the early morning fire, with something to drink, she turned to me.

"I know you think that Peter should have stood up to James and defended you, but you need to understand their different personalities."

"Sara, there isn't a single one of you needs to explain yourselves to me, we all know what I am."

She smiled. "You are what we all are, fallen, but at least you seem to be doing something about it." Her

225

eyes indicated Esther. "You might not be cut out for preaching in the market place, I don't think I'd take you seriously, but you're doing what you can. We all make our offerings from the gifts we have."

As we spoke she was preparing bread and figs and a few scraps of a meat that could have been cold mutton for an early breakfast, and for a while was silent, concentrating on the work. I let her be, she hadn't got to her point yet, but in time she did.

"It's all to do with self confidence." She said. "James and Matthew, and Judas before he died, were all educated men, they could hold their own in any company. But Peter and Andrew aren't like that, they're just fishermen. They know that every time they open their mouths their accent makes them sound like country bumpkins, so when a man like James makes some cutting remark they have no immediate and clever response. But if we're to grow and spread the word to all people, we don't need cleverness; we need truth, we need strength and we need dogged determination. Those are Peter's gifts."

That was it, she'd said her piece, and said it simply and directly. Whether it was true or not, time would tell, but at all events it required no embellishment from me. I kissed her on the cheek and left her with Esther.

At the stables, Saul was organising everything and everybody, he was a small man but a very forceful one, none of the doubts I'd seen earlier were on display here. This man knew exactly what he wanted to do and now he was going to do it. There were two servants, six men at arms, his man Samuel and myself, a total party of eleven of us. Our numbers and the fact that we were on horseback should make us immune from bandits, if we couldn't outfight them, we could outrun them. By the time we were mounted the trumpet was sounding at the gate, signalling the fact that it was now open. We spurred our animals and set off, the rest of them apparently easier on their mounts than me, and a lot less likely to fall asleep.

The journey was not quite as uncomfortable as my memory of the last one, perhaps we were mounted on better horses, or had better saddles, or even more probably I was entirely focussed on what I knew must come.

My determination was that Saul should not reach Damascus, I would not allow him to do to Mary and Lydia and the others what he had done to Esther. My problem was the presence of the six men at arms. The two servants I could deal with, Samuel I could deal with, I imagined Saul himself would be a fiery little fighter, but he lacked my expertise in the brutal business of blood letting. No, my problem was those six men at arms, two or three of them looked like serious fighters, and the sheer weight of numbers would tell.

If the worst came to the worst I would simply knife Saul in the back, as we rode, and let the dice fall where they would. The worst they could do was kill me, and I'd already been there. It's difficult to frighten a man who's been ready for crucifixion. However, for the time being I was prepared to let the journey unfold, the longer we shared each other's company the more relaxed and less guarded my companions might become. There was always the possibility that *something* might turn up, something that might remove the requirement for my noble and inspiring sacrifice.

The third night we spent at Jezreel, mixing a little business with our business, but the place was no longer home to me, I had no interest in my old haunts and not a lot more in the tent yard. I wasn't sorry to move on the next morning. There were three more days and two nights left on the road, the sand was running out of the glass, I watched and waited.

Moving up past the eastern shore of the Sea of Galilee the scenery changed from the short hilly country of Galilee and Samaria into the longer views and wider valleys of Syria. Once again the snow capped ridges and peaks of the Antelibanus range could be seen stretching away to the north on our left hand horizon. But despite the splendours of the scenery my mind was on other things. My stomach was already knotting up in anticipation, not so much of the deed itself, but of the possible escape afterwards. In such cases it's probably better to know that there's no hope of survival, and just go ahead with the killing in the full awareness that you're going to die with him. It's when there's some chance of escape, some chance of survival - that's when you start to fret about it.

As it was, I had decided to do nothing until we were within galloping range of Damascus. If there was to be no distraction and I was obliged to act in cold blood in front of everyone, then that could offer at least a vague prospect of escape. If I could do the deed and leave the scene, and if I could reach Damascus before the men at arms reached me, and if I could lose myself in the crowds. Then perhaps I would live a long and happy life. That was a lot of ifs.

On the first day after leaving Jezreel I found myself riding alongside Saul, he had become more and more withdrawn as we made our way north, but I was beginning to lose my inhibitions. Unlike everyone else in our group I knew that we were never going to reach Damascus; I knew that my actions were going to lead to at least one death, perhaps more, perhaps my own. Saul thought he was going to Damascus, but I knew he was going to hell - even if I had to go with him. Which meant that as long as I didn't alert him to this fact, then I could say what I liked, I would no longer be dependant on his goodwill.

228

"Is it true that you were taught by the Rabbi Gamaliel, the man they call the greatest Pharisee?" I asked. He looked at me curiously, he was unused to scholarly enquiry from this quarter, but could see no harm in the question.

"Yes, I studied The Law under Gamaliel. He's not just the greatest Pharisee, I would call him the greatest teacher. Many people suggest that the exactness of his judgement surpasses even that of his grandfather, Hillel."

He would have imagined that to have dealt with the matter, but showed his good breeding by politely raising his eyebrows, in case there was anything else I wished to ask. There was.

"You must excuse my ignorance but I'd heard it said that when the man Simon Peter appeared before the Council to answer for his heresy, Gamaliel spoke in his defence. Saying that if his beliefs were false they would fail anyway, but that if his views came from God then anyone opposing him could find themselves in conflict with that very God." His eyes were locked on mine, but only because he was afraid that if he looked away it would be an acknowledgement of my point.

The sharpness of his responses, the speed of his anger and the ruthlessness of his actions made Saul a dangerous man to challenge, and I had never before dared to do it. I waited for the outburst to hit me, but although his mouth began to move as if to answer, he didn't actually speak.

Being of very limited intellect and not knowing when to stop, I was unable to leave the silence alone and pressed on. "It's just that of all my many sins, I feel that killing my own master could have been the greatest." This was a lie, but I wasn't going to tell him about the children. "And I wondered if acting against the judgement of your own master was not a step in that direction?"

This time I had provoked him sufficiently to draw a response, an infuriated one. "It seems I may have misjudged your usefulness Jesus Barabbas. You know nothing and you understand nothing. I shall speak to you again in Damascus."

Then he urged his horse forward to draw ahead of me. As I looked at his tense and angry back, rigid in the saddle, I smiled to myself. Every time someone had ever told me that I didn't understand something, what they had actually meant was that I understood it all too well. It's like the man who says his wife doesn't understand him.

For the first part of our journey four of the six men at arms had ridden at the front of our small column and two at the back; but the next morning, as we moved further into the desert country of Syria, Saul changed things round. In order to avoid the dust thrown up by the leading horses he sent all the men at arms to the back, and rode alone at the front, followed by Samuel and myself.

This seemed to reinforce his view of himself, Saul alone, against the world. He was not normally a taciturn man, the very opposite, he always had some point or other that he wished you to understand. Some point that he could see clearly, and if only you would pay closer attention - so might you. Yet since our brief encounter after leaving Jezreel he had relapsed into silence, engrossed with his thoughts, or possibly even, his doubts.

It was in this formation that we set off on the morning of the sixth day, our last day on the road. Already we could see the shining white walls of Damascus, and their surrounding belt of cultivation, standing out in front of us like a huge oasis in the desert landscape

Samuel and I, as Saul's two senior assistants, were next in line behind him. As it would have been demeaning for us to have ridden alongside the servants, and a problem of precedence for us to ride one behind the other, we rode side by side. Despite our early difficulties together, the daily routine of us each running our separate but adjacent businesses, had produced a rough acknowledgement that we might as well make some attempt at politeness. That, and the joint requirement for us both to try and organise our affairs to take account of Saul's volatile temperament. So although I wouldn't have trusted the man out of my sight there was a degree of superficial civility, but it was only ever wafer thin.

"Saul's man in Damascus, Eliezer, I assume you must have met him while you were there?" His rising intonation made it a question.

I hesitated for a moment, genuinely puzzled. "It's a big city, Damascus, and even if I'd known what he looked like we could have been there all year and not run into each other."

He nodded, as if accepting my answer, before continuing. "It's just that you were both looking for the same sort of people, in the same sort of places, at the same time."

I shrugged, he could follow this trail all day long and it would get him nowhere. "Then we shall just have to ask him - if he ever bothers to turn up."

"That's the point, I know the man better than Saul, and I know that he hasn't just walked off, he's not that sort of man. If he's gone missing then something's happened to him, something nasty." There was hostility and suspicion in his voice. "It would have needed a man like you to have dealt with him, a man with a long record of brutality."

I swung round in my saddle to look at him directly. "The real problem is you can't accept that I found the information your friend couldn't, I did the job I was paid to, and he didn't. If you ask me politely I might help you to look for him, we could start by searching the taverns. He's probably under a table in one of them."

He didn't rise to my sneering tone, he just carried on gnawing away at it, like a dog at a bone. "Perhaps he found out that you weren't quite so keen to root out these Jesus people, that you were planning to tell Saul and me a pack of lies, Perhaps he found out that you were as cosy with them as you were with Esther. You would have had to keep him quiet, wouldn't you?"

As we spoke I'd been watching the walls of Damascus coming closer, and we were now within two or three miles of the Gate of Mars, my nearest possible point of safety. This was it, close enough that I might just about hold off my pursuers - any closer and the watchers on the city walls might see what happened. The only thing that could stop Saul was death, his death, and there would never be a better time.

I smiled at Samuel, tired of this entirely pointless argument. "We'll soon be there and then we'll find out if I'm telling the truth." I reined my horse back, and gestured in front of me. "You go first, you're the senior one - I'll follow."

He looked uncertain, he thought I had something in mind, and couldn't work out what. But not wishing to look timid, he rode on as I'd indicated, and I fell in behind him. As he moved forward I turned back to the servants. "Saul says that you two and the men at arms are to drop further back. You're to keep on following us, just from a longer distance. This is a big moment for him and he wants to enter the city with just Samuel and myself, apparently it has a special significance for him." I didn't wait for an answer, they'd got their orders and this wasn't going to be a debate. I spurred up to resume my place behind Samuel. I would take him at the gallop, a slashing sword cut across his back, killing him wasn't important I just had to put him down. Then without pausing I would take Saul, with luck the first thrust of the sword would go cleanly through him and then I would ride for the city as if my life depended on it. Which is exactly what it would do.

I made myself trot meekly for a minute or two as we widened the distance between the three of us and the escort. I looked down to loosen my sword and make sure that my dagger was ready to hand, then I glanced back, the guards were more than a furlong away. Perfect. I dug my heels in and prepared myself for action. As I did so, there was an almighty flash and a peal of thunder. My horse reared up with a whinny of terror and I was thrown from the saddle.

I landed on the ground with a bruising jolt and an astonished awareness that there was a light far brighter than the sun shining down on me. I scrambled to get to my feet, but had got no further than kneeling in the road on my hands and knees, when I realised that my shadow, there on the road below me, was far blacker and the surrounding light far brighter than they had any right to be. I didn't dare look up, whatever was producing this much light would certainly blind me. Strangely, in those first seconds I didn't think about the others, or even of what could have caused it, I was just afraid of the light.

Then a voice came, or was it a voice? For a moment I didn't know if it was inside my head or if I was hearing it through my ears. But no, it really was a voice, and it was speaking in Hebrew.

"Saul, Saul, why do you persecute me?"

Saul's reply was hesitant and frightened, as mine would have been. "Who are you Lord?"

"I am Jesus who you are persecuting, but get up and enter the city and you will be told what to do."

For what might have been the most important few moments in my life, my wits had left me. Although the voice continued, I couldn't concentrate on the words, all I could think was: 'Yes, that is the voice of Jesus, it might be three years since I heard him, but that is certainly him.' I should have been paying closer attention to the detail, I should have noted every word, but the awareness that I was listening to the voice of God was too much for me. I stayed there, crouched in the road, too frightened to look up.

Then I realised that the voice had stopped and the light had faded, we were left simply in the brightness of the noon day sun, and that was only bright enough to dazzle you - not blind you. As I rose hesitantly to my feet I realised that my lack of understanding might not be due solely to my own stupidity, the rest of the message hadn't been for me, it had been for Saul. I looked around me, Samuel was still prostrate on the ground, but Saul had, as Jesus instructed, come to his feet and was now staring about himself in a dazed fashion.

I went up to him, but he didn't look at me, he just stared about as if trying to see something that wasn't there. I grasped his arm. "Saul, can you hear me?"

He turned his face to my voice, but his gaze was blank and unseeing. "Barabbas, did you hear?"

"I heard Jesus tell you to enter the city where you would be told what to do. I think you must have looked at the light and been blinded - can you see anything at all?"

He shook his head. "It makes no difference, I've been blind for years." Then after a pause he said in a quietly astonished voice: "But I can see things more clearly now than I ever could before."

Then Samuel found his feet and his voice, and came over to us demanding to know what was happening. Saul was silent and so I answered for him. "The voice you just heard was the voice of Jesus, there will be no more persecution and no more arrests, at least not by Saul. Go and dismiss the servants and the men at arms, they're not needed any longer."

Before he could make any comment Saul grasped my own arm. "You're one of them - aren't you?"

"Yes, I'm one of them, thank God."

"Will you help me? I have to get to the city."

"I was just about to help you when I saw the light, you're not the only one who's just been saved from the darkest folly. But yes, I'll take you to the city."

I thought again about Jesus' words to me in that miserable basement in Jerusalem, about me being given time to find repentance, it had just happened again. Does every man get this many chances? It seems unlikely, though why the light should shine on me I had no idea.

Saul was in no condition to ride, and so with a quietened and confused Samuel leading the horses behind us, I took Saul's hand and led him down the road I had planned to gallop along. For the most part he stumbled along in silence, just the once asking me in a puzzled and horrified voice, "Do you know some of the things that I've done?"

I remembered once asking someone that question myself, so I gave him the most honest answer I could. "Yes, I know a lot of the things you've done, and it's lucky for you that God is more forgiving than me."

That, of course, and the memory of some of the things that I'd done.

We were met at the Mars Gate by a man who seemed to be expecting us, and who led us to a house on Straight Street, where I left Saul with another man called Judas. He was polite, but made it clear that my role was over and that he would tend to Saul. There was a completeness about the timing of these events that made them seem natural and obvious, rather than astonishing and incredible. We left the horses at a stables and I took Samuel with me to get a room at the same inn by the market where I'd stayed last time. If Lydia or Mary wanted to find me then that's where they would look.

CHAPTER TWENTY

I sent Samuel back to Jezreel, with instructions to tend to the business, mine and Barnabas's, as well as Saul's. Then I spent my days waiting and thinking. Nobody made contact with me, nobody spoke to me, and that made sense. The church community in Damascus had been given a warning to make themselves scarce, and they'd heeded it, they would have been mad not to. I just wondered what was happening to Saul.

Then after three days of waiting and thinking, and trying to imagine how I could ever have thought that murder would solve my problems, I had a visitor. It was Lydia, the local Deacon who had baptised me into the church, she was looking wary and ill at ease, and didn't delay communicating that fact.

"How can we be sure this isn't just another of his schemes to trap us? The man's known for his savagery, not his honesty. You told us yourself about his behaviour in Galilee."

Despite being sure, I didn't rush my answer. Too many of the people who trusted me had ended up dead, I didn't want to add to that list; but no amount of thought could lessen my certainty. "I'm sure that he would rather die than harm you or any other follower of Jesus."

She looked at me, searching my face for any trace of doubt - there was none. "What happened on the road left no room for doubt in anyone's mind. That was the genuine voice of Jesus, speaking from somewhere beyond this life. Saul's not a stupid man and unlike me he doesn't need to be told a thing repeatedly."

Then after a moment I added an extra thought. "Your problem isn't going to be dealing with his opposition, it's going to be dealing with his support. Now he's found the truth he'll want to shout it from every roof top, and he'll expect you to be doing the same. I think you might have caught a tiger by the tail with this one."

Satisfied with my sincerity, if not his, Lydia took me back to the house of Judas, on Straight Street, where she said Saul had been fasting and praying since our arrival. Having been told in a dream that it was safe to do so, Ananias had overcome his misgivings and baptised him earlier that day, Lydia, myself and some others were to join them for a celebration meal.

The Saul who greeted me was a gaunt creature who looked as if he hadn't slept, much less eaten, since I'd last been with him. But the most immediate change was that he could see me now, and although I'd seen his eyes burning with passion before, this time it was a very different passion.

"Jesus Barabbas, my friend." He hugged me with what seemed to be a genuine pleasure at our reunion, and it was certainly the first time he had ever called me his friend. "The scales fell from my eyes when Ananias laid his hands on me. But now - I can scarcely imagine the amount of work I must do to make up for my earlier life." He was distraught, but determined. As I thought, the old Saul was still there, just pointing in a different direction.

"How could you ever have let me come to Damascus to attack your friends? You knew what was going to happen."

I hadn't intended to discuss the matter, but his accusation was made in earnest and caught me unprepared. "You were never going to reach Damascus." I said, before I could stop myself. His eyes narrowed as he struggled to digest the full meaning, but a sharp intake of breath from behind me indicated a faster brain at work. I turned to see that Mary Magdalen had entered the room in time to hear my remark. Her face and stance made it clear that this subject would receive further comment.

"You were going to kill me?" He sounded surprised.

"What else should I have done? I only said that I was a follower of Christ, I didn't say I was good at it. And like I said on the road - you weren't the only person to be saved from folly that day."

From that point I stepped back to let Saul greet his new friends and fellow believers. My presence seemed too much like having a mourner at the feast, but every so often I caught him giving me sideways glances, as if he couldn't believe I'd meant it. I just wished I could tell him I'd been joking.

The meal was a scene of relief: at the passing of the threat of persecution, and joy at the conversion of so great a prize. I'm well aware that we should feel the same joy at the conversion of the most humble individual as we would at the conversion of a King. Any one soul has the same value as any other. The truth of the matter is that the followers of Jesus are also human beings, and we all felt that the conversion of such a prominent member of the Sanhedrin, and so great a danger to all our lives, was a cause for rejoicing, and so we did.

It took another two or three days before there had been enough meetings, and enough assurances given, for the full community of believers in Damascus to accept that Saul, or Paul as he now wished to be called, was fully accepted. Personally I felt that if he was going to change his name to mark a new beginning, he could have picked something with a little more difference than Saul to Paul. However, nobody asked me, and more and more people were now just calling me

Barabbas, possibly feeling that I wasn't a suitable holder of the Jesus part.

Most people in Paul's position would have started their preaching career in a small synagogue in a quiet part of town, to see how things went, but that wasn't the man's style. Three days after his baptism, in the main synagogue, next to the Tetrapylon in the very centre of the city, Paul stood up and began to preach of his belief in the new Messiah. There wasn't exactly a riot, but it was touch and go for a while. The man was unstoppable. If Paul was a General then I was a foot soldier, we were not natural bedfellows, it was time for me to return to the relative calm of tent making and leave him to conquer the world.

However, before I could arrange this, an interruption occurred to prevent my immediate return to the world of neat stitching and carefully folded seams. The interruption, unsurprisingly, was Mary Magdalen. Her disapproval of my intended actions had yet to be voiced, though from her manner I felt it would be more in sorrow than in anger. She joined me in the street outside the synagogue.

"You were right about the man's energy, the only question is whether it will attract more people than it repels. There are lots of Pharisees living in Damascus, and they might not be too comfortable to find one of their own preaching in direct opposition to the Council's edicts."

"Paul's view will be that any discomfort they suffer will be their own problem, his job will be to tell the truth as clearly and publically as possible. That's the way he is."

She thought about it for a minute, and then said. "That's fair, we prayed to be spared his persecution, and we were. It just hadn't occurred to me that it could happen in this way. But what about you? I heard that you were planning to go back to Jezreel."

"I don't think I could keep up with Paul. I respect his determination; I always have, even when I disagreed with him, but I could never live the rest of my life scurrying round in his shadow."

"So where does that leave you, are you going back to the tents?"

"I think so; it's the only honest skill I have. It isn't given to all of us to be public preachers, I admire what Peter and Mark and the others are doing in Jerusalem, and what Paul will probably do here, it's just not for me. I think it's time we stopped hiding, we should live openly and honestly, saying who we are and what we believe in. Now they've lost the services of Paul, the Sanhedrin can't harass all of us everywhere, and the Romans couldn't care less."

"Ananias said you'd mentioned something about Esther."

"Yes, before I settle down to work again I'm going back to Jerusalem to see if she feels able to resume her position in the church at Jezreel. If she does, I'll take her back with me and settle her into a new house, Barnabas won't mind me taking the money out of the business. One of her brothers used her imprisonment as an excuse to steal the old house, and now he's settled his entire family into it - there's nothing like a tragedy to bring the cockroaches out."

"You're not tempted to kill him as well are you?"

"Well obviously I considered it, but I couldn't stand you shouting at me again."

"I haven't said a word about it, yet."

"That's even worse."

It turned out that Mary had intended to visit Jerusalem herself, for a meeting with James and Peter, and it made sense for us to travel together. So that

241

afternoon I said my farewells to Paul, a surprisingly emotional affair considering what I'd had in mind for him, and promised to speak up on his behalf with the apostles, or at least as many as would listen to me.

The next morning Mary and I met again to join an escorted south bound group of travellers. She arrived at the meeting place accompanied by Lydia and Ananias, with a serving girl carrying a baby. She no longer bothered to deny the child was hers, and named her as Sophie, I even took my turn at kissing the child. Thinking about it; that could well have been the first child I ever kissed in my life. Within the hour we were on the road, I seemed to spend my life in permanent motion and would soon be qualified as a tour leader on this route.

The long awaited admonishment for my frustrated plan to deal with Saul, or Paul - take it as you wish, turned out not to be as bad as I'd feared. Her main point being my presumption in taking God's role in the allotment of vengeance.

Once clear of the city and in open countryside I pointed out to Mary the place on the road where we'd experienced our meeting with Jesus. Though interested, and curious to hear the story told again, she used the opening to revisit my moral shortcomings.

"It doesn't seem to have crossed your mind that Saul was serving God's purpose, his activities led to the distribution of Jesus' teachings throughout Palestine. It was the scattering of disciples that led to the foundation of so many churches from Egypt to Cilicia, even as far as Rome."

"And you think that I should have stood by while he did to you and Lydia what he was already doing to Esther?"

"That's an unfair point, Lydia and I would have accepted whatever was in God's plan for us. Which is exactly what Esther did."

"Nonsense, Esther should have ducked when she saw what was coming. All that I planned to do was what any soldier would, in defending his native country from an invading army. Paul was the invader and you were my home country. The Torah tells us that when peaceful means fail, we should put our enemies to the sword."

"That's a clever argument Jesus Barabbas, but that's all it is. Esther knew the danger, but was still prepared to sacrifice herself to give an example to all the rest of us, about standing firm in the face of danger. As for you - I don't deny that you meant well, but that's not enough. Rescuing Esther from prison was a good example of your own courage, but planning to kill Saul was not only stupid, it was sinful. Do you understand this?"

She looked me straight in the eye as she spoke, I couldn't avoid the question and found it impossible to lie. I was out of my depth in this sort of argument, especially with the disciple referred to as Jesus' closest companion. So I abandoned my clever argument and after a heavy sigh, agreed that I understood. Then we rode on, both relieved that the matter had been dealt with. Six days later we were back in Jerusalem.

Mary made her own way to visit another Mary, Jesus' mother, and I found my way back to Peter's house. Esther was recovered, physically, but still not sure if she could cope with meeting Paul face to face again. I knew how she felt. It was agreed that we would return to Jezreel together in another day or two.

It had been a pleasure to see Peter's wife Sara again, but I was relieved that Peter himself wouldn't be back till later. It wasn't that I disliked the man, but I was never sure what to expect from him. Following the uncertainty and turmoil of the crucifixion and resurrection he had matured into a fearless and effective public preacher, which proved how wrong I could be, and yet he was still an unpredictable companion. Which way his opinions would fall seemed to depend on who else was present.

According to Sara most of the main group of the apostles were away on various missionary trips around Judea and Samaria, though I would still find Barnabas at Mark's house, which was where he now lodged. In so far as the Jerusalem church had a formal meeting place, John Mark's house had gradually become that place. It was the place where messages for other disciples could be left, and meetings arranged, the place where you were most likely to meet whoever you were looking for. Mark's mother, yet another Mary, and her servant Rhoda were both committed followers, which meant that it was one of the few houses in the city where the disciples could speak freely and in confidence.

That second evening in Jerusalem Mary Magdalen, Joanna and Esther had joined us at Mark's house for their evening meal, eating together was always an important part of the church life, especially in those early days. With us were the normal people of the house, Mark and his mother, with Barnabas and Matthew. There was a sense of togetherness, of us all being engaged in a joint enterprise, it was sense of excitement and happiness. As the least involved of all of those present I might have been more detached, and yet even I was caught up in the thrill of this new beginning. We were all infected with the same feeling of optimism about the things we were about to accomplish. But then we had visitors and the mood changed.

The two brothers Peter and Andrew, accompanied by James joined us. At first there was a surface dressing of politeness, greetings were exchanged, with Mary as the first to be acknowledged and me being the last. That seemed a fair order of priority, but then they got down to business.

James addressed me. "I understand that you are now to be welcomed to our ranks, without further reference to your background Jesus Barabbas, and so I welcome you as our companion in Christ." I was about to thank him for this, but he continued. "However, there are some things that need to be made clear between us. Our work in Jerusalem is so vital and the conditions here are so carefully balanced that we cannot allow unauthorised adventuring like your trickery at the praetorian prison. Had I known about that I would never have permitted it."

I wasn't standing for that. "As I understand it, Esther's last remaining fellow captive from Jezreel has now died in prison. Is that what you wish had happened to her?"

I had imagined this to be a killer blow, but I wasn't used to dealing with a Temple trained Rabbi. "The only reason for that death was as an act of revenge for your own attention seeking actions. Your foolish behaviour enraged the authorities and you were directly responsible for that man's death."

"At the time I released Esther there were only two of them left, out of an original group of fourteen, was I also responsible for the deaths of the other twelve?"

"What I'm telling you, is that if you think that you can come to Jerusalem and use our name to carry on as if you were still some cheap roadside bandit, then we will want no further part of you."

There was a sob, as Esther found this talk about the human cost of her freedom more than she could bear.

I'd been ready for further argument, but Esther's presence made that impossible, and I was reduced to glaring impotently at James and Peter.

At first Mary had been content for me to speak up for myself, but now she was moved to join in. "James, your language and your suggestions are not an acceptable way to address your brothers and sisters in Christ. Jesus Barabbas did what he sincerely believed to be for the best, with the result that we have at least saved one life out of the captives from Jezreel."

James turned to face her, he'd been waiting for Mary to speak. "Thank you for that correction sister, although I'm surprised that you would take the part of a supposedly reformed murderer. It brings me to the subject we came here to discuss, namely the man Saul."

There was a long silence as we waited for him to continue, but he sat in silence. I hadn't previously realised that silence could be aggressive, but his was. I was in no mood for polite formulas of address, this man had all the arrogance of the old Saul. "What about Paul?" I stressed the P of Paul.

James waved a dismissive hand. "He might have changed his name, and that might have fooled you, but it comes nowhere near fooling me. I stood and watched as he organised the stoning of Stephen, the crowd weren't sure at first, but he urged them on. He can change his name as often as he likes, but the leopard doesn't change his spots. I've seen him and his bully boys dragging away innocent men and women to their deaths - what have you seen?"

"Yes I've seen that as well, but I've also seen the light of God and heard the voice of Jesus. That was enough for me, why isn't it enough for you?"

"He's a liar and so are you. Mark thinks that you've been gathering information to protect us, he thinks it's alright for you to be a spy, as long as you're our spy.

Well I think that any man who's sold out one lot of friends will sell out anyone else he mixes with. Which is exactly why we should be very careful in allowing you to mix with us."

Mary came to her feet, bristling with outrage, I'd thought it was only me that could make her this angry. "James, the fact that I allowed you to usurp my position as our Lord's successor gives you no right to speak in this way. You have allowed that position to go to your head. Do you honestly intend that the church in Jerusalem should be your own private property, and that you, and you alone, should take all decisions - is that what you think?"

That might have dented his smugness, but it didn't go deep enough. "I know that we should devote our precious time to offering salvation to those who wish to receive it, there are some people so far sunk in sin they have little hope of redemption in this life." He was answering Mary, but his eyes were fastened on me. I thought his remarks weren't just bad theology, they were also unfair.

Although Peter and Andrew showed no signs of joining in, Matthew couldn't hold back. "I shouldn't need to remind you that our Lord came to minister to the fallen of Israel, not the righteous. And that includes Saul and Jesus Barabbas. No one is beyond the grace of God; or do you wish to rewrite our Lord's words?"

"That isn't what I said." It actually was, but at least he was backing off, if only slightly. "What I meant was that some people's sin is so great and their signs of redemption so small, that it is impossible to imagine them coming to the knowledge of God without divine intervention." A typical lawyer's answer, but Matthew had been a tax collector, and they're also good at balancing the books.

"Which is exactly what is reported to have happened on the Damascus road, or do you doubt the evidence of every man in that party, all of whom testify to the blinding light?"

"But nobody else claims to have heard the voice speaking to Saul, just Saul himself for his own reasons, and this creature." A pointing finger stabbed aggressively in my direction.

"Of course nobody else heard," I shouted, losing patience, "they were too far back to hear, but they saw it all perfectly clearly."

James picked up the scent of a problem and focussed his gaze directly on me. "And why, exactly, were your armed guards so far back, when their place should surely have been by your side?"

I couldn't answer that without opening up a whole new area of difficulty, the sort of difficulty that he would love to exploit. "They just were." I said. As a reply it was completely inadequate, and it provoked a predictable snort of triumph from James. "How very convenient."

"James, it is only recently that I had to counsel a brother on the need for humility, must I counsel you in the same way?" Mary failed to say that I was that brother, and I didn't think it worth mentioning. "I saw these men when they came in from the road. Jesus Barabbas was leading Saul by the hand because he was blind, there was no trickery. My colleague Ananias was told in a vision that he should go to Saul and baptise him. And now Paul preaches daily in the synagogues of Damascus, despite his fellow Pharisees trying to shout him down. How can you possibly doubt all this?"

How he could possibly doubt it was apparently quite easily. "Sister I mean no offence, but you give the testimony of your sex, influenced by emotion and feeling, above facts. What we have is the man who poses the greatest danger to our church, parading himself as a convert to win our trust, and when he's done so he will strike again. This plan of Jesus Barabbas and Mark's to divert Saul with false information about our followers in Damascus was pathetic. He's seen through it and is now doing whatever he can to discover the truth for himself, and worst of all, one of our own has decided to help him."

"James, you're a sad and barren creature." All heads turned to look at Esther, who had come to her feet, the better to confront the man who thought she should have died in jail. "You can see nothing but your own self righteousness. I pity you and I shall pray for you."

There was another silence, but this time a shocked silence, Esther's words had come straight from her soul, and it would take a braver man than James to argue publically with that.

Eventually Mary leaned forward to address Peter, she spoke softly. "What about you Peter, what do you think?" She put out her hand to touch his, but he withdrew his own, as if frightened of being burnt. "I . . . " He struggled to find any sort of words. "I'm not sure, I don't think that I could trust Saul." He flicked a sideways glance at James, perhaps wanting approval. I agreed with his wife's verdict on his strengths, they were far greater than my own, but playing him off against James in this way only exposed his weaknesses. It was like tormenting a blind man and I could see no point in prolonging it. If Peter was going to come into his own, it wasn't here and it wasn't now.

I looked at Mary, she was our leader, but she had turned to Esther. "Will you be ready to travel tomorrow morning?" Esther nodded, too filled with emotion to speak. Then Mary looked at James. "Whatever our Lord said about the leadership in Jerusalem, James, I'm now leaving it to you. My friends and I shall be leaving the city tomorrow, I shall pray for your work every day, as I hope you will pray for ours." Then she simply smiled at him, she was finished with him. As he rose reluctantly to his feet, realising that no clever answer could deal with this, Peter and Andrew rose with him. The three of them left in silence.

As the door closed behind them there was a collective release of breath, the tension had been unbearable.

CHAPTER TWENTY ONE

The rest of our evening together was a celebration, Though I'm not altogether sure of what. There was an atmosphere of gaiety that can sometimes be missing from gatherings of the exclusively devout. It must have been Mary's relief at the discovery that, from her point of view, the church in Jerusalem was now a lost cause. There was no longer anything to struggle for. It's as I mentioned earlier, the usurper to any position can't wait to get rid of all trace of the person being replaced. James hadn't simply taken Mary's place as head of the church in Jerusalem, but was now removing all connection with her. His attacks had never truly been aimed at me or Paul, they had all been aimed directly at Mary, with Paul and myself as no more than a flimsy excuse.

This bald repetition of the facts makes the man sound manipulative and unpleasant, yet being a follower of Jesus teaches me that it could have been my own fault that I failed to spot his many excellent qualities. All I can tell you is how it looked at the time, and his many excellent qualities were remarkably well hidden.

Our arrival in Jezreel was less of a let down than it had been when travelling with Paul. On that occasion my mind had been filled with what I was going to do to stop him, whereas this time I had the responsibility to help Esther to re establish herself at the heart of a new church in the town. This time it was a new beginning, and I'm better at those than endings. Despite my earlier opinion that her troubles were at least partly of her own making, I was now wondering if there would be some place in her organisation for a tent maker. It wasn't quite on Paul's level but it was still quite a transformation.

And what then? Well to be honest, in story telling terms, for quite a while there was an awful lot of nothing very interesting to hold your attention. The tent yard went back to its original size, as Samuel moved Paul's part of the business up to Damascus. Paul was always very particular about paying his own way in the world, and frankly, whenever he found the time he was very good with a needle and thread. I went to the Legion barracks to renew my acquaintance with Sextus Flavius, the centurion in the Tenth who had gradually become my friend, and with whom I did most of our business. He wasn't there, having received an unexpected posting back to Rome. I found myself disappointed to lose a friend, but that's always a danger with the military; they come, and they go. I introduced myself to his replacement and began the lengthy process of making a new friend.

When everything was added up and the accounts were cast, I was relieved to find that even if my boys hadn't been making the profit they should have, at least there had been no disasters.

I found a new house for Esther, and even moved back in as her lodger, except that this time I stayed in for the evenings when she had her meetings, instead of going to the tavern. I didn't bother seeing Hannah at the bakery, the sex wasn't worth her stupidity, nor did I try to murder her mother again, despite my promise to do so. In fact I became that oddest of all things, a worthy citizen, I almost fitted in. My attachment to the strange new religion marked me as different, as did my unmarried state, I was almost thirty and still single. To the average Jewish mother the second condition was probably odder than the first.

Mary and Joanna, for she had come with us, had continued on to Damascus and there was a regular exchange of letters between us, detailing our comparative successes and failures in expanding our groups. With Paul's brash approach to spreading the word setting an example, Esther and her new Deacons became more expansionist themselves, her days of reticence were over. She shared a certain feeling with me, once you've been at the point of dying a nasty and protracted death, and are then suddenly saved by fate, or me, it's a lot more difficult for someone to frighten you the next time. You tend to ask yourself - what can they do to me that I hadn't already come to terms with and prepared myself for?

Life in Jezreel became so predictable that a year later someone suggested that, as a prominent local business man, I should stand for the Citizen's Council. If it hadn't been for the fact that Esther burst out laughing when she heard, I might have actually done it. What was worse was when she saw how offended I was she insisted on apologising, and it didn't sound particularly sincere.

There was no temptation to return to Jerusalem, although Barnabas and Mark and I kept in regular contact. Every six or seven weeks I would visit Damascus for a few days, and once or twice Mary and Joanna visited Jezreel, complete with the growing infant Sophie. Paul's conversion didn't stop the persecution of Jesus' followers, but it was dramatically reduced, and our own growing numbers and confidence made us a harder target. My own role in the church was more involved with providing the funding than preaching in the market places, we each do what we're best at, and public speaking didn't seem to be my area.

Paul continued to preach the word of Jesus, but with a slight change in emphasis. He had previously copied the work of the apostles in Jerusalem, preaching mainly in synagogues and to Jewish crowds in the street, but not actively presenting himself to Gentiles. But slowly at first, and then with increasing and deliberate intent, Paul, Mary, Lydia and Ananias turned their attention to the non Jewish people of the city, who made up the majority of the population. Before his crucifixion Jesus had concentrated mainly on preaching to the Jews, but after his resurrection had specifically said that the apostles should make disciples of all nations. The church in Damascus, effectively cut off from their one time heart in Jerusalem, began to do exactly that, and for the first time there were now more baptisms of Gentiles than of Jews.

This change in emphasis was enthusiastically followed by Esther and her friends in Jezreel, and also by the newly founded church we were in correspondence with in Antioch. There were now two separately developing strands to our church, a move I thought could lead to problems. It would only be a matter of time before one lot claimed the other lot were doing it all wrong, human nature never changes.

It was at this time that I received an unannounced visit from Mary. I arrived home one evening to find Sophie playing with the girl from next door, and Mary sat talking to Esther, a scene of domestic normality. Except that I knew it couldn't be, or she would have told us she was coming. I didn't know what was happening, but I had finally worked out that someone would tell me sooner if I didn't ask, so I went to wash myself as I usually did, and changed into clean clothes, before sitting down with them.

In my old age, I sometimes can't work out if I'm having an original and intelligent thought, or if it's just my mind wandering. It's like that when I try to remember the details of the conversation I had with

Mary that evening. I occasionally wonder if I would have been such a keen follower of Jesus if that belief hadn't kept me so frequently on the move, with a succession of new faces and places.

Left to myself in Jezreel, I would probably have grown lazy and settled into some sort of comfortable niche. Esther and her group were trying to spread the word more actively than before, and yet it was still with nothing like the determination shown in either Jerusalem or Damascus. However, there's a fault line in my personality that needs the stimulus of regular bouts of excitement. It's not that I'm tempted back to the life of banditry, that part of me is gone for good. So when Mary told me what she wanted that night, I was ready to agree before I even knew the details.

I sometimes wonder how the others would have reacted if they'd realised that a part of my belief was propped up by my enjoyment of adventure, a feeling that we were engaged in something that was disapproved of by the rest of society. Would I have been a church member if it had been what respectable people were supposed to be? If our campaign to spread Jesus' teachings ever became that successful would I have to go off and find something else to believe in? I smiled to myself at the improbability of the idea.

We were sat with our meal, we never do anything without food, when Mary came to her reason for visiting. "The church in Damascus is Paul's church now, Lydia and Ananias are Paul's assistants, not the other way round. His personality is so strong there can never be any doubt about his leadership. He might be right or wrong, though he's usually right, but whichever the way of it, people follow him. He's God's gift to our church."

There was nothing about this to surprise me, that had always been how it was with Paul. The man was a leader not a follower.

"Which means that I'm standing in his way. You know of my connection with the Lord, Paul knows, everyone knows. This means that outside Jerusalem, a place I can never return to, it's impossible for me to be just another disciple, another helper. I stand apart, in many people's eyes I'm too special."

This hadn't occurred to me, but with a pang of sympathy I recognised that she was telling the truth, she was another person carrying her past with her every single day. Unless she retired into virtual seclusion, like Jesus' mother Mary, then she could never be just one of the crowd, she would always be a marked out for special attention.

"Has Paul said anything to you?"

She shook her head almost violently. "No, absolutely not, he wouldn't dream of acting like James." She stopped herself, shocked at having openly criticised another apostle, but then sighed as she realised the futility of trying to maintain the pretence that we all loved each other in equal measure.

"The fact is that I'm standing in Paul's way - I'm drawing attention from where it should rightfully be. It means it's time for me to move away - a long way away."

Then Esther spoke. "You know we'd be delighted if you and Sophie were to join us here, and Joanna too, I would like nothing more than to act as your helper in any way I could."

I would have joined her in this sentiment, but Mary's response was immediate. "Thank you Esther, but I don't think I'd be using whatever gifts I have to their best advantage if I stayed here in Galilee, my future lies elsewhere." Then she looked at me. "Which is why I've come to ask for your assistance Jesus Barabbas; I would like you to travel with Joanna and myself to Rome, as our escort. Once there we can lodge with friends in the city and be able to work without attracting the attention I receive here."

"Will you want me to stay with you in Rome?" My question must have sounded almost eager, but she shook her head.

"No, but as a party of two women and a child, even with the serving girls the journey would be much easier with a male escort."

I couldn't stop myself smiling, another adventure, I have the emotional range of a five year old. "Just tell me where and when, and I'll be there."

"What about the tent yard?"

"My senior cutter, Simon, can hold his own for two or three months, he managed well enough the last time I was away. And besides, Esther's picked up a lot of knowledge about the business, he can always ask her for advice."

We spent the rest of the evening talking about how best to organise the matter, but the main decision had been taken, Mary and Joanna were going to Rome - and I was going with them.

As it was already spring, it was decided that if our arrangements were to include not just Mary reaching Rome, but also my return to Palestine, then we had best leave without delay. Ships can and do sail the Great Sea throughout the year, but a prudent traveller will avoid the winter months. I'm told it's not just the storms that are to be avoided, but the cloudy skies in winter make the ship's navigation more difficult, and they say that's more dangerous than the storms. Even the dangers of the deep were not enough to overcome my intention to go, though I still don't honestly know if that was caused by my desire for adventure or my wish to be near Mary. Perhaps the two were the same.

*****

Where once I would have picked up my cloak and walked out of the house, bound for any adventure that took my fancy, I was a man of affairs now and it took me almost a month to settle those affairs securely. I corresponded with Barnabas and Mark, I made sure that all was in order with the Legion and I ensured that Esther had sufficient funds to survive my absence. The only thing I failed to do was to advise those in Jerusalem exactly why and with whom I was travelling to Rome. I knew my friends well enough to know they could work out for themselves what was happening, but that if I hadn't actually told them, then they could with good conscience deny any knowledge of Mary's whereabouts. My opinion in this respect was confirmed when their reply to my original letter noticeably failed to make any enquiry about the details of my trip. It merely wished me, and my companions, God speed and recommended who we might seek out when we got there.

The arrangement with Mary was that we should meet in the city of Tyre, the Phoenician port on the coast by Galilee; and so when I was ready it was to there that I made my way. Although I don't think it was as far as Damascus, the group I was with were slow moving and the road was bad, so it was late on the fourth day before we trudged down the peninsula on which the city was built.

There was a time when the Phoenicians were a great people, matching the Greeks in their command of the shipping trade, but that had been a long time ago. Now, along with its sister city Sidon, further up the coast, there wasn't much left but the memories. Phoenician territory had been reduced to a narrow coastal strip, and wasn't even big enough to grow the crops to feed themselves. They relied on importing grain from Egypt and buying food at exorbitant prices from Herod, paid for by their exports of glass and purple dye.

They had two harbours one on each side of the town centre, and in line with the general air of dereliction they were both too silted up to admit more than small coastal ships. Anything bigger, the Egyptian grain ships for example, had to anchor in what they called the roads, which was an area of water protected by the long mole. Then a shuttle service of smaller boats ferried cargo and passengers to and fro.

I was walking the dock side of the old north harbour, where most of the merchants worked, wondering how best to set about finding passage to Rome, when I noticed a small representation of a fish painted by the side of a ships' chandler's door. It wasn't much to look at, just a pair of curved lines to make the outline of a fish, unless you already knew what it might stand for you wouldn't have paid it any attention. It might have represented a soothsayer's zodiac sign, it might have represented the goddess Aphrodite, or it might have been put there to say the ships' chandler was a member of the local church. I'd heard that our people in Antioch were using the sign, but this was the first time I'd seen it for myself.

It was dark and cool in the warehouse and smelled strongly of the pitch they put on ropes. Draped from the rafters like huge curtains were fishing nets and wide brown sails, standing on the floor were the coils of tarred rope and stacks of barrels, and then hanging from hooks on the wall was a collection of wooden blocks for the ropes to pass through. Beyond those simple objects, I could identify none of the other mysterious and presumably nautical items piled up around the place. This wasn't just my first visit to a ships' chandler, it was my first sight of the sea, the proper sea; when you think about it the Sea of Galilee and the Salt Sea are really no more than large lakes.

"Good day to you master." The voice took me by surprise, I'd been too busy examining his stock to notice the owner's arrival. Not being a particularly cautious man in such matters I stepped towards him, clasped his hand and came straight to the point.

"Good day. My name is Jesus Barabbas and I am a follower of the risen Christ, am I amongst friends?"

He smiled, a warm and non commercial smile. "Welcome to my house Jesus Barabbas." Then having repeated my name he paused, and looked thoughtful. "Are you the one who avoided crucifixion and was riding with Saul of Tarsus on the road to Damascus?"

He didn't say what had happened on the road, all he'd have heard so far would have been third and fourth hand rumours; now he wanted to hear the story first hand - from me. So within the hour I was sat with Demetrios, for that was his name, his wife, their two sons and three daughters and their servants at the midday meal. As we ate I told them what had once happened to me in a Jerusalem basement, and what had happened on the road to Damascus, and how Saul had become Paul. As I spoke of seeing the light and hearing the voice, I realised that no matter how long I lived, or how far I travelled, people would always want to hear this story. I was less important, and considerably less interesting than some of the things I'd witnessed, and the story was travelling faster than me. Followers of Jesus often talk of bearing witness, but they don't usually mean quite as literally as this.

The ships' chandler and his family made me welcome and I earned my keep by helping them with their sail making. Sewing sails wasn't so very different from sewing tents, and I agreed with Paul that a man should pay his own way in this world; taking charity was fine - but not every day.

However, when Mary and her party arrived, three days later, I was put back in my usual and distinctly subsidiary place as all attention turned to her. I might have been a witness to great events, but everyone knew that Mary was a part of those events. The way that family and business life came to a standstill as all eyes focussed on her would have unnerved me, but she seemed accustomed to it and was endlessly patient with their questions. What did Jesus say about this, and how did he feel about that? If this was her normal routine, I could understand her desire to move to Rome.

Having quickly established that my knowledge of sea travel was non existent, Demetrios took over all arrangements for securing our passage, we had both decided that I was better employed sewing sails. I was happy to be fully occupied, it helped keep my mind off the dangers involved. I found it both surprising and slightly disturbing that none of the people I was mixing with made any reference to our chances of drowning. The dangers of travelling by land are an everyday topic of conversation: robbers, sandstorms and flooded rivers being regularly mentioned. Yet the same people who say how frightened they are of highway robbery will happily trust their lives to leaky old ships, in the optimistic expectation that their captains and crews will know what they're doing. I've heard otherwise sensible travellers suggest that no ship's crew would take untoward risks, as their own lives, as well as those of their passengers, depended on the outcome. This view ignores a fact which I had established for myself since arriving in Tyre, and that was that a disturbingly high number of the ship's captains I had met in taverns were heavy drinkers and incompetent gamblers. What this said of their navigational and ship handling skills I didn't like to think.

Less than a week later, through the good offices of my new friend Demetrios, we were able to take passage on a huge grain ship, called the Swan. I had managed to subdue my reservations about taking a long sea voyage, or even a short one, in the general excitement of going to Rome and my pleasure at being with Mary. However, when faced with the reality, my unhappiness came rapidly to the surface, which was exactly what I feared I might not do when we sank. And a part of my mind was sure that it was *when* rather than *if*.

Assurances from the ships' chandler and his friends, most of whom had been to sea and returned unharmed, were of no interest to me. Just because they'd been lucky a few times didn't mean I'd be lucky the next time. I might not understand ships, but I knew all I needed to know about drowning. There was only one thing that persuaded me to go ahead, and that was the sheer impossibility of telling Mary that I wouldn't.

Unfortunately my proper respect for, or perhaps abject fear of, the dangers of the sea wasn't the only thing held close to my heart. I didn't know if my feelings for Mary were a powerful but still rational attraction to a fascinating and compelling woman, or had they spilled over into a sickness, an obsession. I was sure it had nothing to do with her position in the church, and everything to do with the fact that whenever she walked into the room I had difficulty in tearing my eyes off her. I'd gone to great lengths to keep this feeling to myself, and though Esther had made a lucky guess on the subject, I was sure that no one else had a clue. Even acknowledging to myself the absolute pointlessness of the fixation did nothing to end it, and was probably responsible for my inability to establish a decent relationship with any other woman. I dreaded the embarrassment of anyone discovering my stupidity in yearning so desperately for someone so unobtainable.

As far as the voyage was concerned, even before we set sail my fears seemed to be fully justified by the simple process of getting onboard the ship. Being too big to enter the inner harbour and sit safely alongside a quay, it was anchored in what I was assured were the relatively calm waters inside the breakwater, but this still meant transferring from an unstable small rowing boat and up the high side of the ship. I courteously waited for the women to be taken aboard first, they were hauled up one at a time, perched on a wooden seat and then Sophie followed them in a basket. I waited for the wooden seat to be lowered again, but nothing happened so I looked at the two boatmen.

"Where's the seat?"

They looked puzzled. "The seat?" Said one, as a question.

Holding on to the side of the pitching small boat with one hand, I used the other to gesture up the ship's side. "Yes, the seat, to hoist me up."

The man replied by pointing at something I hadn't previously noticed; a worn and frayed rope ladder hanging limply down the ship's side. A final look at the boatmen confirmed this wasn't a joke, this was how you did it. With deep breath I took my life in my hands and jumped for it.

CHAPTER TWENTY TWO

"I know that you're normally a private man Jesus Barabbas." I blinked in surprise, is that really how I appear to others? I was surprised that anyone could take this message from my loud and often insensitive behaviour. "But on the voyage it will be best if we stay together as a family group. That way we can share our sleeping space and cook all our meals together."

I nodded, as if I'd given serious consideration to whether or not I would object to being in a family group with Mary. "Where would you like to sleep, on deck, or below?"

"Joanna's been on ships before, she says that the lower deck will smell, because there will always be someone being sick, or not getting to the latrine fast enough. It doesn't sound very pleasant."

She screwed her face up in distaste. "Given a choice between a foul smelling and slippery floor below and the risk of getting wet on deck, I would rather chance the deck. If it gets too cold we'll just have to squeeze in closer and hold onto each other."

I agreed with her, thinking with some relief that she obviously had no idea how I felt, or she would never have suggested us spending our nights like that.

One of the ship's officers, he announced himself as the Mate, came to speak to us and the other new arrivals. "Listen carefully, this is important. You're not allowed to light fires anywhere on the ship, at any time, for any reason - is that understood?"

"But we were told we could cook our own food." Said one of the women.

"You can, but you do it on our stove in the galley. You'll be allowed in there twice a day, apart from that there will be no fires, is that clear?" He looked around at us, his expression demanding an answer. We all nodded and said we understood.

"Enough water for drinking will be handed out from the galley, and everybody has to use the latrines up by the bows, no shitting in buckets and spilling it everywhere. Any questions?"

"Yes, what happens if we hit the rocks?" It was the same woman.

He smiled at her. "That depends on whether or not you can swim."

"But I was told there were boats."

"There are, two of them - but you won't be getting in either. So like I said it all depends on how well you can swim." Then with a not unfriendly nod, he left us to make our own amusements

This was every bit as bad as I'd feared, their attitude to the passengers was like a cattle dealer's view of his cows. It was in his interests they should survive, and he would take all reasonable steps to ensure they did; but if the worst came to the worst and they died then, unlike them, he could still walk away from it. The only difference with the sailors being that they would presumably row away from it, in their specially reserved boats.

With the group that had joined at Tyre there were now about two hundred other passengers, a diverse bunch, whose social status covered the whole spectrum. At the top was a Roman Senator, with three aides and a twenty four man Legionary bodyguard; unlike the rest of us the Senator and his aides had their own cabin. Although he didn't confide in me personally, the gossip amongst the passengers said that he was on his way back from a trade visit to Nubia; rather him than me. I felt vaguely comforted to have him onboard, it seemed unlikely that God would have the nerve to drown someone as important as a Roman Senator. At the other end of the social scale were a group of thirty prisoners, but as they remained manacled in the hold with the rest of the cargo they weren't a regular feature on deck.

Our route lay initially from Tyre to Cyprus, where we had cargo and passengers to discharge at Paphos and then on to Syracuse in Sicily, before finally heading for Rome. Our Captain, a weasely little Cilician from Tarsus called Andros, showed no particular interest in our welfare and that suited me very well. I had no intention of asking if he was acquainted with the only other person I knew from Tarsus, it was a big city, and anyway I preferred it if he kept his mind on avoiding rocks and finding our destination.

We came to Cyprus in two and a half days, but it was only a brief stop, with the ship once again anchored offshore. We bought some more food from one of the trader's boats that came out to us, but apart from that all we saw was a glimpse of a rocky barren place with small stunted trees. Barnabas had always said how beautiful it was, but that must have been some other part of the island. It was only as we left Paphos that I fully appreciated how long this voyage might last.

I had been too preoccupied with the novelty of finding myself on a sea going ship to notice the effect when we sailed from Tyre, but this time, as we drew away from Cyprus I was able to see how slowly we were moving. Even with both our main sails filled with wind, it took forever before the island finally disappeared into the haze. Despite me asking the Captain directly how long it might take to reach Sicily, he'd been unwilling to commit himself and had just shrugged, muttering, "It's in the hands of God." The Senator's Centurion, who'd travelled the route before said it could take anywhere from ten to twenty days, unless of course we met with a storm. In which regrettable circumstance, his outspread hands and vague smile suggested, he followed the Captain's example and transferred the responsibility elsewhere.

The days at sea were a curious mix of routine housekeeping matters, made tedious by our circumstances; washing ourselves and our clothes in buckets of salt water, queuing to use the galley stove or the latrine; followed by periods of absolute boredom. Looking after Sophie helped to fill some of the time, and staring vacantly at the unending sea and sky occupied several more hours every day, but I have to admit that despite my fears, it was more boredom than terror. The two serving girls took their turns with Sophie, and spent long hours sewing various unidentified garments. Joanna and Mary walked the deck and talked quietly together, they would probably have included me if I'd asked, but I've spent too much of my life *doing things* to settle easily into *not doing things*. It was into this void that Mary sought to insert some furtherance of my education.

She had eventually satisfied herself that the repentance I expressed for my former life was as genuine as it could be, for someone of my limited moral range. The trouble had started, as so many things in my life seem to have, with an incautious remark of mine. At a meeting in Jerusalem, someone had requested our prayers for their endeavours, and as Mary and I had walked back to Mark's house I had voiced my opinion to her.

"I'm happy to say the prayers we agreed to, but I really don't think it will make any difference, her success or failure will depend on her own efforts." Mary had turned her head to look at me as we walked on, but for a moment said nothing, so I continued.

"In fact it's not just that I don't think our prayers will make a difference, it's more than that. I don't think that our prayers ought to make a difference."

This time Mary stopped. "How can you say that, when Jesus specifically told us that we should pray, and regularly? He even gave us his own prayer to use."

"I'm sorry, I didn't mean to offend you, it's just that if prayer works then it means that our success in any venture depends on how loudly and persistently we can shout at God. It means that the person or group with the loudest voice will always win, and I don't think that can be right."

"You haven't understood, perhaps I haven't explained things clearly enough for you, but God isn't somebody different, he's part of you, and you're part of him. If you're honest and sincere in your faith and what you're praying for is just, then when you pray to God you're no longer just a solitary individual, you're connecting yourself not just to God but to that part of every other human being where God exists. The possibilities are too powerful to ignore."

I realised that I was in danger of upsetting her and I didn't want to do that, but I still felt this was unfinished business. "When Peter appeared before the Sanhedrin he was faced with seventy devout and religious men, all of whom believed they were doing God's work, and all of whom no doubt prayed regularly. Peter told them that no matter what they said he would follow what he saw as the will of God, rather than the laws of man. If all of them prayed for him to fail, and he prayed to succeed - which of them would God listen to?"

"That's easy, God listened to Peter because of the justice of his cause, no matter how many voices were raised against him. Which is why Gamaliel stood up to tell his colleagues that persecuting anyone acting on God's behalf was a waste of time."

"No one stood up to save Stephen, and he must have prayed."

"We can't know the mind of God, or what uses he has for us. But look at Paul's past career and compare that with the work he's doing now. Do you still wish that you'd managed to kill him?"

I looked at her and knew that my reluctance to continue the argument was only partly based on my belief that she was right, it was also based on my confused fascination with the woman, and a determination that I wouldn't do anything that might sever the connection between us. It was this unsatisfactory conversation in Jerusalem that she used to open the discussion between us in the long days onboard the ship, as we butted our way steadily and uneventfully westwards.

I followed almost all her explanation and instruction without demur, accepting all she had to say as being no more than a confirmation of my own experiences. I was a captive audience and anyway would have happily sat and listened to her reciting the names of whoever begat who in the Torah, just for the pleasure of her voice and company. Where she didn't know a thing, she said so, such as the time of Jesus' coming again. But we returned routinely to the unresolved subject which had started this; not just does prayer work, but more significantly - should it work?

Mary said that she felt it was her inability to explain the subject that was at fault, but I think we both knew that was an excess of humility. I didn't tell her I thought that too much of that attribute was almost as bad as my noticeable lack of it, that would have been an insult too far. The fact of the matter is that I'm a partly reformed bandit who thinks the Sabbath is a good day to get over a hangover. The miracle isn't that I failed to understand all of Jesus' teachings, but that I managed to understand

and accept any of them. I just happen to have been lucky enough to experience certain events that most other men haven't, and I suppose that makes me something of an abnormality, a freak. Other men acquire belief by being told of these things, I was actually shown them and still found it difficult. It's almost a though I've been cheating and still haven't won.

In the end I had to admit to Mary that, to my mind, one of the attractions of being a follower of Christ was the fact that we were a prohibited and subversive organisation, a position I'd always enjoyed. She laughed. "That might not be the best way to come to faith, but if it works for you then I'm happy enough to see you here." Then astonishingly she hugged me.

"You'd be a terrible evangelist Barabbas, telling everyone exactly what it is that you don't understand, but if you're content to support those who do the work, then that's also worthwhile. We need supporters and witnesses working peacefully in the community as well as the highly visible public performers. Don't let the parts you don't understand blind you to the value of your role. Live your life honestly, do your work fairly, and let the people you meet know what you believe in. That's all it takes."

I'd always thought there was more to it than that, but perhaps she was just giving me a simplified version. If nothing else, my continuing conversations over several days with Mary and Joanna had not only taught me things but had also passed the time. The only other person with whom I spent much time was Quintus Severus the centurion of the Senator's bodyguard. My years of dealing with the Tenth Fretensis Legion had given me a working knowledge of recent campaigns and postings, and we came to be on quite good terms - if only because neither of us had anything better to do.

Against my gloomiest fears, the mountainous blue line that turned into Sicily showed up along the western horizon on only our twelfth day out of Cyprus. There had been no storms and a marked absence of giant monsters from the deep, it had all been rather uncomfortable, but very undramatic. My strongest emotion was one of relief that I hadn't told Mary how I felt about sea travel, she might have guessed I wasn't keen, but at least I hadn't shared my fear of imminent drowning.

Unlike the shabby grandeur of Tyre and the lack of anything worth looking at around Paphos, the port city of Syracuse was impressive, especially when seen from the sea. With the help of an oared galley we worked our way round the end of an island, which formed the northern arm of the bay they called the Great Harbour. The island was covered with shining white marble buildings, mostly in the Greek style, and was almost big enough to be classed as a city in its own right, although in fact the city continued in equal style on the mainland.

This time there was a proper quay for us to tie up alongside, and this time our ship wasn't the biggest thing in sight; we were just one of a row of six large cargo vessels, all tied up and either loading or unloading. Walking along the quay we passed sacks of grain, amphorae of wine, barrels of oil, anonymous rolls of something that Joanna thought might be linen, and bundles of Spanish timber, all being lifted ashore and loaded onto a waiting line of ox carts. Then at the end of the quay, being carefully hoisted into one ship, there were huge blocks of white marble, the same material that so many of the local buildings were faced with. From the probable weight of the blocks I imagined that if the hoist rope parted, the block would almost certainly go straight through the bottom of the ship. I tried very hard to stop myself from hoping that if it was going to happen at all, it would do so whilst I was there.

Mary and Joanna were less interested than me in this display of international trade, and unwilling to stop and stare, a passing glance was more than enough. I would have been more than happy to spend the afternoon just loitering around the wharf and watching the activity, but as their supposed escort in a strange city I scurried after them. None of us knew of any followers of Christ in the city, and even Demetrios the ships' chandler hadn't heard of any, so instead we decided to examine the local landmarks. We looked at the Temple of Apollo, and we walked around the Temple of Athene, the pair of them together would have fitted into the Courtyard of the Gentiles in Jerusalem, but they were still beautiful buildings. Although Syracuse was now a Roman city, it had originally been Greek, and that's what it still looked like. Even with my lack of interest in architecture, I've spent long enough in Jerusalem to tell the difference between a Greek and a Roman column.

Eventually feeling that this was more than enough culture for one afternoon, I insisted on taking Sophie down onto a small sandy beach near one of the short bridges to the rest of the city, where she and I spent an hour or so splashing water at each other. Then at dawn the next morning we set sail once more.

"Are you ready for Rome?" Joanna asked me, as we stood on the deck, watching the coast of Sicily sliding past, with the smoking summit of Aetna dominating the landscape.

"Why d'you ask? We survived the Romans and the Sanhedrin in Jerusalem, at least in Rome there won't be any Sanhedrin. We're just an anonymous bunch of provincials that nobody will even notice."

"You should pay more attention to what's going on in the world. Tiberius died early last year and the new Emperor, known to everyone as Caligula, is still feeling his feet. He's only a young man, I heard twenty five, which means that a lot of the senators and generals will regard him as not much more than a boy. They've grown used to Tiberius ruling in absentia from Capri, so they won't welcome interference from some unknown youngster. He'll have to make his mark, or go under."

"Surely that doesn't matter, high class politics isn't going to have any effect on us."

"High class politics involves low class manoeuvrings. If a weak Emperor wants to secure his position, a good way to do it is to focus everyone on some external enemy. It's been the Jews before and it could be again, and if the church in Rome gets any stronger it could be their turn next. Don't forget I spent my married life at Herod's court, I've seen this sort of thing at first hand. If sending a few thousand Jews to the arena makes his position stronger, he'll think it a cheap price to pay."

Suddenly the breeze across the water didn't feel quite as warm, and I remembered Peter, after the crucifixion, using the same technique to divert the disciples by turning them against Judas.

"Do you see this as a serious danger?"

"I'm sure of it; that's why I advised Mary against going to Rome at all, until we've seen how things are developing there, but she wouldn't listen."

"So you only asked me to act as an escort when everything else had failed?" My question was part serious and part sarcastic.

"I would rather it hadn't been necessary, but I agree she can't stay in Jerusalem without forcing the disciples to choose between her and James, and however that turned out the division would inflict serious damage on the church. I can also understand how she feels about allowing her own personal fame to distract people's attention from Paul in Damascus, but even so I didn't want her taking this sort of risk."

I couldn't think of any answer that would improve the situation and so made none. Then on the third day we docked again, and this time, if not in Rome itself, at least in the nearest large port to it.

There are two main ports for Rome, the first is at Ostia at the mouth of the River Tiber, the same river which flows through the centre of Rome. The trouble with Ostia is apparently that being situated on a large river estuary it's susceptible to silting. According to the Mate, with whom I now had regular conversations, they kept moving the harbour at Ostia from this side of the estuary to that, then upstream, and then downstream. But none of it made much difference, it still kept silting up, and now could accept only coastal vessels. In typical Roman fashion they had simply decided to build a whole new port somewhere else.

They had chosen to move a lot further south in order to get the best possible site, which was at a place called Puteoli, on the same bay as the volcano Vesuvius, and it was there that we made our final land fall. Where Tyre had been interesting and Syracuse beautiful, Puteoli was simply busy, very busy The inner port was an uncountable mass of shipping, wedged together in such numbers that it looked as if you could walk across the harbour on them. After a good deal of careful manoeuvring, with the assistance of a smaller vessel, we tied up on the outside of another grain ship, which was itself tied up to another ship, and another and so on. We had to clamber across five ships to reach the quay, it would have been easier to climb Vesuvius.

Joanna and Mary had decided that even though it was still only mid afternoon it would be more sensible to find an inn for the night and set off early the next day. Quite why we should all be so tired after spending two weeks doing nothing very much I have no idea, but I was grateful for the decision. The actual city of Rome was four or five days walk away, but travelling with Sophie was hardly calculated to increase our speed and so, at Joanna's suggestion, we booked places on a horse drawn cart.

I'd heard of the Appian Way, who hasn't, it's one of the most important roads in the the empire. However, already knowing that it was world famous for being even straighter and smoother than other Roman roads, meant that arriving to discover exactly that, was a bit of an anticlimax. The Appian Hills and the Pontine Marshes, which would have taken weeks to go over, or around, were crossed with ease. You can see why the Romans are so successful, they don't let anything stand in their way - whatever it is, they just build a road over it or through it.

Yet our destination itself was no anticlimax; despite having heard all my life of Rome as the centre of the biggest empire the world has ever seen, I was still unprepared for the breathtaking size and urgency of the place.

Our arrival began badly, when the carter said he could take us no further than the city gate, as no wheeled vehicles were allowed within the city walls during the hours of daylight; he then dumped our bags at the roadside and prepared to leave. At first I'd thought he was cheating us because he couldn't be bothered to complete the journey, but when I looked around I saw that all the other carts were doing the same thing. When I asked him where we should go for the centre he looked at me as if I were a half wit and gestured to the huge fortress like gate. "You paid me to

bring you to Rome - that's Rome - enjoy yourselves."
Then he clambered back on his cart and left.

Feeling distinctly inadequate as an escort, I smiled weakly at Mary and Joanna and bent down to pick up our bags. Then we joined the rest of the new arrivals, most of whom looked every bit as simple as I felt, and began to elbow and push our way into the city

CHAPTER TWENTY THREE

Priscilla, our contact in Rome, had told us to look for them in the area called Trans Tiberim, which she said lay across the river, to the west of the city centre. 'Entering the city from the Appian Way, you should go directly ahead of you to the Circus Maximus', her instructions had begun, 'beyond which you will find the Aurelian Bridge'. We followed her directions, none of us wishing to admit we were intimidated by the place, but all of us keeping very close together - because we were.

At first I thought we must have strayed into the site of a major construction project, there were workmen everywhere, carrying shovels, hammers and saws; with bags of sand and piles of bricks all around. Men on scaffolding were manhandling planks of wood and shouting at each other. It only dawned on me quite slowly that it wasn't just one construction site, but an almost endless series of construction sites, there was building work going on wherever you looked. Even the enormous racetrack of the Circus Maximus, when we came to it, had workmen rebuilding part of the stands which appeared to have burned down.

The language spoken by those around us was mainly Greek, with a background hum of Latin and an uncountable mix of other tongues. Jerusalem, once unimaginably grand, was beginning to look very small and provincial. The common people on the street were more western than I was used to, they were louder and stared at you more directly; they looked and sounded aggressive even when I don't think they meant to be. This didn't seem to be a place that had much use for subtlety, whatever social skills I might have weren't going to get me far around here.

That first trip through the centre of Rome was not memorable for the details, there were too many details and too much grandeur. I was left with just two abiding impressions, the first of them trivial; no wonder Pilate was unhappy to have been sent to a backwater like Palestine. The second was that there was no doubt we had reached the centre of the known world. I looked round at the others, they were equally wide eyed. The idea of converting this seething mass of busy and preoccupied people to our belief that an executed Galilean preacher was the Son of God and had risen from the dead, seemed to be more of a fantasy than a plan. It wasn't just that these people hadn't heard of Jesus, most of them hadn't even heard of Galilee, and they probably thought that Jerusalem was a type of spiced meat ball.

Trans Tiberim, our destination, was the name of a slum area across the Tiber, a maze of narrow twisting alleys and back streets and the home of most of the city's unassimilated immigrants. It was here that Rome's Jewish community had set up home and even opened their first synagogues. As we followed the directions from the Aurelian Bridge, the streets became narrower and the neighbourhood grew steadily less attractive and more threatening. Nobody attacked us, but the eyes of young men loitering on street corners followed us as we passed and noted our direction. We were being identified and tagged as unwary strangers; people who didn't belong here, and who would make convenient victims - once the sun had gone down. I found myself glancing over my shoulder with increasing frequency.

Arriving at the address, off Via Collina, it shouldn't have surprised me, but it did, to find that Priscilla and her husband Aquila were tent makers. If the followers of Christ ever decide to adopt a symbol for their church it will no doubt be the outline of a Roman army tent, it's where we earn most of our money and could well be why I was selected as the party's escort. I imagined that their decision to locate the large area required for tent making inside the city walls, was a comment on the depressed state of the area and thus the low level of the rent.

Joanna and Mary, and Priscilla and Aquila hugged and kissed each other first, as was proper, and then Sophie was hugged and kissed in turn - which she absolutely hated. After which attention turned to me; as my name was given I could see that momentary flicker of recognition pass across our host's faces. It's partly annoyance that I got away with it, leaving the wrong man to be crucified, and partly interest that they'll now be able to get a first hand account of what actually took place. Nobody's ever sure if they're pleased to meet me or not.

From the way she behaved, I think Mary must have already known, but it was slightly surprising to me. In most households where the dominant figure is female, that person is usually the strong minded widow of the previous master of the house. It might not be rare to find a wife leading her husband, but it is comparatively so to find it done openly and publically. I'm not sure how this manifested itself, but you had only to see them together to know it was so. When I came to think of it, that must be why they were usually referred to using her name first, as in Priscilla and Aquila. I tried to imagine what would happen if Mary set up house with me, and smiled at the impossibility of the image, no matter what I might secretly long for.

"Welcome to our house." Priscilla used her arm to shepherd us in from the street, and into a different world. The exterior had been a rather scruffy and mainly blank wall, with just a painting of a tent next to the door and a pair of torch brackets with scorch marks on the brickwork. Inside there were clean white walls and tiled floors, with windows opening onto a central courtyard. The street outside had been hot and had smelled of too many people living too closely together, inside was cool and smelled of flowers. We must have been staring, because Aquila laughed.

"Let me guess Jesus Barabbas, you're thinking there must be more money making tents in Rome than there is in Damascus."

I looked around me. "It had crossed my mind."

"This isn't just our home and our workshop, it's also the centre of our organisation in Rome. This is our meeting place, and any visitors, like yourselves, can stay with us. Were you followed or threatened as you came?"

"Nothing more serious than surly glances, but it isn't an area where I'd care to be on the streets after dark."

Aquila looked more serious, but addressed the rest of his remarks to the women, in company like this I took a step backwards. "We'd like to move to a better area, but there are enough Jews around here to enable us to blend into the background, and we can afford the property prices. As for being on the streets after dark - you should try to avoid that anywhere in Rome. Behind all the white marble there's a great deal of blood on the stones of this city."

"How is Caligula settling in as Emperor? Are there any indications he might planning some further persecution of the Jews?" Asked Joanna.

Aquila looked at Priscilla for her to answer. "The basic fact is that he's an unstable young man from a violent background. His siblings either died or were murdered, his mother was exiled, flogged and starved to death on Tiberius's orders. He then accepted an invitation to go and live with Tiberius in Capri, as his make believe grandson - all as the price of being named his successor. The only sane people he's ever met have been his slaves. Despite all that, his early months as Emperor were all sweetness and smiles; tax cuts to the people, and bonuses and land grants to the military, everyone was happy."

"Yet something in your voice tells me you don't think this will last." Said Mary.

Our two hosts didn't even bother looking at each other for confirmation, but both shook their heads, and Aquila said. "Last November he was taken seriously ill and although he recovered he was a changed man. He had his cousin and one time rival for the throne Tiberius Gemellus executed. Since then he's been killing family members routinely; his grandmother, his father in law, his brother in law. One of his sisters died supposedly of a fever and another two were exiled, people are saying that when he runs out of family he'll start on the rest of us."

"Is there anything we can do to protect ourselves?" Asked Joanna.

"The trouble with an empire is that a mad Emperor can plunge us all into bloodshed and darkness, and I fear that's exactly what we've got, a madman." Said Priscilla. "We have no protection and will have very little warning of coming trouble. Our best hope is to stay hidden in the back streets, at least until we're strong enough to stand on our own."

I didn't know whether to laugh or cry at her idea of standing up to the Roman Empire, it would be like standing up to an avalanche. Fortunately I kept my mouth shut.

"Then the sooner Joanna and I can begin to help, the more we might accomplish before the storm comes." Mary had all the energy of Paul, but wasn't quite as pushy or loud with it. A combination of her and Priscilla at work was going to be exhausting for anyone standing nearby. I'm a typical country boy - the grass is always greener across the valley. When I was in Jezreel, Rome seemed exotic and desirable, but now I'm in Rome the peace and quiet of Jezreel begins to seem more attractive.

*****

The next morning I woke up with a plan, or if not a plan, then perhaps just an idea. As we ate our breakfast in the central courtyard, I raised the subject with Mary.

"Naturally I'm available to help with anything you need, but unless you have something in particular in mind then there's a friend I'd like to look up while I'm in Rome. Would today be suitable?"

Mary had been deep in conversation with Priscilla and my question had broken her chain of thought, she was distracted for a moment. "What - this morning? No, I don't think we'll need you for anything. Will you know where to find your friend?"

"Yes, I have the address, I'll have a word with the doorman on the way out to confirm the best way to get there. Then I'll see you again this evening."

"Yes, that's fine - we'll see you this evening." Then with a brief smile at me, she turned her attention back to Priscilla. I'd been dismissed, my time was my own.

The streets were still as crowded and busy as they had been yesterday and once I'd left our small side street the noise was still deafening, so it hadn't been my imagination. The buildings were much taller than anything I was used to, several were five or six stories high and looked dangerously insecure. Every so often there would be an ominous gap between two buildings, where there was just a pile of rubble to mark the spot where another building had once stood. I didn't know and didn't like to sound foolish by asking, if the conversion of the previous building into the present rubble was deliberate or accidental; if accidental, what had happened to the occupants - were they still in the rubble?

All along both sides of the street were small shops, often little more than alcoves in the wall, with a wooden shutter let down to act as a counter. Along with the crowds and the noise, there was the expected smell of human waste, the famous system of Roman public sewers didn't seem to reach this far, but every so often a more immediate smell would take over. Bread from a bakery, meat frying on a brazier in a food shop, anchovy sauce and stale spilt wine from a taberna; but as soon as you'd passed that the sewage would come back.

The doorkeeper had warned me that as my destination lay on the very furthest side of the city it would take me more than two hours, and he was right it did, it took three hours. The route took me directly through the city centre, past the Capitol Hill and past the Forum; all places I'd heard of but never imagined seeing. Once across the Tiber and into the heart of the city the smell receded, and the sheer scale and magnificence of the place swamped your senses. At first, from the throng of the crowd, I thought there was some special event, and only slowly realised that this was what the heart of an empire felt like; this was a normal day. As well as the general press of people, there were additional hold ups as we were repeatedly held back, or barged out of the way to allow some important person to be carried past in a curtained litter, borne by slaves and surrounded by guards. But the purpose of my story is not to describe the glory that is Rome: public splendour and moral squalor, there are

285

enough people employed on that story, but rather to describe my own actions.

The doorkeeper had told me to head north west from the centre and make for the Viminal Gate, he'd said that when I got there I couldn't miss it. "It's right next to the gate and it's one of the biggest things in Rome." The man was right again, the Praetorian barracks was extremely big, and no attempt had been made to beautify the place with marble columns and cornices, it was a huge square red brick fortress - and ugly with it.

The Senator's escort, our companions on the voyage from Tyre, had been a unit of the Praetorian Guard, the Emperor's personal and politically active bodyguard: and this was their base. The gatehouse troops were immaculate in deep crimson tunics and gleaming plumed helmets, and initially suspicious of my enquiry. Happily their efficiency proved to be greater than their arrogance and I was escorted in to see Quintus Severus, the centurion from the ship. He didn't know Sextus Flavius, my partner from Jezreel, but rapidly summoned another man who'd served with the Tenth Fretensis who did know him.

"Yes, Sextus was one of fifty or so brought back from Palestine, they were part of a group that Tiberius was going to use as the basis of a new legion to go to Britain. He was assembling groups of experienced men from several legions, but that all came to a standstill with Tiberius's death, nobody's sure what's going to happen. As far as I know they're all still camped at the Field of Mars, wasting their time on exercises and urban support duties."

Seeing my face remain blank at this intelligence, he helpfully continued. "You're new to Rome, and you don't know what I'm talking about do you?"

I agreed, so he drew me a diagram, and then gave me military style instructions. "We're here," he said, tapping one side of the map, "and if you proceed along this road . . ."

Three hours later, Sextus Flavius and I were sat down together with a flagon of Valerian wine and catching up on our recent activities. I might not like most Romans, and don't think they should be in Palestine, but I have to admit that they're a lot better organised than us. Even so, to have a Jew discussing religion with a Roman was always going to be difficult, and doubly so when I was trying to hide the true purpose of my enquiry. But as that was the whole point of me arranging this meeting, I thought I might as well get on with it.

"You remember how we talked about how some of the Jews had become followers of Jesus?"

"Yes, I'd assumed that you were one of them, but didn't like to embarrass me by saying so, as we'd just crucified him."

With a sigh I leaned back in my seat. "There doesn't seem to be a lot of point in me being discreet."

"Your difficulty is that you think of Pontius Pilate as a typical Roman, but he never was, and the circumstances in which you met him were hardly likely to lead to friendship. Even in our eyes he was a brutal thug, which was why he was replaced as Prefect in Judea. Pilate was recalled to Rome for his crimes to be judged, whereas I was recalled to be part of a new legion. The difference between us is that my honour is intact and his in shreds, but the death of Tiberius has left us both hanging in the same wind. Nobody really knows what Caligula's going to do, and in the meantime Pilate and I, and a lot of other people, are just sat waiting for something to happen."

"The point is, Sextus, that I have friends in the city, and naturally . . ."

"Naturally you would like to know if our magnificent and universally loved new emperor has any plans to start another purge against the Jews, or even the followers of Christ."

The way he said it wasn't a question, more a statement of the obvious, but I still nodded my agreement.

"I heard that Saul tried to implicate you in the arrests he made in Jezreel, was there any truth in that?"

I hesitated, which was an answer in itself, but then told him. "Not deliberately, but I was careless about who I talked to, and they gave Saul the information he needed."

"So now you're frightened of giving away another group of Christ followers, but would still like to know if they're in any immediate danger?"

"That's exactly what I came here to find out."

He pursed his lips in thought for a moment. "We both know that I'm in your debt over the arrest of the Zealot, but you might not have heard that the transfer to the new legion was going to involve a significant promotion, and that was largely thanks to that arrest. I'm a man who pays his dues."

I shrugged. "You were a friend to me when you didn't have to be. I'd welcome your help now, but let no man say you're under an obligation - you offered me half the reward, which was fair, and I refused it."

Although the conversation so far had run more smoothly than I might have hoped, it now took a completely unexpected turn. "I'll see what I can find out about any possible threat to your friends, but for now tell me about you and Saul on the road to Damascus, about when you saw the light."

So I told him, the whole story, just as I'd told Demetrios and his family in Tyre. When I stopped he asked me questions, and then he wanted the details of my baptism in Damascus. Again I told him everything, and when I'd finished we sat looking at each other in silence for an eternity.

"Don't tell me their names or where they live, these friends of yours, I would guess that they're somewhere in the warren of Trans Tiberim, beyond that I don't want to know. What I need from you is some taberna or inn where I can leave messages for you to collect. Then there can never be another suggestion that you've betrayed anyone."

That was our arrangement, and it was a good one, it takes the military mind to organise this sort of thing. The unsettling part wasn't the danger of secret dealings with the Romans, it was the extent of his interest in the details of my belief. I'd recognised Saul's uncertainty and doubt before he had, and I think that in Sextus I'd just recognised the first hesitant footsteps of a convert. However, I'd also recognised that this was a time to tread softly, and so we parted with a meeting place arranged and a clasped hand of friendship, but nothing more.

As I walked back across the river, towards the crowded warren of poor immigrants, I thought of Pilate. My one meeting with him had seen him as the implacable and unchallenged ruler of all he surveyed, with even the grey beards of the Sanhedrin finding it prudent to seek his favour. Yet here he was in Rome, where even at the height of his grandeur he would have looked petty and provincial, now no more than a disgraced colonial administrator. There would be no cohorts of troops rushing to his command in Rome, and perhaps not even to his defence. I wondered if the reckoning there had been with the Zealot, Jairus, could in some way be visited on Pilate. Not in the same way of course, but one man with a sword might seek him out. But even as I thought it, I knew it to be a fantasy, a child's dream of revenge. There wasn't an incentive powerful enough to make me consider risking my friends' security with some self indulgent wild adventure - that was the reality.

I told Mary and Joanna about the meeting, and my hope of obtaining an early warning of any threat, but there wasn't anything sufficiently definite to merit me naming Sextus as a possible convert. If anything came of that he could make his own announcement.

The days passed peacefully, I accompanied Mary and the others to services at the nearby Macedonian Synagogue, I would worship downstairs whilst the women sat on the balcony. It was still the case in Rome in those days that most of the followers of Christ, at least in Priscilla's group, were also observant Jews and attended to all the proper requirements that went with that. Priscilla introduced Mary and Joanna to the members of their local church, and a series of meetings flowed from that. If I say that I'm no longer sure what most of these meetings were about, other than repeating the teachings of Jesus, then it isn't because I wasn't interested, but because I was usually busy. Quite apart from helping out with their tent work and telling Sophie stories about all the dragons I'd fought and killed, I had also volunteered for any other jobs that were needed. The employment they found for me was unspectacular but suited my abilities.

Priscilla and Aquila led the largest and most active church group in the city, but there were other groups, each usually forming a part of the congregation at the different synagogues. As each of the synagogues ran independently, the associated church groups often had very little direct contact with each other; there were known to be at least seven or eight separate groups all trying to make their own way. Mary and Priscilla had decided they should be unified into one church, and needed someone to relay messages to and from their leaders. The messenger needed to be a man, to allow the freedom to move alone around the city, and clearly had to be someone they could trust. As all the other men in their own group had better things to do, and I didn't, the job had my name attached to it from the start. Luckily it was a role I enjoyed, finding my way to a series of random addresses all over the city was the best way to explore the place.

I had been on an errand to the Augustan synagogue at the Quirinal that day, it was my third visit in as many days and my contact there, Solomon ben Asher, had asked if I could do him a small service by taking a letter to a friend at a patrician's house on the Palatine Hill. He asked me politely and it wasn't much of a detour, so naturally I agreed. Apart from anything else it would be interesting to see a patrician's house at close quarters, and I might even get inside.

Following his instructions I went past the Temple of Vesta, I was finally beginning to tell one temple from another, then along the Via Sacra and through the Forum. At this point he said that the house would be facing me on the hillside, with white walls and red roof tiles, a description that would have fitted most of the patrician's houses in Rome. There was indeed a house of that appearance where he'd said, but it was far larger and grander than I'd imagined, none of Esther's congregation lived in this sort of style.

Clutching the sealed and folded paper of the message, I knocked firmly enough at the red painted front door to show that I came to this sort of place on a regular basis, whilst privately wondering if there was a back door for people like me. The porter must have been close at hand for it was opened almost immediately.

"Good day, is this the house of Quintus Fabius?"

"It is." His tone was neutral - I clearly wasn't social, but too confident for trade.

"I have a letter for the Lady Procula."

He held out his hand. "I'll see that she gets it."

I held it tighter to my chest, as if fearing he might try to snatch it. "My instructions are to deliver to her own hand, and no other."

He looked at me for moment, debating whether or not to tell me to go to hell. Eventually he decided that hell could be postponed for another day. "Wait here." Then he closed the door and left me standing there.

Minutes later the door reopened, and he stood to one side. "Come this way please."

The interior was every bit as grand as I'd hoped, with a beautifully worked mosaic floor showing dolphins leaping from foam flecked waves. Over to my right the wall had a vividly painted mural showing a lifelike view across a bay with pine trees framing each side, you could almost smell the pine cones and hear the seagulls.

The porter looked over his shoulder, his expression indicating that I was supposed to keep up with him, and not loiter admiring the artwork. Then after passing down a short corridor we were in an open courtyard, with a shady overhang of roof around each side; it scarcely needs saying that there was a fountain in the middle - but of course there was, it was that sort of house. The porter had stopped in one of the shaded areas, beside a small table at which a middle aged woman was sitting.

He announced, in formal tones, "Your visitor my lady." and then left us.

There has never been anyone worth bowing to in Kerioth, and in my estimation not that many in Jerusalem, but I wasn't sure what the correct form was in Rome, nor how important this *friend* of Solomon's was. In the event I gave a small bow and handed her the letter.

She smiled politely. "Thank you." and then broke the seal. She skimmed the contents quickly, presumably to see if an immediate reply was called for, then deciding a closer reading could wait, carefully refolded it.

She gestured to another chair at the table. "Please, be seated." and as I did so she asked. "Are you a friend of Solomon's?"

"Not really, I'm a stranger in Rome and was simply delivering some messages to him when he asked if I could bring this letter to you."

"Your accent sounds Judean, is that where you're from?"

"That's very accurate my lady, I didn't think that our simple country ways would have made an impression in Rome."

She smiled. "Probably not for most people, but I was there with my husband for a while. I presume that since Solomon ben Asher trusted you with my letter that you and he have similar views."

I thought that was a suitably discrete way of asking if I was a follower of Jesus. "He and I share a certain belief, as it would seem do you."

"May I ask your name?"

"Certainly, my name is Jesus Barabbas." I have grown accustomed to people occasionally raising their eyebrows at my name, or even looking slightly puzzled, not sure if or why it sounds familiar. But never have I seen it produce the reaction I now witnessed.

She stared at me, her mouth open, her eyes wide. As I looked I could see the colour drain from her face. "Jesus Barabbas." She whispered to herself, in horror. She stood up abruptly, her chair falling backwards to the floor, and then she said it again, still in an astonished whisper. "Jesus Barabbas." Then without any further comment she turned and rushed away, leaving me alone.

Except that when I looked around I saw that I wasn't alone, a sharp faced man was stood, scarcely an arm's length away. I hadn't seen or heard him arrive and had no idea how long he'd been there, but surely long enough to have heard my name. So he knew my name, and I - yes - I knew his face.

He stepped towards me, his face and his stance that of a man ready to strike me. "Tell me your name again." His voice matched the rest of him.

I took half a step backwards, I hadn't come here for a fight and had no idea what was happening. "I've just given my name - it's Jesus Barabbas."

He took another step towards me. "You're lying - who sent you?"

I couldn't place him but I was sure we'd met, and it wasn't a happy memory. It was a safe bet that he wasn't one of the people I'd killed, but had I robbed him at some time? There were so many of them, I couldn't remember them all.

He looked to one side. "Arton, Vermilius, come here quickly." He was calling for help, which could only mean that he intended to detain me, or kill me, and I didn't want either. Fortunately, my wits hadn't completely deserted me and I charged him with my shoulder, sending him flying. Then I turned and ran.

As I came to the decorated vestibule the porter stepped in front of me, crouching slightly, with his arms spread out, as if to catch an escaping sheep. But it takes a lot more than that to stop me in full flight, and I barged him aside so forcibly that he nearly landed in the painted bay. I wrenched the front door open and pelted down the hill without a hint of a backward glance.

Once amongst the crowds around the Forum I slowed down, partly to catch my breath and partly to avoid the Lictors, the public security officials, wanting to know what exactly I was running from. I turned and looked back up the hill, the red front door was closed and nobody was chasing me. I leaned against a column, waiting for my breathing to return to normal, and filled with the self righteous pleasure of a sane man who has just escaped the clutches of mad men. What on earth were they thinking of? Even by my own inflated standards I'm not sufficiently important to merit that sort of response, I'm not even a threat any more.

But then with a sudden gasp, as the realisation knocked the breath from me, I remembered where I'd seen the sharp faced man. But surely not? I turned to two men stood talking nearby. "Excuse me, but I've just been to the house of Quintus Fabius," I gestured back up the hill, "And I thought I saw someone I recognised there. Do they have any particular guests with them at the moment?"

The two men looked at each other, puzzled by the unexpected question, but they were cultivated Roman citizens and polite with it, so they considered the matter. "I don't know." Said one of them slowly, looking for guidance from the other. The other one screwed up his face a little, to indicate his brain working, and then suddenly smiled. "Well there's Pilate of course, the ex Prefect of Judea, he's staying there with his household. When Tiberius summoned him back from Palestine his wife's family, the Proculi, wouldn't take them in. So Quintus Fabius gave them shelter, thinking it would only be for a month or so, but then Tiberius died and now no one knows what to do with him. It looks like he'll be there for ever."

Now I knew for sure, the sharp faced man had been Pilate's assistant at the trial of Jesus and then at my own trial. He'd been the one standing behind Pilate's chair and whispering in his ear.

"Yes, I remember." Said his friend. "That goes to show the sort of care you need to exercise with these colonial appointments, you bring in someone who's no more than a colonial himself, purely on the strength of his wife's connections, and this is what you end up with."

"There was that case in Galatia, two years ago . . ." I interrupted this new and interesting flow of the conversation by thanking them both and leaving them to it. Of all the crucifixions that take place in the Roman Empire every year, I had thought my connection with that particular crucifixion was over, I should have known better. One way or another, it was going to be the death of me.

CHAPTER TWENTY FOUR

Priscilla was annoyed, in that very restrained and controlled sort of way that the followers of Christ sometimes are with each other, but still annoyed. The most interesting point, however, is who she was annoyed with, and it wasn't me.

"Solomon ben Asher should have known better, he must be aware of my conversations with Procula, he should never have sent you anywhere near that house. Did he fully understand your background - who you are, and were?"

"I'm not sure, I gave him my name but it didn't seem to mean anything to him, but then it doesn't to everyone. Is Procula a possible convert?"

She sighed, "Procula is the strong one in that household, Pilate was a minor Hispanic nobleman who used his good looks and charm to inveigle her into marriage, and then used her family name to secure a colonial posting. But his lack of breeding soon showed through and there were stories of his cruelty causing unnecessary offence to the locals. Now while the Romans consider cruelty and brutality to be legitimate tactics, they only do so to the extent to which they achieve local cooperation. His trouble was that he didn't know when to stop."

"But how does that involve me?"

"Because, although Procula had little option but to stand by him in Jerusalem, once they returned to Rome she was being increasingly troubled by visions and nightmares. She was seeing the dead rising from their graves every night and thought she was going mad. She'd consulted soothsayers and made sacrifices but it had done no good. Then one of them suggested that it must be because of some innocent party her husband had condemned, rising from the grave to taunt her."

"I think she was right when she thought she was going mad."

"Either that or she was being spoken to by God."

"How d'you tell the difference?"

Priscilla laughed. "That's the difficult part, that's what we'd all like to know. How did you know when it was time to be baptised?"

That stopped me for a moment. "I'm not sure, it just seemed to be the right thing to do, everything seemed to point to it."

"Well that's what asking for guidance is all about: you ask God and you ask yourself, and an answer usually seems to become obvious and right. That's the stage that Procula's at now. She'd decided for herself that her problem lay with the death of Jesus; and the fact that with only three crucifixions arranged for that day, and four condemned prisoners, her husband chose to release the wrong man. She thinks that you should have died instead, and so when you turned up in front of her she must have thought you'd been sent by the Gods to deal with her family's wrong doing."

"That almost makes sense, not quite, but almost. So what happens now?"

"I'm afraid it could be a problem for us. I had a meeting arranged with her for later this week, but it was supposed to be completely secret, she'd said that if Pilate found out what was happening he would forbid her from meeting any of our group, and even possibly accuse her of treachery. But now that his secretary has seen you and even the staff will have heard your name, a weak man like Pilate will feel that he has to do something, and it will probably be violent."

I turned to Mary, who'd been listening to our exchange. "It was always the intention that I would leave Rome soon anyway, so with this trouble looming would it be better if I left immediately?"

She glanced at Priscilla, the two of them and Joanna all seemed to work well together, and the exchange of looks had apparently settled my future. "Yes, you've been a great help so far, but there's nothing further you can do here. It would be best if you went back to Galilee and carried on your work there."

That settled the matter as far as they were concerned, and frankly my two weeks in Rome had probably served to settle my own curiosity for a lifetime. The Imperial capital could run very well without me, and I without it, there was just one small thing left to do. Later that afternoon, when everyone's attention had turned to more interesting matters than Jesus Barabbas, I put my cloak back on and slipped out to do it.

The Field of Mars was only half an hour's brisk walk away, and I was lucky to find my friend Sextus Flavius was available. I'd wanted to let him know that although I would be leaving one of our group would still keep in touch with the arranged meeting place, for any warning of planned action against the church groups. But most of all I wanted to let him know that I thought he was poised on the brink of committing himself to joining our movement and that I could put him in touch with someone to talk to. Instead of which what actually happened was that I was given a hurried lesson on the Roman legal system.

"The Senate's position on provincial religious beliefs is simple, Rome is happy that they should grow and thrive; that's how the empire works. For every five thousand colonial citizens we have less than one colonial administrator. Most of the actual governing is done by the local client ruler; with the support of the religious hierarchy. In Palestine that means the Herod family, supported by the Sanhedrin. All we ask in return is that they do nothing contrary to Rome's interests."

I wondered why he was explaining something I already understood, but nodded my agreement. However, he was only just starting.

The law of treason, the *lex maiestatis* is the only capital offence that can be privately prosecuted. This means that any citizen can accuse another of treason, and actually bring the case to court."

"I'm not planning to overthrow Rome, I'm not that stupid."

He looked at me, like a schoolteacher faced with a stupid child. "Be quiet and listen. This document," he tapped a rolled up scroll lying on his desk, "Names Solomon ben Asher, yourself, and numerous other persons, 'so far unknown', of engaging in meetings and actions hostile to the state. We're just one of four units that have been put on standby to take part in a search, which will probably be ordered for tonight. The Senate will put a stop to the proceedings as soon as they hear of it, but by issuing the warrants late this afternoon and acting on them overnight the damage will be done before the Senate has a chance to react. The use of torture is permitted in treason cases, so by tomorrow morning several of you could be dead and they could have a full list of all surviving members of your group; and once you've been identified you'll be vulnerable to anything else they want to do to you."

"Who is our accuser?"

"Pontius Pilate. I would expect him to be directing the action himself tonight - he was always getting himself involved in operational matters in Jerusalem."

"So what should we do?"

"Hide, keep out of of the way tonight, if my men are ordered into action then I'll be with them and I'll have to obey lawful commands. I wouldn't like to find I was caught between my duty to the law and my duty to a friend. Then tomorrow morning you can have your lawyers appeal to have the action cancelled. But by that time Pilate won't care, he'll have what he wants."

I stared out of his office window for a moment, not really seeing the parade ground and the rows of tents. This had to provide an opening, it would probably be the last opening I would ever take, but nobody lives for ever and it had been a good run so far. I stood up and held out my hand.

"You're an honourable man Sextus Flavius, and if we don't meet again, then you should understand that I've been glad to have known you. In the coming days or weeks you might be contacted by someone who says they come as a friend of mine, if so then I think that you'll be interested to talk to them. Thank you."

We clasped hands and I left, there was a lot to do.

It might come to nothing, and if that was the case then tomorrow morning I would leave none the worse and return to my provincial obscurity, but I couldn't do so without at least making the effort. First of all I warned Priscilla and Mary of the planned raids and to send word to all the separate groups that they should sleep away from home tonight. Then I settled myself down to write a brief note, the hook with which to catch the fish. It all revolved around the fact that there was nowhere in Rome that I could be safe from a squad of Roman legionaries, they're the best troops in the world. Any man thinking that he on his own could outfight or outwit them would need to be mad, and the very fact that everybody took that for granted was my best hope.

I took my note up onto the Via Collina, the permanently busy street that cuts through the heart of the Trans Tiberim district, I wanted its source to be untraceable. There I found a bright looking lad to hand deliver it - personally to the addressee, and paid him double the going rate. Then I went back to the house to pack my things and share a last meal with the rest of the household. The arrangement was that tonight I would hide like everyone else, and then tomorrow morning I would set off for Ostia to find passage on some eastbound ship.

Back at the house, Priscilla and Aquila had a letter of their own to a woman called Phoebe, the leader of the church at Cenchrea a port near Corinth, and wanted to know if I could arrange my return to Palestine by that route. I agreed, all roads led from Rome, and that was where I wanted to go - from Rome.

We ate early, well before sunset, the legion wouldn't strike until we could all be counted on to be safely in our beds; and that last meal in Rome lives with me as one of the happiest in my life. Mary had finally found a place to live and work, where she was not immediately recognised, and was not taking anyone else's light. A place where James and his friends in Jerusalem were not actively seeking to isolate her, and downplay her role in the story. Whatever the dangers in Rome you could see that she felt this, at least for the time being, was going to be her home. The stranger who didn't fit into the picture was me, but that was going to be sorted out tonight. Then with final hugs and kisses that we should all have a safe night, and I should start a safe journey tomorrow, we parted, each of us going to different houses to spend the night in hiding.

The information from Priscilla, and the bystanders in the Forum, had shown a very different Pilate to the one I had encountered sitting in judgement on Jesus and me. This Pilate was another outsider, a man thought to be without family pedigree. The Romans say that no matter how much money a man has, it takes three generations to be considered a nobleman, and Pilate had neither that nor the money. What he had was a rich and well connected wife, a member of the Proculi family, and anyone questioning that connection was attacking the very ground he stood on, which struck me as an extremely good idea.

I had been sent to spend the night with friends of friends, I knew no more and didn't ask, it was enough to know the address would not appear on any list of church members. They were carefully incurious about the arrangement, guessing there was something non kosher in the air and not wishing to be told the details. Waiting long enough to be sure the other occupants were asleep, or at least would not think it prudent to challenge me, I left my travelling pack on the bed and climbed out of the window. Although as followers of Christ we were generally unarmed, I felt it might be a challenging night and so strapped on both a sword and a dagger, and thus equipped crept down towards the river.

My note to Pilate had given a meeting time of the first hour, what we Jews would call the sixth hour of the night, which meant I needed to be in position as soon as possible. There was no prohibition against being on the streets at night, but they were unlit and dangerous and so I walked quietly, watching and listening. Any of the patrolling Vigiles, the city's night watchmen, could be heard coming a mile away and were easy to avoid, this wasn't a night when I wanted to explain myself. In the event that I came across burglars at work, then we would probably both run away from each other.

As I approached it, the river bank was noticeable first from the smell, the Tiber is not a clean river, it serves as the city's drain and main sewer, and regularly carries dead bodies. This well known degree of filth in its waters was to be another of my defences tonight.

In the days when I used to tell lies, I usually found it helpful to keep those lies as close to the truth as reasonably possible, and always, always to pander to people's prejudices – no matter how irrational. That way their desire to believe you will outweigh your story's imperfections. In line with these two useful maxims my note to Pilate read:

'I write as a friend to warn you that the Proculi family look down on you as an intruder and would happily see you dead, to avoid being tainted by your disgrace. There is someone in your household, a serpent, whose actions will bring about your downfall. I can help you to be rid of them. For fear of betrayal I will deal only with you - come alone to the middle of the Aemilius Bridge in the first hour of the night watch, with the price of a fatted bull. Signed – a friend.'

I hadn't been sure of the price to ask, in Jerusalem the going rate for a betrayal seems to be set at thirty pieces of silver, but here in Rome it could be more. I hoped the price of a fatted bull might sound suitably ambiguous, perhaps even sophisticated. From my point of view it was irrelevant as I would probably have to dump the money anyway, but one strives for verisimilitude.

I assumed that Pilate would regard the supposedly unexpected presence of troops in the area to be his guarantee of safety. He would assume himself to be within quick and easy reach of massive reinforcements. He would assume that should things turn ugly with his informant on the bridge, then that man would find himself trapped; and these were all perfectly reasonable assumptions – it's just that I didn't share them.

My approach to the western end of the Aemilius Bridge, from the slums of Trans Tiberim, was between a jumble of tenement blocks with lots of dark corners for a man to hide in. I passed narrow, overhung entries that were dark in daylight, and were now blacker than pitch; an entire army could have been waiting down any one of them. Not wishing to appear nervous I didn't stop and look down each alley, but simply took it for granted that I was walking into a trap. This affair was going to end badly, the only question was: for whom?

The night hours in Trans Tiberim were never entirely silent, there were always half heard voices from behind shuttered windows, giving birth, fighting, having sex noisily, a reassurance that life continued. But not tonight, the silence was loud enough to ring alarm bells, I ignored the warning and strode on. Then I saw the bridge, clearly visible in the light of a half moon, a set of six huge stone arches floating improbably above the black water. I paused and looked around, there was nobody visible, it would have been strange if there had been at this sort of time - even the toll booth was closed and shuttered. So I squared my shoulders and marched down the middle of the road and onto the bridge, there was no point in going fishing without the bait, and that was my job. Here I am – come and get me.

At the midway point I stopped by the parapet and looked down into the river. From this close you could see the moonlight reflecting on the ripples as the current broke against each of the bridge piers, like the bow waves of ships at sea. In fact when I stared down at the water meeting the stonework I could imagine it was the bridge moving and not the water, I'm not often so fanciful, perhaps the pressure was affecting my senses. I crossed over to the far side, that was the side I needed to be on, and there I waited.

"You - you have something for me?"

It was his voice, even after a gap of five years I could still recognise it, but then being sentenced to be flogged and crucified is the sort of thing that sticks in the memory. I turned to face him, and as instructed he had come alone, although I could see a couple of burning torches where his escort waited over at the cattle market end of the bridge.

"Yes Pilate I have something for you, and you have something for me."

He squinted at me in the pale moonlight. "Do I know you? Have we met before?"

"You sentenced me to be crucified, but don't worry I don't hold it against you, after all I was guilty as hell and deserved it."

"Then why should we talk about it? Your message said there was a serpent in my household who would bring about my downfall. I have the money you asked for," he held up a purse, "So tell me - who is it?"

"I'll come to that in a moment, but first do you remember Jesus of Nazareth, the prophet and preacher?"

"Of course I do, the whole of Palestine has been in an uproar ever since." Then he paused and stepped even closer to me, examining my face. "You're Jesus Barabbas, the robber, the one that I released instead of Jesus Barabbas the preacher. I'm right aren't I?"

"You're right, but tell me – why did you release me? I never understood at the time."

He laughed, a sneering and unpleasant laugh. For a man supposedly alone in the dark at midnight with an unknown blackmailer it was also a very confident laugh. "That's easy - the pair of you were just troublemaking Jewish scum and I wanted you both fed to the dogs, but I had a riot brewing in Antonia Square and I had to do something about it."

"Or more likely you couldn't afford another complaint to Tiberius about corruption and civil unrest interrupting the tax flow."

"Put it how you like, my job was to keep order and Jerusalem was packed to the seams for the Passover; I needed that crowd to disperse peacefully. They were all shouting that the preacher had been falsely convicted and should be released, but the Sanhedrin wouldn't hear of it. They said that if I released the preacher they would produce an even bigger crowd than I'd already got. Whatever I did there was going to be a riot - that's exactly the sort of situation that sorts the men from the boys."

His tone of voice was that of a man extremely pleased with himself, he must have told this story a hundred times to his friends, and each time he reached this point they would lean forward and ask: 'So what did you do next Pilate?' But I wasn't one of his friends so I just stared at him in silence, nothing I said could stop him finishing the tale of how clever he was.

"You two having the same name was a gift from the Gods, all I had to do was go out onto the balcony and give them what they wanted. I asked them if they wanted me to release Jesus Barabbas, and they all shouted Release Him, Release Him. So I promised them, on the word of honour of a Roman nobleman, that if they all went home peacefully I would do exactly that, and I did. Of course the point was that none of them had ever heard of you - they all thought I was talking about the preacher."

He laughed again, he found this whole subject quite amusing. "You Jews think you're so clever, but I ran rings round you. I gave them ten minutes to disperse and then sent him off to be crucified anyway. Then once we'd got him nailed up his few remaining friends all ran away. That's how you deal with mobs: you show them who's boss and they soon get the message. My only regret was that I had to release you to fulfil my word, but you don't matter so it was a small price to pay."

He stood beaming in my direction, I thought for a moment that he was expecting my congratulations, but then realised that he was actually looking over my shoulder and I turned to follow his glance. A group of ten or more men had crept up behind me from Trans Tiberim as he talked, and were now standing in a line across the bridge less than thirty paces away.

"You have only one chance to survive the night, and that is to give me the thing you promised, and if I consider it worthwhile then I'll release you. You know you can trust me, after all I've done it before."

Behind me I heard swords being drawn from sheaths, they sounded even closer.

"Tell your men to hold their positions, I didn't come here to fight them, and to prove I am no threat I'll surrender my own sword." I drew it before he could stop me, and in one sweep threw it across the road where it clattered against the far wall. "For what it's worth I also have a dagger, and you can have that as well." I brandished it visibly and them threw it after the sword. Then I threw my cloak to the ground to show that I was visibly unarmed.

Pilate called to his men. "Stay where you are."

Then he looked at me through the semi darkness. "So tell me Jesus Barabbas, who is the serpent in my household, the one who will bring about my downfall?"

Without saying a word I took a pace forward to bring us face to face and chest to chest, and only then did I speak, and then quietly, as if we were friends. "You're the serpent Pilate, your actions have already brought about your own downfall. You're a dead man."

Then I seized him round the waist and swung him up onto the top of the parapet wall, he was only a slight man so the effort wasn't great, but the way I felt I would have done the same if he'd weighed twice as much. A hardened tent maker, with a burning anger, against a soft patrician is no contest.

He was shaking from the shock of my sudden onslaught. "You fool if you drop me, it will take me a minute to die in the river; but they'll crucify you and that will take days."

His men were now surrounding us, but didn't wish to close in the final few paces for fear of making me drop him. "I was rather hoping you'd think that." I said

I swung myself up onto the parapet next to him, clutching him closer than a brother. "You crucified the wrong Jesus," I said, "you should have killed me." And then I pushed us both off the edge. Like inseparable twins, like Castor and Pollux, we tumbled through the air in close embrace, and then we hit the water.

CHAPTER TWENTY FIVE

There were several assumptions implicit in my plan, all of them perfectly reasonable. If I list them you'll see what I mean. First we needed to be on the downstream side of the bridge, to avoid being banged against the stonework by the water. Second, I'd taken it for granted that Pilate couldn't swim, hardly any Romans can, and certainly not in a cloak and long tunic with a sword strapped to him. And finally there was the fact that, despite my distrust of sea travel, I'm an excellent swimmer and was now wearing nothing but a short tunic. Throughout my childhood I'd been visiting the Salt Sea, it was only a day's walk from Kerioth and we frequently had goats grazing in that direction. My friends and I would swim for hours, and I think I can modestly claim to be quite good at it.

Unfortunately there seems to have been one assumption that I failed to address in sufficient detail, I had assumed that the River Tiber would be filled mainly with water, it never crossed my mind that there was an alternative. Unfortunately the filth that I already knew was in the river seemed to comprise most of what we landed in, together with dead dogs and a lot of other unidentified floating lumps. Even what water there was seemed thinner than I was used to, so thin in fact that I doubted anyone could swim in it.

Pilate had struggled as we first submerged, his bony hands scrabbling to get a grip around my throat, but I'd been ready for that and hit him in the face until he stopped. It's not easy hitting someone under water, but my flailing efforts seemed to do the trick, and then I kicked against his still twitching body to propel myself in the direction I hoped was up.

The bridge had disappeared when my face reached the surface, or at least I think it had, there was so much floating debris clinging to my hair and face that it wasn't clear if my lack of vision was caused by the darkness or the fact that my eyes were clogged with filth. Whilst considering this point I found myself sinking again, but this time my mouth was open as I went under. What I swallowed was vile beyond belief. The good sense of the troops in not following me was clear and I realised that this could be the end of me, I was swimming as strongly as I ever had, but still sinking. Despair at my own stupidity was my last thought.

*****

I was lying on my back, and hands, coarse and rough hands, were trying to pull my tunic over my head, and then something rested on my belly, I think it was someone's knee. I retched violently, almost explosively, which is a thing you should never do whilst lying on your back with your tunic half pulled over your head. The contents of my stomach were now in my mouth, nose and hair, I was in danger of suffocating and began to panic and lash out wildly.

A stream of obscenities indicated the surprise of the man kneeling on my belly, but at least he got off me. After a minute's confused struggling I managed to get the tunic off my face and stagger to my feet. Two wretched rag pickers stood looking at me, disappointment written all over them, it was easier work stripping corpses that were actually dead. I looked about, it was early morning and I was on the river bank, but most importantly I was alive. My mouth and throat

312

tasted disgusting and I stank like a week old carcase left in the sun. Then I retched again, even more than the last time.

It took me an hour to do it, but at length I made my way up to some houses, and eventually to a public well. Two women were sat talking, but soon stopped when they saw me, then one of them said something to the other and they both burst out laughing. Seeing me look put out at this, she repeated for my benefit that it would have been easier if I'd just paid the ferryman like everyone else. To make up for laughing at me they agreed to pour buckets of water over me, it might not have made me look human, but perhaps less like a dead dog.

As I made my way slowly, to allow for the still regular retching, back to the house where I'd left my travelling bundle, I smiled to myself. It was a long slow contented smile, if I lived to be a hundred the memory of last night would still keep me warm on cold nights. There was no possibility that Pilate had survived, I was still a comparatively young man and had been ready for it and dressed for it, he'd been none of those things.

He was dead and I was glad, God alone knows what Mary would say if she ever found out. She would probably tell me that Pilate might also have seen a great light and become another Paul, she would certainly tell me that I shouldn't have killed him. I knew I was wrong and that she'd be right to tell me so, but I also knew that if the circumstances were ever to be repeated then I would do the same thing all over again. Where this left me as a follower of Christ I didn't know, not the sort of specimen the others would want to boast about, that's for sure.

The docks at Ostia were nothing like those at Puteoli, they were crowded and busy, but the ships weren't on the same scale as the huge grain carrier we'd come in on. That didn't bother me, I wasn't scared of drowning any more. The death of Pilate had taught me two things. If the open sewer of the Tiber couldn't drown me than nothing would, and that I still had more work to do on my religious observance.

I caught the first ship I could, a coasting vessel making its way down Italy and across to Greece, I didn't mind how long it took, I wanted to be out of Rome. If Mary looked me in the eye and asked if I'd been involved in the disappearance of Pilate, then I knew I'd have to tell her. And she would ask, the whole thing had my footprints all over it. I found myself smiling again as I remembered my last contact with him, when I'd kicked against his drowning body to push myself to the surface. Mary had been right about my state of grace not lasting very long.

It took us six weeks to reach Corinth, I could almost have walked it as fast, but never mind. I found Phoebe, Priscilla's friend, and gave her the letter, which delighted her. She then wanted me to tell her every single thing I could about the church in Rome, exactly what they were doing, how they were organised, who their leaders were. This information was given to a roomful of people, as her deacons and other church members crowded in to hear the news. Like Priscilla, Phoebe had a husband, but also like Priscilla he was the helper rather than the leader. I was slightly surprised to find that neither of them were tent makers. I stayed with them for a week and then took passage once more, heading further east; as long as you keep heading east in the Great Sea you really can't miss Palestine.

Coming to Jezreel again was not just a homecoming, but also a blessed relief from the dangers and discomforts of travelling. Esther welcomed me like the prodigal son, and once again I found myself giving lengthy descriptions to crowds of people, about where

I'd been and what I'd seen. I was almost completely honest with them, right up until the events of that last night, when my honesty began to wear thin. This discretion lasted for three days before I had to tell Esther, not just about the fact I'd deliberately killed Pilate, but that I'd been pleased with myself for doing so, and would happily do so again. Her first comment was that she was glad I'd told her openly instead of having to listen to me shout out bits of it in my dreams, as I had about the dead children.

I think that Mary Magdalen is the most compelling and fascinating person I've ever met, but I know she has better things to do than mix with me, and she can sometimes be direct to the point of aggression. Whereas Esther takes a much softer line, and is more inclined to ask why you thought some course of action was a good idea, rather than simply telling you it wasn't. So we talked about things, and we talked about vengeance, and we talked about repentance and I think we got there in the end. But I still suspect that deep inside I'm as grubby as I always was.

*****

That was really the end of my adventure with the leaders of those who have come to be called Christians, and that was more than thirty years ago, practically a lifetime. The realisation that I was no more than a hanger on to their coat tails made me remember Mary's advice: live your life honestly, do your work fairly and let men know what you believe. She said that was all it took to be a decent man, and I suppose without really meaning to, that was what I ended up doing.

Jezreel held too many memories and there were still people who thought of me as the man who betrayed Esther and her friends, most of whom were never seen again. Despite the bond between Esther and myself there was too much unfinished business on every street corner, it was time for another of my fresh starts.

I handed over the reins of what had been Barnabas's tent yard in Jezreel to Simon, who'd been running it in my absence, and as the lawyers say I put my affairs in order. Then I went up to Damascus to say goodbye to Paul, only to find that he'd fled the city the week before, to avoid a mob of enraged Pharisees who blamed him, quite rightly, for half the Jewish population of the city becoming followers of Jesus. Lydia and Ananias were unperturbed by his sudden departure, the man was a tireless worker and deeply committed to the cause, but he was also quick tempered and volatile. They assumed that when things quietened down, he would probably be back, and if not - then he'd already given their membership a tremendous boost.

I found the Syrian ways and customs to be to my liking, and having already discovered that tent making was closely related to sail making I had no difficulty in choosing Antioch as my next destination. I settled into a yard by the harbour and combined the two trades, being by then quite used to the idea of calling anywhere I rested my head - home. I had no way of knowing just what a centre of Christianity the city would become, but then I do have quite a knack for falling amongst friends.

Down the subsequent years I have seen a regular procession of the great and the good of our movement passing through Antioch, it's one of those places of which people say that if you stay there long enough you'll eventually see everybody worth seeing. But then they say the same thing about Jerusalem and Rome.

To my great happiness Barnabas was sent by the disciples to bring some order to the competing groups of Christians in the city. As in Rome a collection of different congregations had sprung up, each more or less independently of the the others, and Barnabas's job was to join them into a unified body under a single leadership, before they found themselves disputing points of doctrine. There were already false prophets claiming to act in Jesus' name promoting a wide variety of suspect causes, somebody needed to say who was with us and who wasn't.

Barnabas, Mark and Paul remained my friends throughout the rest of their lives, and Barnabas in particular would always stay at my house whenever he was in the area. Even Peter, about whom I once had doubts, came to accept me during his time in Antioch. It was recognised by all of us, though politely not mentioned, that I would for ever be regarded as more useful than honourable, and that didn't bother me. I had been close enough to the cut and thrust of high level religious manoeuvring to know that I was happier making tents. In keeping with my modest place in their ranks I never joined in with any of the controversies that occasionally erupted, usually involving circumcision or eating with Gentiles, two subjects absolutely guaranteed to raise an argument in those early days. My unwillingness to debate these points was not just because I thought them irrelevant, though they were, but more because I valued the friendship of those close to me, above doctrinal purity. Perhaps that tells you something about my moral standards, or lack of them.

And now where are we? Thirty eight years after the death of Jesus, all our early leaders are dead, all the people who actually met the man are gone; well that is all except me, and I haven't been much help. Peter was killed in Rome four years ago, then a year later Paul suffered the same fate, then Mark died in Alexandria, and it must be ten years since Barnabas died in Cyprus. Despite all this the church has not just survived but is growing more strongly than ever; having successfully weathered the loss of these founding fathers I'm sure that nothing will stop us now.

The fact that the Romans killed both Peter and Paul can't change the fact that it's their own empire that will be used to spread the word, and that alone will ultimately change them beyond recognition, or destroy them. The same roads they built to move the legions will also move our own people, the same ships they built to carry grain across the Great Sea will also carry our disciples. They might have established this high speed communication network for their own purposes, but once in place there's no way of stopping other people using it for their own ends. Am I really the only one who can see this so clearly?

I'm a family man now, happily married to Ruth who I love dearly; we have five children together, and now even grandchildren, and I love all of them. It was only the fact of having children of my own that brought home to me the enormity of my earlier crime, and with it the knowledge that, despite what Esther had so often told me, I could never make sufficient atonement for something of that nature. Somewhere there was a bill waiting for me, a bill that was going to need paying. Even if he'd been wrong about everything else, James was right about me being damned.

But I'm avoiding the issue; what about the person I'm not mentioning? None of the details of my present life make any difference to the fact that since the day I met her, the woman I dream about at night is Mary, and I don't think that will ever change. After I fled Rome, with Pilate's finger marks still on my throat and the stench of the Tiber still in my hair, Mary stayed on in the city, helping Priscilla to establish the church there. I never heard any more about Pilate, it seems that his disappearance had gone strangely unremarked, no warrant for my arrest followed me to Corinth or Antioch and no awkward questions were ever asked of me. Perhaps his family, or more accurately his wife's family, had been as glad to see the back of him as I'd suggested. I never knew the truth of the matter, I was simply happy to have escaped.

Two years later Mary moved to Ephesus with Priscilla and Aquila, where with Paul's help they took over the leadership of the fledgling church there. She and I corresponded, but I was always aware that as well as the responsibilities of her work, she had a young daughter, Sophie, to bring up, and that I was an unhelpful distraction in her life. Besides which I didn't want her letters, I wanted her presence, although to exactly what end was never clear - even to me.

Then ten years ago I had a letter from Priscilla saying that I should rejoice that our beloved sister Mary had been called to her eternal home. I read it again, part of my mind refusing to recognise the meaning, and then I read it a third time before finally admitting that my shouting 'No, No, No' to the letter would change nothing. I was unable to join Priscilla's rejoicing, instead regrets washed over me and through me, for the years I'd spent making excuses. Excuses about how I was too busy to go to Ephesus - maybe next year? About how I didn't want to intrude into her already busy life, about how I didn't want her to ask if I was responsible for Pilate's disappearance. A parade of excuses to avoid facing what I felt about the woman, and my inability to deal with it. A turmoil of confused emotions that might not bear close scrutiny, and certainly wouldn't be reciprocated.

I must have spent hours that afternoon sitting on the sea wall, staring out over the water, reliving every moment of the time we'd spent together. Eventually Ruth came out looking for me, and having found me sat beside me. I gave her the letter and when she'd read it she held my hand for a while without speaking, and then we walked back. I admire people who are good with their hands or their brains, but best of all I appreciate people who are good with their emotions. Ruth's like that.

And so the years have gone on - and although there's still that bill to be paid one day, Antioch's a fine and beautiful place to make your home. Life is good, the days are sunny, I'm happy with my wife, the business prospers, our children are all I'd hoped for; no man could ask for more. But there was still something missing. I wouldn't have been so bothered if I could have worked out what it was. Eventually it came to me - just six weeks ago the answer walked through the door.

I was on the sail floor at the front of the building when a figure walked in from the quay, coming through the open double doors, silhouetted by the bright sunshine outside. The outline was clearly female, and as she came towards me I wondered if there was something about the walk or shape that was familiar. I screwed up my eyes to cope with the glare, it wasn't one of my daughters, or anyone else in my recent past, so I stepped forward to get a better view. However, even with the light on her face I was still puzzled, I half knew her, but half wasn't enough.

She smiled at me, a warm friendly smile, recognition came closer with the smile; but before I could make the connection she turned and beckoned someone else to come in with her. I honestly don't know if I sat down deliberately or just collapsed backwards onto a conveniently placed chair. A girl of thirteen or fourteen walked hesitantly through the door, and she was Mary Magdalen, younger and less worldly wise, but unmistakeably her.

I wasn't so much speaking as gasping, but still managed to climb to my feet again and threw my arms round the older woman, lifting her off her feet in the process. "Sophie, I didn't recognise you."

She laughed. "Well I was only six when you left and I might have changed a little since then. But I can still remember when our ship stopped at Syracuse and my mother and Joanna had dragged us all round some boring temples, then you said you'd had enough history and were going to take me to play on the beach."

I nodded as the memory came back and then turned to look at the girl again. "She's so like your mother, it would delight me every time I looked at her."

Sophie snorted. "She's a thirteen year old girl who thinks she knows everything, she certainly doesn't need you telling her how delightful she looks."

The girl was embarrassed. "Mother!" was all she said, but I didn't need any more, it was her voice.

I took her hand, and though I didn't often use my full name, this seemed like a suitable moment for it. "I'm Jesus Barabbas, and even knowing exactly who you are I still don't know your name."

She smiled. "Mary, of course, who else could I be?"

I took them through to the house and called for the family. A full hour was spent introducing and explaining everyone to everyone else, before we even began to discover the reason for their arrival. "My mother talked of you often," said Sophie, "but I think she knew that you would never come back; and though she would have loved to see you again thought it best to leave you to build your new life here. Whenever we had visitors who'd met you or knew anything of you, she would always want to know how you were and what you were doing. We knew all about Ruth and the children."

I was astonished. "She talked about me? What did she say - did she ever come to approve of me?"

"It wasn't quite as simple as that, sometimes she approved and sometimes she was angry with you, particularly after what you did to Pilate."

"How did she know about that?"

"The guards on the bridge reported that his attacker had told Pilate 'You crucified the wrong Jesus, you should have killed me', before throwing them both into the river. My mother said that you were the only person she'd ever met who would have said and done that. Then she and Priscilla said that you'd been seen leaving Rome the day before, and so it couldn't have been you."

"They actually lied to protect me?"

"My mother claimed later that she was just confused about the date, but really she couldn't have coped with hearing that you'd been executed. She said that since Jesus had said you were being given time to find repentance, you would probably need to live to be a hundred. For what it's worth Priscilla thought Pilate was a blood stained tyrant and that your actions could probably be justified, it was a subject the two of them used to talk about."

"Was there anything else she said about me?"

Sophie paused, considering her answer for a moment. "Yes, she said that if ever I needed a friend, someone outside the circle of the disciples, a person who could be relied on, then I should think of you."

For a moment I smiled with simple pleasure at the trust she had in me, but then realised the implications and grew more serious. "So that means you have a problem, something that you need a friend for?"

"Yes, I think there is a problem. I didn't understand my mother when she said that I might one day need such a friend, but that's a good description of what's happening now. Things are being changed, accounts of events that I have personal knowledge of are being given, which I know to be untrue, and there's nobody to stop it happening."

"What sort of things?"

"D'you remember the apostle Thomas, one of the original twelve, who was living in northern Syria before he disappeared?"

"Yes, he came to Antioch once and I met him, but nobody's seen him for more than twenty years. There was talk of him going to the far east, but I don't think anybody really knows."

She shook her head to indicate a lack of interest in his current location. "Before he left Syria he wrote a list of Jesus' sayings, I've seen it myself and my mother had a copy and said that most of it was correct. The point is that in the last year, a new version has begun to be circulated, and this time someone has inserted extra quotations, which were never there before. They say that Jesus appointed James to be his successor, and that women are not worthy of eternal life."

I raised my eyebrows. "That doesn't sound like any of Jesus' sayings that I ever heard."

"That's because he never said them, and neither did Thomas. And that's not the worst of it, a new version of Mark's story of Jesus' life has been issued, and the earlier versions seem to have been replaced in all the churches I've spoken to. Supposedly on instructions from Jerusalem."

"What are the differences between them?"

"The new one stops when my mother and the other women found the empty tomb. After it says that they were afraid, it just comes to a complete stop and doesn't make any attempt to finish the story. It leaves out the resurrection and our Lord's instruction to make disciples of all nations, and it also leaves out my mother being named as his successor."

We stared at each other as I tried to think who could be responsible. "I have to admit that I disliked James from the first time I met him, that first day after the crucifixion." I remembered the meeting: a group of tense and frightened men who were so ashamed of their own behaviour that they united in calling Judas a traitor to make themselves feel better.

"Though as much as I disliked him," I said, "I wouldn't have thought him capable of this sort of thing - which is probably why it's only started after he's safely dead."

"My mother never hated James, she simply thought that he was the wrong person to lead the church, he lacked the breadth of vision - but once he was appointed she always accepted his authority."

Sophie's daughter Mary raised her hand, a little nervously, as if asking permission to speak. "Don't forget that there's even a new version of Paul's letter to Timothy, saying that women shouldn't be allowed to teach."

I looked at Sophie helplessly. "You've come to me for help, and I'll give you anything I can and gladly, but I don't know where to start. I can't go around every church removing false texts. This isn't the work of just one man, I think this is a joint effort by the Jerusalem leadership to re-write the history of the church. They're hardly likely to stop just because we ask them to."

"I'm not suggesting that we ask them to stop doing anything, what I'm suggesting is that we should start doing something ourselves. You should tell your own story, set down the facts of the matter as you saw them."

I laughed, and even Ruth smiled at the idea. "Nobody wants to hear from me, the word of a convicted criminal against the church leadership."

For the first time in our conversation the steel of Mary Magdalen pushed through the politeness and friendship. "Don't waste my time or yours with ancient history - you might have been a vagabond once, but that was a long time ago and a long way away. Look at you now, you're a well fed pillar of the community with a successful business and a happy family. If you were any more respectable you'd be on the synagogue council."

"I already am on the synagogue council." I admitted, embarrassed by her accuracy.

"Exactly, you just use your background as an excuse to avoid doing things, don't you?"

Ruth looked at me with an expression that said, 'she's got you there'.

I kept my mouth shut and waited to be told what to do next.

"You're the last person on earth who met Jesus, who was there at the crucifixion, who watched the apostles dispute the leadership and who was even present at Paul's conversion. You're not a stupid man, did it never occur to wonder how it happened that you were there for so many crucial events?"

The honest answer would have been no, but that wasn't the point, so I struggled to go deeper. "I'm a witness, is that what I'm supposed to be?"

She stepped forward and put her hand on my arm. "No Barabbas, you're not *a* witness, you're *the* witness. It's time for you to make sense of your life, it's time for you to find the repentance that you alone were given time for. And the way you're going to do it is to set out the events of your life, fully and honestly. Don't try to favour anyone, just write exactly what you saw and heard. Then when people read it they will recognise the truth."

As she was saying this I knew she was right, and not because she was her mother's daughter, but because it made sense of everything that had ever happened to me.

"I'll do it, and when it's finished I'll call it: Looking for God - From Kerioth to Antioch."

"And did you find him?"

"Did I find him?" I thought for a moment. "No I couldn't honestly say I *found* him. I just woke up one morning and realised that he'd been there all along."

Sophie spoke softly, almost reluctantly. "One of the last things my mother said, when she knew she hadn't got long, was to make a confession of something that had troubled her for years. She said that despite all she'd said to you, the one sin of yours she could never fully condemn, was when you planned to kill Saul on the road to Damascus. She could never make up her mind if a sin born so directly from loyalty and love was truly a sin."

With a sigh, I turned to Joshua, my eldest. "You'd best take care of the tents son, I could be busy for a while."

Postscript

It is an old and true saying that like all mankind I entered this world between the piss and the shit and have rarely risen higher, but if nothing else I believe that having finished this manuscript I finally have a worthwhile legacy to leave. As I prepare myself for the end of this life, I feel like a leaky old ship that has somehow survived the storm and is now passing the breakwater into calmer waters; rather breathless and quite astonished to have got this far.

As Sophie said, all the other witnesses to these events are now dead, all that remains is the word of a convicted killer, but I hope to have played some part in securing a true record of the great betrayal that was attempted, and even now lingers on in places.

It's too late to right the wrong that was done to Mary and our movement, but now that I've told my story I hope that those who come later will know what was done, and perhaps avoid making the same mistakes. And now, if you'll excuse me, I'm going out to sit on the sea wall for a while, to watch the waves come in.

###

COROLLARY

This narrative makes no attempt to cover more than a small portion of events in the early church, a snapshot, the view of one individual. It was written in the first person, and thus as a work of fiction, because that was the only way I could look at the atmosphere of the time and how it felt as these events unfolded, without it becoming a mere catalogue of maybes. There comes a point where one simply needs to tell the story, and that's what I've tried to do.

Although a practising, and occasionally puzzled, member of the Anglican church, I suspect my primary motivation to explore this subject was intellectual rather than religious. On the subject of women priests and bishops, I was always fascinated by the argument against them which started from the position that Jesus could have picked women disciples, but chose not to. But then He could also have picked Gentile disciples and chose not to do that either, and how many Christian clerics do you know called Israel Goldstein? Alright, there might be a couple, but you take my point - they're thin on the ground. That, and the discovery that as well as Jesus calling himself The Son of the Father, Barabbas in Aramaic; the man that history calls Barabbas had the given name of Jesus. Two men called Jesus Barabbas - who could resist?

Another point that sent me back to re reading the New Testament was the story of Judas. I never could understand how he moved quite so rapidly from being one of the twelve Apostles to being the most hated man in Palestine. The betrayal for cash motive never made sense, he was already the disciples' treasurer and had access to easier funds than the chief priest's blood money. He seems to have been acting out a pre-destined role, a role that somebody had to act out for the rest of the story to work. It seems clear that he was operating with Jesus' knowledge and if not His agreement then at least His acceptance. However, as this sort of thing is so speculative, all that I put into the story was a note of doubt about his motives and the suggestion of some other way in which a man might be given thirty pieces of silver.

If you're interested, there's a fascinating essay on Judas in the Collected Works of Thomas De Quincey; best known for writing 'Confessions of an English Opium Eater'.

The story of James assuming the leadership of the church in Jerusalem after the crucifixion is well known, as is Peter's astonishing acquiescence to that fact. But then despite his devotion to Jesus, Peter had a record of bending with the prevailing wind. Consider not just his three times denial on the night before the crucifixion, but also his wavering and eventually vanishing support for Paul, which caused such lasting and deep ill feeling, when discussing the requirement for circumcision. I say none of this to suggest that he was not an infinitely better man than me in every possible way, but simply to remind you that before he became a saint he was also a human being.

James was, by all surviving accounts, the least active of the disciples and could never have been seen as the 'dearest disciple' mentioned in gospels, the only serious candidates for that position being John or Mary Magdalen. The behaviour of James, an exclusive and hard line Rabbi, in resisting calls for equality between Jew and Gentile, between circumcised and uncircumcised, and between men and women, would have ensured that Christianity became no more than a very brief and soon forgotten cult. Despite Jesus' focus on primarily addressing the Jewish community, He made it clear (John 10:16) that his mission also included the Gentiles, and He says so even more explicitly after the resurrection. James chose to stay in Jerusalem speaking only to other Jews, and although this was not without its dangers it certainly wasn't 'Spreading the word to all nations'. Yet without the tireless missionary work of the various evangelists, of whom Paul is the most famous, but who included Peter, eventually justifying Jesus' description of him as 'The rock on whom I will build my church', neither you nor I would ever have heard of any of these events.

The Gospel of Thomas, which is no more than a list of Jesus' sayings, quoted individually without any supporting narrative, is widely accepted to be 'substantially' accurate. Of the various non canonical gospels it was much earlier and has always been treated more seriously than the rest, and was a much debated and borderline case for inclusion in the New Testament. However, it is known, by the varying phraseology and word use, and the sheer improbability of some of the quotations, that significant alterations have been made to the original. A sensible question is whether those alterations made it more or less likely to be included in the collection of books which became the Bible.

It is worth our while to spend a moment looking at the disparities in this otherwise valuable document, as they seem to show a uniform bias. The sayings are given as a numbered list: 1 – 114 and for the sake of brevity I will refer to most simply by their numbers. If we are to ignore the duplicates, e.g. no. 56 is the same as no. 80, and if we also ignore the contradictions e.g. no. 14 contradicts no. 27 on the value of fasting, then we are left with two interesting problems.

The first is to be found in saying no. 114 at the end of the list, which has Peter saying to Jesus: 'Let Mary (Magdalen) leave us for women are not worthy of (the) life'. To which Jesus replies that He would make her male so that she could enter heaven. The immediate impression is that this is a bizarre and later insertion and unlike anything in the New Testament. But dislike of its oddity is not enough to dismiss it out of hand, further reasons for its dismissal should be given, and modern gender sensitivities can be ignored as they are, in this context, irrelevant.

The fact that Jesus' alleged response is in such a contrast to his known relationship with Mary Magdalen, and the respect He showed her, both in his life and after the resurrection, is in itself probably enough to reject this item; but we can dig further. Sayings 21 and 61 name Mary and Joanna as followers to whom mysteries are being explained. Then in saying no. 62 Jesus says; 'It is to those who are worthy of my mysteries that I tell (them)'. There is no suggestion that He plans to change Mary or Joanna's sex. All we are left with is the clear imprint of some later hand trying to downplay Mary's status.

The second anomaly to leap off the page is no. 12, which has Jesus naming James as his successor to be head of the church. The different tone of this item is striking. Most of the rest are explanations or corrections, the only other person named as being one to revere is John the Baptist, and whatever you think of James he isn't in that category. On a more detailed level no. 14 argues against the avoidance of impure foods, saying that it isn't what goes into the mouth that defiles a person, but what comes out of it. Then in no. 53, when asked if circumcision was necessary, Jesus replies that if it were useful then children would be born in that state. James as a strict and orthodox Jew disagreed strongly on both points.

His views on these subjects can have been no surprise to Jesus, who had known James all his life, as a disciple and close family member. These points together with his unwillingness to convert Gentiles, despite Jesus' instruction to do so, makes the possibility of him being chosen as sole leader of the movement quite literally unbelievable.

This prompts the question: if it was felt necessary to make this alteration to Thomas's list of Jesus' sayings, then what well known fact of the time was being overturned? Who was being written out of the story? It seems unlikely that any specific nomination of Peter would have been needed, as Jesus' earlier remarks about him: 'On this rock . . . etc.' would seem to have made further comment unnecessary. The presence of such an unlikely nomination as James gives the strongest possible indication that someone other than

Peter was specifically named as Jesus' successor, and that name was later changed.

At this point in the search for a probable original version one would need to be wilfully obtuse to avoid stumbling over the name of Jesus' closest companion, a companion whose gender would have made her unacceptable to the church elders in Jerusalem - amongst whom James must now be counted.

It would be evasive if we were not to look directly, if briefly, at that favourite subject of religious conspiracy theorists: was Jesus married to Mary Magdalen? Was the wedding at Cana their wedding? Like so many things in the New Testament one can produce semi rational arguments to support all sorts of theories, including that one.

Even if we accept as unprovable the suggestion that Mary was at the Last Supper, which it seems clear that Leonardo believed, it would have been extremely odd for her not to have been. (If you'll excuse an old joke: the reason she doesn't appear in Leonardo's famous picture is because she was the one holding the camera.) She was undeniably Jesus' very close and long term companion, and was beyond all possibility of doubt the person to whom the revelation in the Garden of Gethsemane was made, with all that implies for her chosen position. In terms of closeness to Jesus, this places her ahead of all the other disciples and even his own mother.

For Jesus to have been married would have made sense of His taking to Himself humanity in all its forms, and after the crucifixion it is believed that Mary his mother lived, at least for a time, with Mary Magdalen. Perhaps the grieving mother and the grieving widow offering mutual support.

My suggestion to you would be that, endlessly fascinating though such a notion is, until someone turns up a two thousand year old wedding invitation it remains unverifiable and so, at least in this situation, futile to pursue. In terms of the nominated succession, it simply doesn't matter. The point surely is that the provable degree of closeness between them was such that they must have been of one mind with respect to the core teachings of Jesus' ministry, which is considerably more than can ever be said of James, or even Peter. They simply couldn't have been any closer even if they were married. These conclusions require no flights of fantasy, but rather a careful reading of the known facts and a degree of sober reflection.

Mary Magdalen features much more frequently and prominently in the Gnostic and other Gospels not included in the New Testament canon, than she does in the included texts. The difference is quite remarkable. In view of the known changes to the canonical gospels and even, as we have just seen, to the non canonical Gospel of Thomas, it seems likely that the attention paid to her in those books was at least partially responsible for their non inclusion in the New Testament. And the centuries long repetition of the claim, only recently abandoned by Rome, that she was previously a prostitute would have needed a level of textual confusion unworthy of a well informed schoolboy - unless, once again, there was some other motive. A political commentator might describe this sort of thing as 'spin'.

The ending of Mark's gospel, which is agreed to be the earliest and most authoritative, and the very source which might have been expected to comment on such events, has been deleted by an unknown hand. It ends abruptly and in mid flow at chapter 16 verse 8, and no trace of its original ending is known to exist. Various alternative versions have been attempted, none of them more than tidying up exercises. The gospels of Luke and Matthew, which may be confidently assumed to use Mark's account, with the now lost 'Q Source' and possibly, the Gospel of Thomas as their guide, make no mention of who was designated as leader following Jesus. However, the frequency of allusions to Mary Magdalen might have made that unnecessary. Whereas, in terms of mentions, even James' mother scores more highly than he does.

Academic consensus is that in the late first century the only reliable and widely circulated accounts of Jesus' life were Mark's Gospel, Paul's letters and the Gospel of Thomas. Which is why I refer to these documents as being the objects of contemporary revision, they were the only ones available: Matthew, Luke and John hadn't been written yet. The so called 'Q Source' was also probably in circulation then, but we know only that it existed and was used as a source by later writers; we don't know its authorship, date or contents.

Paul's letters to the various new churches around the Mediterranean are a fascinating mine of information, both about the writer, and the state of the early church, but they do contain inconsistencies and anomalies. Anyone interested in a deeper study of Paul would be well advised to get themselves a copy of 'The Life and Epistles of St. Paul' by those two eminent Victorian gentlemen W.J. Conybeare and J.S. Howson. It looks a little heavy at first and most of the illustrations are terrible, but I promise you, to quote the Michelin Guide, it's worth a detour.

The fact that some of the early churches that Paul either founded, or was in contact with, were led by women sits very uneasily with one or two of his high profile and frequently quoted comments about women. e.g. 'I do not permit a woman to teach or have authority over a man'. Yet in almost direct opposition to that is the lengthy description of marital equality to be found in First Corinthians chapter 7. A brief extract of which is: 'For the wife does not have authority over her own body, but the husband does; likewise the husband does not have authority over his own body, but the wife does'. I expect that for a lot of you, like me, that's not what you thought to hear Paul saying about female equality, yet the remarks feel genuine and, unlike some of his other alleged comments, it serves nobody's agenda to have added them separately. Paul also writes in Galatians 'There is neither male nor female because Christ unites us'.

There is a serious difficulty in contrasting one part of his supposed sayings with another; and a further difficulty in contrasting those sayings with his actions. A sufficient difficulty to make one wonder if both positions came from the same man. Paul's strictures against female leadership are a genuine concern for the modern reader, especially when they are so clearly contradicted by his own actions. Yet if he didn't mean it - then why did he say it?

There are two obvious possible answers, the first being that perhaps he never did say some of the things attributed to him, perhaps the bigot was a later insertion. I'm not a conspiracy theorist, the butler usually did it, the cock up view of history is almost always preferable to any sort of conspiracy. And yet, again and again I seem to return to the point that a degree of discernment needs to be employed when reading even the New Testament, the uncritical acceptance of every single phrase seems unrealistic. I have never heard this point made from the pulpit and it feels arrogant to find myself suggesting it - but if a passage of scripture looks and sounds like a cuckoo in the nest, then that, conceivably, is exactly what it is. As the Gershwin song puts it: 'The things that you're liable to read in Bible, it ain't necessarily so.'

A second possible reason for him saying that he wished to restrict the role of women is one of political practicality. If you note his instruction that the new churches should avoid speaking in tongues, he nowhere claims this is because the practice itself is suspect, but simply that it is to be avoided because it will make outsiders think that church members are mad (his word, not mine). Note also his instruction that the new churches should be respectful of local laws, customs and rulers. Once again this isn't because it will make them better Christians, but rather because it will enable them to go about their work without provoking unnecessary local antagonism. If you them come to his remarks about women not preaching you can see them as part of a continuum, respecting local traditions and ways, whether you agree with those ways or not.

Paul is saying: 'This might not be what I do - but these things will help you to preach the gospel unmolested'. Such an approach might not be the purest or most rigorously moral position imaginable, but when trying to preach the word of God to a hostile and uncaring first century audience, from a rigidly patriarchal background, it was intensely practical. And whatever else one might say about Paul, you have only to read his letters to see that he was an intensely practical man.

One rarely mentioned fact about Paul, which might argue against his supposed misogyny, is that, unlike Jesus who only might have been married, Paul certainly was. (As indeed was Simon Peter) As closely as we can calculate he was 31 years old at the time of his conversion on the road to Damascus, for an ambitious and orthodox Jew of that age to be unmarried would have been extremely unusual; unusual enough to have raised questions about just how orthodox he was. Even more specifically, his election to the Sanhedrin, which can best be dated as coming after the death of Stephen and more than a year before his conversion, would have required not only that he be married, but that he should also be a father. Paul states clearly in his first letter to the Corinthians that he was unmarried at the time of writing, though whether he had been widowed by death or divorce, and when, is unknown.

Whilst the existence of Barabbas seems uncontentious, the accompanying story of Pilate's appeal to the mob is almost certainly a fabrication, introduced because of the necessity of putting the Romans in a good light. The few historical facts known about Pilate show him to be an opportunist thug, even by the brutal standards of his time. The suggestion that he would have agonised over the death of an innocent man, particularly a Jew, doesn't stand up for a moment.

The situation in first century Palestine was one where the orthodox Jewish authorities were opposed to the spread of Jesus' teachings both doctrinally and on the grounds that they would dilute Jewish identity and the coherence of Jewish nationhood. Their opposition could be taken for granted, whatever the apostles said. The Romans, the dominant military and political force in the then known world, maintained an officially neutral view of alien religions, just as long as they didn't disturb the Pax Romana. The reality, however, as is so often the case, was much more fluid and ambiguous. Regional Roman officials enjoyed a great deal of autonomy, and the support or hostility of the local administration could be crucial to a missionary campaign. The possibility of gaining the approval of Rome itself would be a prize worth paying almost any, remotely justifiable, price for.

In what looks like a remarkably modern example of realpolitik, it seems that a conscious decision was taken to appease the Romans, and thus ease the passage of the new religion throughout the empire. The unfortunate, but undeniable, fact that it was the Romans who had crucified Jesus meant that another scapegoat had to be found, the High Priest and the Sanhedrin were tailor made for the role. The morality of this position is something you need to consider for yourself.

One rather sad point is the fact that the reason most of us never knew that Barabbas and Jesus shared the same name, Jesus Barabbas, is the result of a deliberate decision, primarily by the early church father Origen of Alexandria in the third century. It was felt it would be less confusing to the layman to use only the first part of that name for the Son of God, and the second part for the convicted criminal. You can see what they mean, and I suspect there was no ulterior motive, but it seems a shame to take someone's name away, especially when that's all they've got.

The revision of the account of Pontius Pilate's behaviour for political and propaganda purposes has nothing to say to us about the state of male/female equality in the early church, but what it does say is something even more fundamental. It tells us that there were people in the early church, and no doubt in today's church also, willing to change the record to suit their own perceptions and requirements. Sometimes such changes were understandable details, such as clarifying exactly which Jesus Barabbas was being referred to, but sometimes the changes were far more serious and altered the very meaning of the text.

Could the anomalies in Paul's Epistles on the subject of equality between men and women in the early church have been caused by the same revising motives that amended Thomas's Gospel, deleted the ending of Mark's Gospel and produced the highly unlikely account of Pontius Pilate's actions? Or are these things no more than a string of coincidences?

It is an established maxim that the plural of anecdote is not fact, a rolling wave of rumour doesn't equal a hard pebble of truth; nonetheless when your three best friends tell you you're drunk, it's probably time to lie down. In other words you have to use your own judgment to establish a line between giving credence to gossip or alternatively ignoring a probably valid, if unsubstantiated belief. It isn't easy and there are lots of grey areas. The Christian churches, the ones with whom I am most familiar, recognise this fact to varying degrees in their different denominations.

Orthodox Christian belief is thus a mixture of scripturally mandated behaviour: you shall not kill, and long standing tradition: Catholic priestly celibacy. Anyone attempting to live their life on a strict and literal interpretation of every word in the Bible will soon find themselves faced with a host of contradictions and Leviticus inspired irrelevance. I would hate the idea of a church that bent with every passing social novelty, but we are no longer a desert dwelling tribe of nomadic sheep herders and it is unhelpful to act as though we were.

For example Jesus had nothing to say about the injustice of slave owning, although the existence of slavery is mentioned several times in the New Testament, this doesn't mean that He approved of it, it simply means that He thought there were more fundamental lessons to be learned. Lessons about our approach to God and our fellow man. The following admonition appears in Mark: *'Love the Lord your God* .

. . ' and *'Love your neighbour as yourself'. There is no commandment greater than these.* The reader is clearly expected to extrapolate general moral standards from these two commandments. If we are expected, on that basis, to use our common sense and judgement on a subject like the permissibility of slave owning, then might I politely suggest that we should be doing so in other areas as well.

Which brings us to the inescapable requirement to decide for ourselves the level of partiality (I'm trying to avoid the word bias) in the New Testament, either from the authors themselves or later revisers. My view is that wherever you feel that level lies, it cannot honestly be seen as zero. Unfortunately I can't give you a pre packaged answer, mainly because I don't think there is one. All I can do is to point out that if careful consideration of this subject doesn't lead us to the view that Christianity should include all people of faith and good will, in full and equal participation, then we might just be missing the point. What do you think?

Acknowledgements of errors:

I'll start with the big one first: St. Augustine said that we should come to understanding through belief, rather than the other way round, and you may feel the thrust of this book runs contrary to that directive. To which my only excuse is that curiosity got the better of me.

In order for this story to make any progress at all, I have had to engage in some guesswork. Where the Gospels offer conflicting or ambiguous information then a writer of this sort of work must inevitably choose one version at the expense of the others. I have always selected what seemed to me to be the obvious or common sense choice, sometimes using the weight of church tradition as a guide. I don't think that any of these decisions have any bearing on the flow of the narrative, and they're only ever used to reduce the breadth of the story to that which could have been seen by a single observer.

Although the names and genders of the church leaders mentioned are correct, and in the case of Priscilla (Prisca) and Aquila their relative leaderships roles; for the sake of convenience I have made unverifiable assumptions about the exact chronology of the church hierarchies in Rome and Ephesus.

One recurring problem was the fact that so many of the characters use two or more different names at different times in the story. It would be pointless to list every occasion where this has happened, and the following cases are just some examples of what I mean. With the obvious exception of Saul of Tarsus changing his name to Paul after his conversion, which is altogether too well known to ignore, I have in most cases selected one name per character, even when this is not strictly historical.

Simon Peter should perhaps have been referred to as Simon his Jewish name, rather than Peter, the Latin version of the name Jesus preferred, having been filtered through Greek from Aramaic. The simple fact is we all know him primarily as Peter.

The identity of the various Marks and John Marks mentioned in the NT can be argued over, some commentators have even suggested that there were as many as three separate people referred to by that name. I think that improbable and have gone with the long established tradition that all such references are to the same person, who also wrote the Gospel of that name.

John Mark should probably have been shortened to John in the early sections of the story, rather than Mark, as the Hebrew John is likely to have been preferred by his fellow apostles to the Latin Marcus, which he acquired later, but it is more consistent within the story to use Mark throughout.

The date at which the man called Joseph by his parents was given the new name of Barnabas by the Apostles in Jerusalem, in recognition of his good works, almost certainly comes after I begin to use that name. Once again I chose the better known name and stuck with it

The precise identities and familial relationships of Mary Cleopas (Clopas) and James can be argued over until the cows come home. I have looked at all the evidence I could find and come to what I think is a sensible decision. If you look at the same evidence and reach a different decision then *tant pis.*

And finally if you think that I have taken too many liberties with the various character's motives, words or actions, I would point out that there are fewer differences between most of my account and that in any particular Gospel, than there are between the Gospels themselves. Beyond that I'm afraid you'll just have accept that's how it goes with works of fiction.

Thank you and goodnight.

Ian Lindsay is the pen name of established author Ian Okell. The change of name is to avoid confusing people already familiar with his previous work, light hearted action adventure thrillers. They are:

Rude Awakening - A man dying in hospital wakes to find himself in the Bronze Age; is it real or has he actually died?

Loose Cannon - A couple run for their lives to avoid a rogue military intelligence operation. Set in present day London.

Charlie Chaplin's Uncle - A Victorian railway caper in a snowstorm, a young Charlie Chaplin meets Sherlock Holmes.

Rendezvous in Paris - A race to snatch a missing radar part ahead of the German Blitzkrieg, set in Paris in May 1940.

Available in paperback or ebook download. Full details available on any major bookseller's Ian Okell page.